Praise for *Private Equity*

Finalist for the New American Voices Award

Named one of the best books of the year by *Vogue* and *Time*

"[Sun is] a keen observer of [wealth's] subtleties and signifiers. . . . The first chapters of the book engage in a form of concealment and restraint— the sort of writing that seems fitting for someone who succeeds in a job that demands compartmentalization and competence. . . . As Sun starts to come apart under the pressure of her job, the writing gets more fragmented, and more experimental. . . . There is a beautifully written section, catalyzed by a weeklong vacation to China, in which Sun offers a portrait of her parents during and after the Cultural Revolution, and tries to make sense of the volatile home she was raised in. . . . It's a smart structure, and well-executed: just as Sun's self-abnegation becomes unsustainable, her writing breaks loose. The maneuver is unusually stylish for a memoir."
—Anna Wiener, *The New Yorker*

"Sun writes clearly about the demands and privileges of the job, though this isn't a tell-all about abuses in the industry but rather a more probing inquiry into what we deem success and the values underpinning it."
—*Vogue*

"The joys of Sun's memoir lie in the absurdity of her tasks: coaxing a famous athlete to a company party, sourcing Mitt Romney's phone number on a deadline, coordinating private-jet departures. . . . It's [Sun's] personal revelations that elevate the book above a typical tell-all." —*Time*

"A riveting, thoughtful memoir delving into questions around the psychological and physical cost of burnout and coming-of-age in the work-

place. [*Private Equity*] surfaces deeper questions around what it means to be successful in America—and whether it's actually worth it."

—*Fortune*

"[Sun's] awakening feels hard-won, and she captures the hollow cultishness that crept over white-collar New York in the Obama years, when Gordon Gekko types started going to SoulCycle. Indeed, the same qualities that nearly reduced her to an automaton have made her an astute, punctilious narrator." —*Harper's Magazine*

"An enthralling memoir about self-discovery, and a look at the dark side of extreme wealth and today's work culture." —*Cosmopolitan*

"Carrie Sun's memoir, about her experience working for a billionaire hedge fund tycoon, might read like fiction, but it all happened to her. It's not only a funny, revealing, and exciting read, it's also a fascinating look inside one of the world's most secretive and powerful industries."

—*Town & Country*

"A penetrating but all the more necessary critique of extreme wealth and toxic work culture as [Sun] questions what it really means to waste one's life." —*Oprah Daily*

"[Sun's] book is about career burnout and the hollowness of pursuing money, but it is also a satisfying story about a brilliant woman moving from self-doubt to self-confidence." —*Star Tribune*

"Those in high-pressure careers or in the financial industry will find this book insightful." —*Booklist*

"Wonderful . . . If you're a fan of everything from Ishiguro to Michael Lewis, this book is worth checking out."

—Jay Caspian Kang, *Time To Say Goodbye* podcast

"Piercing and propulsive. Carrie Sun's examinations of this most rarefied stratum are nuanced and poignant. *Private Equity* is a young woman's reckoning, set at the summit of money and power that asks the most universal of questions: How much of ourselves do we owe our family and work, and how do we find the courage to make our days our own?" —Stephanie Danler, *New York Times* bestselling author of *Sweetbitter*

"*Private Equity* is an extraordinarily gripping and revelatory journey through a world we rarely get to glimpse, despite its influence on our lives. But it is also a moving story of how easily a life can be submerged by work, and what it takes to regain one's soul."

—Oliver Burkeman, *New York Times* bestselling author of *Four Thousand Weeks: Time Management for Mortals*

"Incisive, sharp, and utterly compelling, Carrie Sun's memoir is a damning portrait of the finance industry and one woman's harrowing journey through it. She captures with incredible precision the tunnel vision that wealth and privilege provides—as well as the disillusionment and burnout that can follow. *Private Equity* gives us an opportunity to reflect on our own relationships to work, and to think about how we might make a different way in the world."

—Mychal Denzel Smith, author of *Stakes Is High: Life After the American Dream*

"Carrie Sun's nuanced and shocking memoir depicts a woman's rise in a high-finance dystopia where an employee's life is never private and nothing is equitable. *Private Equity* is the account of years of leashed efficiency that left her a wild and breaking heart and, eventually, the courage to speak its bitter, unsparing truth."

—Honor Moore, author of *Our Revolution: A Mother and Daughter at Midcentury*

"A fascinating memoir, tense and exciting, taking us inside a rarefied kingdom that, more than we'd like to admit, controls our lives. I highly recommend it."
—Phillip Lopate

PRIVATE EQUITY

a memoir

Carrie Sun

PENGUIN BOOKS

DESIGNED BY MEIGHAN CAVANAUGH

ISBN 9780593655016 (paperback)

THE LIBRARY OF CONGRESS HAS CATALOGED THE HARDCOVER EDITION AS FOLLOWS:
Names: Sun, Carrie, author.
Title: Private equity: a memoir / Carrie Sun.
Description: New York, NY: Penguin Press, 2024.
Identifiers: LCCN 2023026566 (print) | LCCN 2023026567 (ebook) |
ISBN 9780593654996 (hardcover) | ISBN 9780593655009 (ebook)
Subjects: LCSH: Businesswomen—Biography. | Finance. | Work-life balance.
Classification: LCC HC102.5.A2 S86 2024 (print) | LCC HC102.5.A2 (ebook) |
DDC 332.64/52092 [B]—dc23/eng/20231127
LC record available at https://lccn.loc.gov/2023026566
LC ebook record available at https://lccn.loc.gov/2023026567

First published in the United States of America by Penguin Press,
an imprint of Penguin Random House LLC, 2024
Published in Penguin Books 2025

Printed in the United States of America
1st Printing

The authorized representative in the EU for product safety and compliance is
Penguin Random House Ireland, Morrison Chambers, 32 Nassau Street,
Dublin D02 YH68, Ireland, https://eu-contact.penguin.ie.

For my mother, my father,

and all those who have the courage to quit

CONTENTS

Prologue: February 24   *1*

PART ONE

July 28–August 18   *7*

September 3   *27*

September 4–30   *51*

Fourth Quarter   *71*

PART TWO

First Quarter   *101*

Second Quarter   *123*

Third Quarter   *147*

Fourth Quarter   *173*

First Quarter   *207*

PART THREE

Second Quarter   *243*

July 1–September 26   *273*

September 30–October 28   *291*

November 18   *313*

Epilogue: July 27   *331*

Author's Note   *335*

Acknowledgments   *337*

PRIVATE EQUITY

PROLOGUE

February 24

A white, serious-looking doctor with graying hair came into my room, checked my chart, discussed it with other hospital staff in hushed voices, and then came back over to me, leaned in, and said, "I'm gonna be straight with you 'cause you're almost an adult." I was in the eighth grade. Hours ago I had seen them label my race, during intake, as *Ontl* and heard them refer to me as "the Chinese girl." "I reviewed your situation and it's not great. We're going to give you one antibiotic now, but for the stronger one, we'll have to wait until tomorrow. Your body has deteriorated so much, it might be too weak to handle everything at once. The plan is for you to fight this and, well, hopefully get a little bit better by morning, 'cause I gotta be honest with you: I can't say for certain if you'll make it through the night."

Six days earlier, my mother had taken me to the doctor for a cough and fever that would not subside with Tylenol. I had waited almost a week to tell her how sick I felt because I was afraid she'd blame me; I did not want her to have to take time off work. Mom had specially selected our family physician, the only one she'd found in our area who practiced Western medicine and was from mainland China. But Dr. Li was away, so we saw a backup doctor, a white woman. She ordered a chest X-ray, saw signs of pneumonia, gave me a shot of Rocephin, and sent us home.

A day later I could not walk up and down stairs.

Then I could not eat.

Then I could not keep down juice.

Then I could not keep down water.

Mom wanted to give me generic antibiotics she had brought over from China. Dad said no, we should listen to the American doctors. Mom objected. They quarreled. I heard yelling. Dad did not believe that I was as sick as I was. Mom took me back to the clinic and demanded treatment. The same doctor saw me, saw how I was wheeled in. She checked my vitals and immediately called an ambulance.

One second, two seconds. A minute. An hour. It was dark and I was awake, staring at the clock. Earlier, a nurse had told me I could press the call button as frequently as I wanted, if I needed anything at all, like an ice cube, which she said would soothe the dehydration in my mouth. I cried at her kindness, then found my body was so dry, it could make no tears. Air traveled through my lungs like crumpled sandpaper; I could not breathe. I remembered Dad, who liked to educate me using Chinese idioms, fables, and phrases, often telling me *kū dōu láibují*. We were the people—Chinese, immigrants, strivers—for whom *crying, there's not enough time*. So, I stopped crying and decided to fight. But what did *fight* mean?

I wanted to live. Still, I had no ability to influence the trajectory of this disease with my thoughts or agency or will. It seemed wrong to think I had any control over the outcome of my life, over what I perceived to be a combination of pure uncertainty and genetic and biological luck. Following the rules—taking the medicine I had been given during outpatient therapy—did not work. Suddenly I became hyperaware of time. Not in the sense of how much time I had left, but the time value of decisions—like when to speak up and when to ask for help, like how an antibiotic today versus one tomorrow might mean the difference between life and death.

I did not practice a religion and neither did my parents, but if there had ever been a time to make a prayer, it was now. I closed my eyes and whispered:

> *Dear God: Thank you for giving me the gift of life. If I am blessed with more life, I promise two things. One, I will make the most out of each and every day and do something of value with my life. Two, I will be a good person. Thank you. Amen.*

My ice cube had melted, so I pressed the button for help. I opened my eyes.

PART ONE

It was the aspiration of all those of us
with professional ambition to work
our way as close to this hub as
we were each of us capable.

—Kazuo Ishiguro,
The Remains of the Day

July 28–August 18

Yuna called me immediately after she got off the phone with Boone. "God, Carrie," she said. "I was so nervous, the first thing I said was 'I can't believe I'm speaking to a billionaire!'"

I had prepped her, of course. Yuna was my best friend from Michigan, from the part of the Mitten where P. F. Chang's was a hot spot and going to Meijer was a pastime. After high school, I went out east; Yuna enrolled at a local community college and dipped in and out of jobs. She had finally achieved her dream of leaving Michigan, working as a field test engineer for Samsung in Kansas, when I asked her to be a personal reference for my interview process with Boone. She was the last of his calls, of which there were ten.

EIGHTEEN DAYS EARLIER, I had gone to meet with a head-hunter in Midtown. Peter specialized in support roles for boldface names. His team placed candidates in positions from receptionists to chiefs of staff at major firms in finance, real estate, media, and other industries. He and I went over my background again and again.

"You're a superstar. *But*," he stressed in his British accent, "everyone will ask you why a math and finance dual degree from MIT, who graduated in three years, wants to be an assistant."

I looked out the window of that small, sterile room and wished the air-conditioning would work a lot harder. Three years before this, I had dropped out of an MBA program because I felt restless with the conviction that I had been wasting my life. I wanted to change paths. So, I enrolled as a non-degree student at various universities and cobbled together a liberal arts education by taking classes in the humanities. When I told my fiancé I wished to go back to school to get a graduate degree in creative writing, he asked, "But who's going to cook dinner?" Like so many aspiring writers and artists, I hoped to get a job during the day that would allow me to pay the bills while working on my craft and getting an MFA.

But finance nudged at me. My yearslong indecision about what to do next—whether I should put to better use the education my parents had climbed mountains and crossed oceans to provide for me; whether I should marry my fiancé, who paid for all our joint expenses and some of my individual expenses and in exchange wanted me to prioritize him and his career and not work myself—had cost me over half my life savings. I paid for anything my fiancé did not want me to do. We argued over my taking a fiction workshop, the reason I was alone in Manhattan for the summer even though he and I lived in Ann Arbor. Three weeks into the workshop, I received a cold email from Peter after one of his researchers had come across my profile on LinkedIn.

I looked back at Peter and explained that my objective was neither maximizing earnings nor status. "I want a job," I said, "so I can afford to figure out my life."

Peter asked about the last line on my résumé, where I had written down some interests: Creative writing. College football. I told him he had to keep them there.

"I get it," he said. "I'm a photographer."

He paused.

Then he inhaled.

"So," he said. Another pause as he looked me in the eye, smiling. Recruiters are one of the main gatekeepers for the hedge fund and private equity industries. Some jobs are posted on employment aggregator sites; many are not. After a résumé screen, a phone call, and the current interview to make sure I would comport myself in just the right way, finally, he let me in. "I'm working on a search I think you'd be perfect for," he said. "Have you heard of Carbon?"

I hadn't—but I had heard of Argon, a hedge fund that had long and widely been seen as financial royalty. I asked Peter if the two funds were related.

"Correct." The founder of Carbon had cut his teeth at Argon. "Carbon, they are a *rock star* of a fund. And yet"—Peter raised an index finger and lowered his voice—"under the radar. We never see any Carbon résumés floating around because once people get there, they stay. Forever. No one leaves." He let a few seconds pass. "The job is the sole assistant to the founder of the Firm, Boone Prescott.

He's a billionaire. And he's young." Peter glanced down at his note-book. "Boone is, from all accounts, the *nicest*. And Jen, who runs his family office and personal life—she's an absolute sweetheart. The job is essentially being Boone's right-hand person: you'd manage his time and business life, help with some research, and also provide support to one of his analysts. This is a once-in-a-lifetime opportunity. Can I pitch you to them?"

I LEFT PETER'S OFFICE and went back home to a dorm room I'd rented through NYU. I was working on a short story about a woman in the middle of a quarter-life crisis when I received an email from Peter: "Pls call me!" Jen wanted me to come in at two thirty, in two hours. Could I make it?

I had had plans to meet someone for lunch, a woman named Ruth. She was one of two Americans who had sponsored my father so he could leave China and come to the United States for his gradu-ate studies in the eighties. I felt I owed much of my life to Ruth's kindness, although I had never had the chance to share this senti-ment with her. Now that I was in New York, I had reached out a week earlier in hopes of expressing my gratitude and catching up. My mother was in awe of Ruth. In Mom's telling: Ruth, after being a homemaker and raising two kids, realized how her kids respected her husband more than herself because he had a career and she did not. So, she got divorced, went back to school, and later taught at a small liberal arts college in New Jersey. It was during those years that she traveled to Anhui, one of the poorer and less-developed provinces in the middle of China; there, she met my dad, who served as her translator.

Ruth was in her garage in New Jersey when I called to cancel. "You really caught me in the nick of time," she said. She did not guilt or yell at me, though I felt her disappointment seep through the phone. I was disappointed too. But I could not say no. You don't say no to Carbon.

I HEADED BACK uptown to meet with Jen in a building near Barneys on Madison Avenue. Never before had I had a same-day, in-person interview after applying for a job. I arrived on the tenth floor and rang the bell. Maya opened the frosted-glass doors. I knew about Maya; Peter had told me that she had once been an assistant to the head of a mini-major film studio. Maya seemed warm and maternal, like someone whose fuse might extend all the way to the moon. After bringing me a bottle of water, she dropped me in a room to wait for Jen.

I had spent the short hours prior to this interview reading anything on Boone I could find. Carbon did not have a website or a Wikipedia page, and Boone was not active on social media. He did not give interviews. He did not sit for photos. Stories about him featured squiggly lines coalescing into caricatures of what appeared to be very different people. All this did not stop the financial press from crowning him Wall Street aristocracy or the society pages from speculating about his wife and kids and homes and money.

About the money: In the early part of the decade, Boone debuted on a prominent list of the youngest billionaires in America. What was special about Boone was his age, his net worth, *and* his industry. If Boone continued compounding his wealth at, say, a rate of 20 percent per year—a conservative estimate given some of his reported returns; a number that does not even factor in carry, the profits he'd receive from owning and managing the funds—he'd have a net worth of over $5 trillion by the time he reached the age of Warren Buffett.

About the Firm: I found a dribble of information. A leading financial publication had called Carbon the world's hottest hedge fund. Another had named it one of the world's top-performing large hedge funds, ranking it among other hedge fund titans and their flagships, like Ray Dalio's Pure Alpha II and Ken Griffin's Citadel. Of note, I could find nothing negative written about Boone or Carbon anywhere—in contrast to Dalio and Griffin and their firms, about which I had read articles mentioning subpoenas tied to possible insider trading, as well as employee turnover tied to a culture wherein the biggest insult was to call someone suboptimal.

About Jen: There was no information. No LinkedIn, no Facebook, no Twitter.

About the position: I received no job description.

A minute later, Jen walked in, apologizing for the look of their suite. She and her colleagues had just moved into the new family-office space. I stood up to shake her hand and noticed her well-tailored outfit, mid-heel pumps, and silky brown hair. My mind flashed to the iconic *The Devil Wears Prada* scene in which a post-makeover Anne Hathaway struts through the office wearing Chanel. I looked down at my suit, which I had bought on sale for my business-school interview years ago and which had ripped on the way there (later, Mom sewed up the tear on the back slit of my pencil skirt); I made immediate plans to go shopping.

Jen mentioned she was from Missouri. As I walked her through my background, her eyes appeared to twinkle. "That makes complete sense," she said after I told her I had tried being on the investment side. That I'd loved it, then hated it, then realized I wanted to do something else.

When Jen asked me the question Peter said she would, about why I would want to be an assistant and not a hedge fund manager myself, I was prepared. "I have other passions that interest me more," I said. "At heart, I'm a nerd. My favorite class in college was optimization. I'd love to optimize someone's life and help someone great do great things."

An hour after I left, I received an email from Peter: "Please call me when you get this." Boone wanted to meet me as soon as possible. When could I come in?

Two days later I made my way to Carbon's offices, which were in an iridescent skyscraper where Midtown meets Central Park meets Upper West Side. Carbon occupied the entire forty-sixth floor of a building home to the behemoths of the money-management industry. After walking through the travertine lobby, past a Brâncuși sculpture, I rode the elevator up.

A receptionist buzzed me in and welcomed me with "How can I help you?" There were actually two of them: Charlotte and Olivia, both blond, super pretty, looking like they definitely shopped at

Barneys. I made eye contact with one and then the other and said that I was here today to see Boone. Charlotte, the one who'd greeted me, sprang up from her chair and said, "Please follow me." As I followed her, I noticed her straight, voluminous hair with curled ends bouncing so perfectly that I wondered whether professional blowouts were a job requirement. I stepped into a large conference room named Paget and took in the early-evening view.

The finishes were opulent—marble, glass, steel, wood, and leather in shades of beige and cream, tinseled with cobalt—but that was not what got me. Most offices I had known had harsh fluorescent lighting reminding you that you were hard at work. Here, the light raying from the seamless ceiling, softened through distance and angles and filters, glowed. It mixed with nature, with its reflection off Central Park, and caused whoever was in the room to feel alive with the same starry force that made the view—the sky, the moon, heaven, and earth.

"Can I get you anything to drink?" Charlotte asked. "We have water, coffee, tea, soda . . ."

"Water, please."

"Sparkling or still?"

"Sparkling."

"Ice or no ice?"

"Ice."

Charlotte walked to the other side of Paget, where eight abstract paintings in sky blue and ivory hung on the wall. Below them, a credenza. On the credenza, a phone, some succulents, an iPad that controlled the audiovisuals of the room, and a tray that held a bucket of ice, a glass carafe of ice water, and a thermal carafe of hot water.

Charlotte slid open the credenza to reveal a minifridge. She pulled out a bottle of sparkling water and a short glass tumbler, filled the glass with ice, set the glass down in front of me on a metal coaster, and walked out of the room.

I sat down on a plush leather armchair. Not at the head of the table and not at the foot, but one chair away from the head so that, if Boone did sit there, he and I would be perpendicular. To the north, my left, was a wall of windows. On the closer end, I saw a meadow. Beyond that, a lake, a lawn, a museum, a reservoir, and the entirety of Central Park, which, from six hundred feet up, looked like a rug of treetops. Even farther away I saw the Bronx and the George Washington Bridge. I saw a pure horizon.

I drank my water and waited for Boone. My hands did not sweat, my pulse did not race. Boone would be the first billionaire I'd meet, but by then—I was twenty-nine—money had lost much of its sheen to me.

WHEN I WAS TWENTY-FIVE, working as an analyst at Fidelity Investments, I made over three hundred thousand dollars. I took my bonus, went to the Bloomingdale's outside of Boston, tried on dozens of pairs of shoes, and left empty-handed. Some part of me felt jealous of people for whom money seemed to bring joy, ease, and happiness. A confirmation that they were on the right path. Gold diggers, I envied them—and anyone else who knew exactly what they wanted. Right around then, I started dating someone with money, the same man who, over time, feared that my career aspirations might conflict with his plans for me to be a doll in his house. We flew in his family's private jet to his family's multiple homes. But the more money I made and the more I was surrounded by wealth, the more I found myself recoiling from it all. I planned my getaway and quit Fidelity after four and a half years, hoping to do a pivot. Two months later I started on a new path at the University of Pennsylvania, enrolled in a joint-degree program between the School of Arts & Sciences and the Wharton School of Business. When I arrived on campus, I found myself steeped in a culture that seemed to prioritize drinking and partying over working and studying. So suboptimal, so ineffi-cient. A colossal waste of time. This was the culture from which I was trying to escape, evinced by an offhand remark a coworker at Fidelity made to me one night: "I basically sit on my ass and do nothing and make millions. What could be better than that?"

BOONE CAME IN. We shook hands. He sat exactly where I'd thought he would. He had moved through the room with an absolute intent—a tight spring to his step, a measured angle to his posture—as I sensed my every blink and breath being observed, judged. I would've felt more heat if not for something I couldn't fully explain: perhaps it was his look, which young me growing up in the Rust Belt might have described as all-American; or perhaps it was how I wondered what it was like to be him, if he thought the story about him, preceding him, was fair.

For an hour, we chatted, though I cannot remember much about the meeting except its banality. He wore a light blue shirt, he car-ried an Evian bottle, he brought a printout of my résumé and did not smile or give me any sign of how well or poorly he thought I was doing. He said he received seven thousand emails a day and needed help organizing his inbox and life.

Peter had told me about what an earlier candidate was asked to do. Boone had left the interview to use the bathroom and asked this woman to compose an email to a colleague (or maybe to his mentor—I can't recall) about some works of art, and to complete the task by the time he returned. It was less a test of writing skills, more a test of how you would perform under pressure with incomplete information and scant guidance. I did not have to write an email. I did have to answer some very broad questions about myself: "Why are you here?" "Why do you want this job?" Boone asked me to explain what I had done at Fidelity; I perked up. I told him how, with no real programming experience, I had learned Java and R and built, from scratch, a custom portfolio optimizer that we used for our quant-investment needs: back-tests, simulations, rebalancings. "Basically an in-house version of Barra," I said. What's Barra? he asked. It was then I realized how wide the knowledge gap was between fundamentally and quantitatively driven finance: here was an investor whom many had called a phenom, who did not know one of the industry-leading providers of optimizers and risk models. This was also the moment I realized I wanted to work for Boone, a billionaire of (relatively) low ego.

Near the end of the hour, Boone stared at my résumé. After a long ten seconds, he looked up and asked, "What's your weakness?"

I had prepared safe answers, the kind that career websites suggest: Turn a weakness into a strength, or describe a non-deal-breaking weakness and show how you've improved. Show self-awareness. Show progress. *I'm impatient. I'm too proactive.* As I searched my drawer of scripted responses, something came over me and instead I blurted out, "Intensity."

Silence.

"I tend to take everything seriously," I said, "and often to an extreme. Not everyone likes to be around that energy." Silence again. I smiled and kept calm. Then I added, "In any case, whatever I do, I give it my all. I aim for the best in the world."

"Do you have more time?" he asked. "I'd like you to meet one of my colleagues."

THE NEXT ELEVEN interviews were a blur.

Minutes after meeting with Boone, I met with Gabe, Boone's software analyst, the person to whom I'd also provide support. He interrogated me for an hour with surgical questions on my psyche and résumé, beginning with the same question as Peter, Jen, and Boone. I answered. Then he asked, "But why?" I repeated what I had said; there was no deeper why. His dense eyebrows and smooth complexion told me he was probably around my age, maybe a few years older, but his forehead, even when his face was as blank as it was then, showed two deep-set creases. "But you," he pressed, "could do so much more." I swallowed an objection and stayed composed. He continued, "With your background, you could be a fund manager yourself or, at the very least, make so much more money. Why wouldn't you?" I remained stoic and breathed, slowly, in and out. I thought about his statements and, without tones of apology, said, "It's just who I am."

Two days later, on a Friday afternoon, I met with Boone's wife back in Paget. This was my fourth meeting at their offices in a week. Peter had told me it was down to me and another candidate and Elisabeth would be meeting us both, one after another. It's a bit odd to interview with your potential boss's wife, but apparently she weighed in on whom to admit into the inner circles. Elisabeth entered the room and turned her body to look behind herself, her hand holding the door until it closed, gently. "He does not trust easily," she told me the minute she sat down. Wearing no makeup, no flashy jewelry, no alligator shoes or crocodile bags, she appeared to be a different person from the young woman I had read about online. She told me she thought of this position as half assistant, half research analyst—she had spent some time in finance too, after graduating from a top college—and how I might be a "perfect fit" for it.

The following week, when Boone was away, I met with Gabe again. Again he asked me, as we drank our beverages in a ground-level espresso bar, how I could be sure I did not want to be a portfolio manager. This is it, I thought, if I have to explain myself to him one more time after today, I'm done. I felt I could not work well with someone whose only line of questioning implied a worldview with no room for revision. "Let's say in a year," he said, "you're given the opportunity to be an analyst at Carbon. Would you take it?" I shook my head, explaining that I had already been on the investment side, how in those years I had come to discover that I loved people and stories a bit more than I did numbers or finance. I mentioned an essay by one of the founders of Y Combinator, a premier start-up accelerator, on how to do what you love; later, I followed that up with an email to Gabe exploring quotes from the essay on how "prestige is just fossilized inspiration" and "you have to like what you do enough that the concept of 'spare time' seems mistaken." In my spare time I wrote, read, and planned. Seeing how the first two weren't exactly moneymakers, I thought it a smidge too perfect that I could get paid (well) to plan someone else's life. Gabe replied the next morning: "Thanks for the thoughtful response!"

The third and final week I met with eight more people. First up on Monday, in a small conference room named Etna, was Jay, the chief operating officer. With a mien like the caterpillar from *Alice in Wonderland*—a soft antagonism tinged with unintentional comedy—Jay wanted to make sure that I knew who I was and what my role would be. "I'm the grease," I said. "I'm here to help the wheels turn more efficiently." He asked me to confirm, and confirm again, that I would never, ever try to be the wheels. "No, I'm the grease," I said.

Next up were Bridget and Emma, a double interview with the women who ran investor relations. Peter had warned me that they were protective of Boone and liked no one. They asked me where I got my will to be of service to others. I thought of my mother—how ever since I was a girl with pigtail braids, I was her best friend, secret keeper, and emotional support—then said, "I was an only child and found that the best way to make friends was to give first." I knew that Emma, at least, liked me when she let slip some things about Carbon's culture. "The goalposts move every day," she said. "And Boone cares about every detail of everything, from periods and commas in investor letters to perfect alignment of text on PowerPoints."

Two days later, on a Wednesday afternoon, wearing a new sheath dress under a new collarless blazer, I had another round with Boone. We took a walk in Central Park, where he flinched at the sight of a rat and I concentrated on walking in heels over uneven sidewalks. "Are you going to get bored in this job and leave?" he asked. No, I said, I have many ways of busying myself outside of work. I told him I wanted to be a writer. "Would you leave if you got a writing job?" No. "Would you stay five to ten years?" Yes. "How are you with positive feedback? Because I don't give it." That's fine: I had a Korean piano teacher who was not one for positive reinforcement; plus, my mom's Chinese. I avoided alluding to Amy Chua because I did not believe I had a tiger mother; not once did Mom (or Dad) ask to see my report card. (Although they did find a way to comment on all other parts of my life—how I chewed at the wrong pace or smiled at the wrong width—I was determined to excel at everything so they would have *méi huà jiǎng*, a phrase used when something was so good, there would be *no words speak*.) Boone reached into his pocket, took out his phone, scrolled through some notes. Then he asked, "If this doesn't work out in eighteen months, what do you think the reason would be?" I think, I said, to be truly effective, I would need buy-in from everyone—analysts, partners, assistants— and if I don't have that, if people don't like me for whatever reason, it would be hard for me to operate at the level I'm sure you need to run your life. "I agree one hundred percent," he said. "Your biggest challenge will be not to intimidate others. The more people like you, the more you'll be able to get done." I assured him I would be quiet and absorb everything like a sponge. At the end of our stroll, after telling me how nearly everyone at Carbon was in their twenties and thirties with the average age somewhere around twenty-eight or -nine, he said, "No one—" He looked into space. "Yes, that's right, no one has ever voluntarily left Carbon."

After Boone and I returned to the office, I met with three assistants back-to-back-to-back in a medium-size conference room named
Meru. Sloane, whom Peter had told me was the queen bee of the
women at Carbon, had gone to the same elite college as Boone. In
addition to her primary role supporting Neil, Boone's partner who
oversaw the public equity side of the Firm, she was the de facto office manager. Sloane and I sat facing each other across the table. We
talked about SoulCycle. I tried hard to toss the image of Regina
George out of my mind but did not succeed.

Courtney was the assistant to Jay and the sidekick to Sloane.

Kelly was the assistant to Ethan, Boone's partner who co-led the
private equity side of the Firm. I tried hard to notice more about
the three women than their hair—Kelly's was red, Courtney's was
blond—but they were answering my questions about the specifics of
their jobs with statements allowing for hardly any differentiation:
"It's intense." "Nonstop." "A lot of work . . . but fun!" I felt embarrassed of my inability to observe much more about the women. Even
then, however, I was starting to sense a flattening, a dimensional-
ity reduction that made it difficult for me to extract meaningful
features, like personality—they all seemed supercompetitive, highly
extroverted, fiercely energetic, and nice.

And at last, on Thursday, I had my fourteenth and final interview, this one with Boone's executive coach. With a PhD in clinical
psychology, Keith was tasked with assessing my mental fitness. We
met over Skype. I made sure to look squarely at digital Keith and
not twitch or shake or blink at the wrong speed. Keith asked about
my family background, life history, values, and dreams. He asked
me questions for which I cannot remember the wording, but this

was what I heard: How was I with stress? Was I emotionally mature? Was I given to anxiety or panic or was I a supreme worker with a bulletproof heart and mind? My reaction to being probed, perhaps even more than the content of my answers, was the real test. There were questions behind the questions: How was I with boundaries? Was I willing to volunteer information about my private self as evidence of my full commitment to the position? Was I going to embrace my good luck at being the chosen one, and was I going to be appreciative of this luck, the luck of joining in conversation with Boone, by being all in—putting work above everything else? Or was I out?

WHILE I HAD been preparing for my psych test with Keith, another process was afoot.

Days before, I'd received a text from Peter: *Got some other things to discuss. Pls circle back.* He wanted to chat about references. I had given three. Carbon's people asked for eleven, eight of which they had chosen. Apparently they had plucked a few names off of my LinkedIn: some were connections, some were not, most were people to whom I hadn't spoken in years. I didn't recognize one of the names, so I crossed it off the list. Another was an ex who was trying to start his own fund. Another was my fiancé, Josh, who was on his way to becoming an ex after issuing an ultimatum: when I told him I wanted to take this job, he demanded that I choose between Carbon and him. "You don't need to work," he said. "Why are you doing this?" I had listed Josh's family's company on my résumé because I had once been on their payroll, mostly for health-insurance reasons (although I had helped them plenty with admin and travel and

logistical tasks and accompanied them to meetings, conferences, and
even tried to help expand their business to China). I wanted to be
completely honest about my history should a future employer, Carbon or anyone else, get ahold of my past W-2s. I also wanted to know
if Josh would keep his word, which he gave me four months into dating, that he would be a supportive partner no matter which direction
I took my career.

Peter told me Boone wanted to call everyone the next day. Could
I make this happen?

If I did not make this happen, my interview process would be
over. So, I asked around to get a couple of numbers I did not already
have in my contacts, then tried to get all seven people on the phone,
one after the other, during an evening in the middle of August. I
asked all these people—most of whom had no reason to help me
out—not only to speak to me to prepare for Boone's call but also
to wait by the phone and, if and when he did call, pick up and
speak positively about me. A test of my reputation, tact, efficacy,
resourcefulness, sense of urgency, and willingness to be all in—and
of whether I had it in me to rearrange the world for Boone.

I understood my job description: to make the world work for Boone.

Suddenly I became too aware of how much I had already remade
my world for Boone. Peter had sent me on interviews with various
funds. All of them, including Carbon, asked about my availability;
the only time I had blocked off was from four to six thirty p.m. two
days a week for my writing workshop. Every potential employer—
I was in later rounds in at least four other places—respected my
window except Carbon, which kept scheduling my interviews right
when I had class. I missed three whole classes out of twelve.

By the end of that mid-August night, I had spoken to everyone save for the ex, whom I nixed from the list because he did not know me. He once told me, when I was twenty-eight, that my biological clock was ticking and to "hurry up" and decide on a career and a man. I replaced him with Yuna. With Josh, on the phone, I told him he was free to say whatever he wanted, but if it was negative, then he would likely be alone in his claims. He threatened to ruin my career if I did not stop this and choose our relationship. "I know you to be many things," I said to him, "but if there's one thing you're not, you are not a liar. The topic at hand is my work ethic, skills, and capabilities, not our relationship. You've told me time and again how you believe that I could do anything I wanted to in this world. I'm asking you now to do the right thing and tell the truth."

The next day at 7:29 a.m. I sent Peter the complete list of references: ten names, along with job titles, email addresses, and cell phone numbers.

"They are good to go," I wrote.

"You literally are a magician," he replied. He told me this was by far the most intense search he had ever worked on. "Thank you for keeping your wits about you."

"WAIT, SO, YUNA . . . tell me what you said."

"Carrie! He was so nice. Never in my life did I think I'd have the privilege of talking to a billionaire!" She took a moment. "I thought he'd be like, you know, uptight and arrogant and all that, but he was *so* kind."

"Aw, that's amazing! Now tell me what you said."

"Well." Yuna exhaled. "I talked about our relationship. I didn't go to a fancy school or nothing, and I definitely do *not* have my shit together, but you don't care about that. You care about people. You haven't changed at all from small-town Michigan."

Yuna talked to Boone right after Boone had talked to Josh, who called and told me not to worry because he could not bring himself to say anything disparaging about me. In total, eight people contacted me after their calls. Two didn't. Maybe they forgot. Maybe they didn't think it was important to tell me. Or maybe Carbon decided that those eight, which included my original three names, had produced enough data. Whatever the number of reference checks—eight or ten or more—I saw how the world, with my help, tuned itself to Carbon.

I WAS AT HOME in Michigan when Boone called. My base salary would be what I had asked for, plus I would be eligible for a bonus after one year. No range was given for the bonus. Would I be able to start in two weeks? The day after Labor Day?

I smiled, said yes, hung up, and screamed. I walked over to my nightstand, slid off my engagement ring, opened a drawer and picked up a journal, and, with that, started packing for New York.

September 3

I woke up at three a.m. There I was, on my first day of work, wired and alone. A week earlier I had signed a lease on a studio in a Midtown high-rise. A six-minute walk from the office, it was not yet ready for move-in, so a friend had lent me his place for a few days. I lay awake on the Upper East Side, staring at the ceiling, ruminating over the events of the past two weeks.

Boone had sent me four books in the mail. "To get us in sync," he'd said. All self-help, no finance—all about increasing optimal performance, productivity, creativity, and efficacy. Two I'd read in college; I read them again, along with the new titles, and took meticulous notes.

Ted, Carbon's director of IT, emailed me: What new cell phone did I want? Which carrier? What area code? Carbon would pay for the device and service and would "not track or charge back" for personal usage. Unlimited calls, texts, and data, including international, at the highest speeds. I used this opportunity to change numbers, switching area codes from mid-Michigan's 517 to New York City's 917.

The main reason I changed my number was so that my ex-fiancé would stop contacting me. After accepting the job, I ended our engagement. The wedding had been planned for November, and I had been feeling an excessive, lingering guilt over its cancellation—not because the relationship was over or that I would miss Josh, but because I hated wasting money. Josh's parents had paid for the venue, an atrium inside the modern wing of the Art Institute of Chicago that had been named after hedge funders Ken and Anne Griffin. His parents had also paid for two silk gowns from Vera Wang. The emerald-cut engagement ring had cost more than the average home in Michigan. I'd be lying if I said I hadn't enjoyed and welcomed many of these perks.

But none of the perks mattered. When Josh met my best friend from college for the first time, he described me as "a fish in a fish tank." My friend's exact words to me after the double date were "What the actual fuck." I shrugged. I had only just begun to understand what had been troubling me so much about our relationship: He needed a say in everything. Josh said he found it sexy when I ate only lettuce. He said he wanted me to wear more makeup, higher heels, skimpier outfits, and, when I said I would prefer not to, he said, "Why can't you do it for me, if you love me?" He said if he and I disagreed—and we did, a lot, debating everything from the problem of free will to whether my nonbelief in seeking retribution meant that I did not believe in justice—then I should change my beliefs to match his because he was, I quote, "the man." Over that summer, I felt like the hand of God had fished me out of still water and placed me in a river. I did not need to be single; I needed a partner who would not try to build enclosures. After I called Josh and told him I was choosing neither him nor Boone but, in fact, myself, he said, "I'll pay you more than whatever Boone is paying you not to take the job." I hung up.

My thoughts during those small hours centered on a different call. "This is the first curveball I'm throwing at you," Boone had said, his opening line when he called me in the afternoon on Labor Day, two days earlier. I was supposed to start work in less than twenty-four hours, but now he wanted to postpone by a day (he and a colleague needed to make a last-minute half-day trip for a potential investment). "Come on Wednesday instead of Tuesday," he said. "How's eight thirty?" I told him that was great. "You'll see, this is typical, things always change at the last second. Oh, and Wednesday is Family Day after work, so wear something casual, not business." After the one-minute call, I spent hours trying to guess what Boone's definition of *casual* was. I settled on skinny black jeans, a dotted silk blouse, and, since I did not feel like assaulting my coworkers with my bare armpits quite yet, a cropped white jacket.

When the sun rose around six thirty a.m. I got up, got dressed, stuffed a pair of heels into my bag, and walked out the door.

TEXT FROM PETER, 7:09 a.m.: *Big day. Thinking of u my friend. Good luck!*

I GOT OFF the subway at Fifty-Ninth Street / Lexington Avenue.
The buildings loomed above me. This area had recently been labeled Billionaires' Row, a reference to the group of ultra-luxury
residential skyscrapers that hugged the southern edge of Central
Park; several of them soared over a thousand feet and altered the
skyline of Manhattan. But this corridor wasn't merely where some
of the world's richest slept. It was also where many of the new kings
of Wall Street—billionaires who had made their fortunes from
hedge funds, private equity, and other alternative assets—worked.
Regardless of the precise address of their offices, they constituted
their own class in the taxonomy of Wall Street. They were uptown
folks.

Take the blocks near Carbon. These were the stores I passed on
my crosstown walk before my first day of work: Fendi, Dior, Chanel, Burberry, Louis Vuitton, and a corner cluster of jewelers for
whom carats pooled like candies—Tiffany, Bulgari, Van Cleef &
Arpels. Before I even set foot inside the building, I had, floating in
my mind, perceptions of quality, rarity, excellence, trust, timeless-
ness, achievement, world-class, and forever. The best investors are
masters of psychology: they buy up your mental real estate before
you realize it's for sale.

What was not on my mind was money. I felt neither rich nor
poor. My salary did not give me much purchasing power on Billionaires' Row, but it did give me a sense that I was being fairly compensated for my position, I think. The negotiation for my pay had gone
like this:

Carbon: What do you want for your base?

I named my number.

Carbon: Done.

Peter had said Carbon would've gone higher had I pushed; I hadn't. The ask, which was my ending base salary at Fidelity, seemed like an appropriate start given that it was also the median base salary for MBAs coming out of Harvard, Stanford, and Wharton that year.

It was not yet eight. I was far too early. So I walked to a Starbucks, ordered a coffee, sat down on a chair, and browsed the *Wall Street Journal* on my phone, thinking about hedge funds.

In 1949 Alfred Winslow Jones created the first hedge fund strategy: long/short equity. His key innovation was combining the concepts of leverage (borrowing for increased exposure, thus higher returns when a basket of well-selected stocks went up) and short-selling (borrowing stocks from a lender to sell and repurchasing the shares when the prices dropped, thus decreasing net exposure and producing returns when the stocks went down). This strategy hinged on picking the right stocks. The result was higher returns at a lower risk because of a more diversified, more market-neutral—or hedged—portfolio. The industry would have its ups and downs; it wasn't until the last decades of the twentieth century that the daring funds began to attract much wider attention for their masters-of-the-universe performance numbers.

The eighties and nineties were the halcyon days for hedge funds. They operated on the fringes of the mainstream financial system without much oversight. Most of their investors were high-net-worth individuals or family offices with healthy appetites for risk. Those were also the years before Regulation Fair Disclosure (Reg FD), a rule the SEC instituted in 2000 to try to level the playing field by forcing companies issuing shares to the public to disclose material information to all investors, large and small, simultaneously. Special and early access was, in theory, gone after that. In 1990 the industry had 530 players managing $39 billion. Fewer funds meant fewer competitors vying for investor dollars as well as less crowded trades. Ten years later the industry ballooned to approximately 3,335 funds with nearly $500 billion in assets under management (AUM). When the tech bubble burst in the early aughts, the average stock hedge fund outperformed the total return of the S&P 500 by a wide margin. The industry had sold their investors on the twin promises of beating the market—what's known as generating alpha—and cushioning the fall during a downturn. On this, they delivered. The world took notice.

In the late nineties, the funds' investor base began to change from individuals (who, on the whole, maintained their allocations in hedge funds) to institutions, led by David Swensen, head of Yale's endowment. Swensen pioneered the endowment model, turning a portfolio invested mostly in marketable securities like stocks and bonds—which convert easily into cash—into a portfolio invested mostly in alternatives like hedge funds, private equity, and real estate—assets that are more illiquid and higher fee in expectation of higher returns. He spun around $1 billion in 1985 into $10 billion by 2000. Encouraged by his performance, others followed suit. Pensions, endowments, foundations, and other institutional money meant new sources of untapped capital, providing significant in-flows. By the early aughts, the investor base had switched from mostly individuals to mostly institutions and funds of funds. Total AUM in the industry swelled to about $2 trillion in the second quarter of 2008.

Then came the financial crisis. Hedge funds suffered in 2008 but not as much as the market, with the average fund down 18 per-cent compared to 38 percent for the S&P 500. Asset allocators lost confidence, redeeming $382 billion that year. There's some debate about the role of hedge funds in the crisis: most narratives say while they weren't one of the main causes of the collapse of the economy, they withdrew assets and sold securities at such large scales that they further destabilized the financial system. Those who sur-vived were wounded but not dead. Several managers made prescient calls and corresponding fortunes. Hedge funds were seen by many in finance—not by the public, who had a strong and justifiably nega-tive view of all of Wall Street—as, still, the place to make your bets; they weren't the baddest of the bad guys. From 1990 to 2009 the average stock hedge fund beat the S&P 500 total return by over 5 percent a year. Yes, there were flops, notably Long-Term Capital Management, a fund helmed by, among others, two Nobel laureates who had mismodeled risk (and as a result, during the 1998 ruble crisis, their fund imploded)—but, by and large, hedge funds contin-ued to deliver. In 2010 there were 7,200 funds managing over $1.5 trillion. They embodied the American dream at its peak: anyone could start a fund; with hard work, and good luck, anyone could get rich.

But after the dot-com crash and the financial crisis in the same decade and the Bernie Madoff scandal in late 2008, the focus of the industry began to change. Hedge fund clients (who are known as Limited Partners, or LPs) demanded more risk controls, transparency, and compliance measures. This, and the regulatory environment resulting from the Dodd-Frank Act, part of which required hedge fund advisers with $150 million or more in AUM in the United States to register with the SEC, made them more expensive to operate. Barriers to entry, like start-up costs, increased. The emphasis for some of the larger funds, which had been on superior performance, might have shifted to gathering and maintaining assets. Suppose you have a $10 billion fund and the typical two-and-twenty fee structure—that is, a 2 percent annual management fee plus a 20 percent annual performance fee. A rough calculation would say that managing the assets for a year with zero return would net you $200 million versus working night and day to try to produce a (pretty decent) return of 10 percent. Returns often get more difficult to generate the more AUM you have; when your AUM gets to a certain level, the incentives can change. At the same time, the digital revolution had begun to democratize financial data, information, and knowledge; anyone could now go online and find a company's forms, reports, earnings-call transcripts. Competition skyrocketed. By the mid-2010s the total number of funds jumped to eleven thousand as the AUM for the industry reached $2.6 trillion.

Eleven thousand funds, however, meant a rash of problems. First, performance got diluted as the supply of public-equity opportunities shrank: the number of listed stocks in the United States had been on a steady decline since it peaked in the mid-nineties. Second, there might have been a herd mentality: it's harder to differentiate your thinking when you have swarms of investors harvesting the same crop of companies for juicy returns. Third, and related, the amount of original research and insight required to beat the market increased. Fourth, there was the shriveling profit pool, since fees had come down due to pressure from institutional LPs, averaging around 1.6 percent for management and 18 percent for performance. Four years into the post-crisis bull market, the average stock hedge fund trailed the total return of the S&P 500 by about 20 percent. LPs were furious; they were missing the upswing. The industry got congested. Alpha vaporized. Hedge funds were becoming the laughingstock of the financial world.

Not Carbon. Carbon's AUM had grown by a multiple of more than five hundred in its lifetime. In its first seven years, it produced compounded annual returns of over 40 percent. One year in the aughts, it returned over 90 percent before fees. Though it suffered in the crisis, Carbon recovered by doubling down on what it was good at: tech, stock picking. And more: whereas other marquee hedge funds had headcounts in the hundreds or even thousands, Carbon ran extremely lean, which meant a huge pot of profits ladled out to a tiny number of employees.

Weeks ago, I had been introduced to a fund of funds (a fund with a portfolio comprised of other funds as opposed to securities like stocks and bonds). Josh had tasked a development director at a university in Michigan with finding me a job in the state, one that would make me want to pass up Carbon. The director connected me to several business leaders in the region. But nothing was a go. Then Josh reached into his network and put me in touch with the cofounder of a local private equity firm, who put me in touch with this fund of funds, whose executives considered me for an investment-side role. I was deep into the Carbon process by then, so I gave the woman I spoke to a heads-up that I would probably be leaving for a job in New York. She asked where. I told her. Doing what? Working for Boone. "Stop," the woman said over the phone. "Don't interview with us. Take that job. He's a once-in-a-generation investor." Her fund was one of the early LPs in Carbon. "Boone," she said, "has made us *so* much money."

And so I walked up to the building, all smiles, hope, and will. It was five minutes before eight thirty. I had worn cheap flip-flops for the commute. Never again. I leaned against a pillar and prayed for privacy as I squeezed into a pair of black patent-leather Louboutins. I hated those stilettos, but I was determined: I instructed my body to reclassify any pain as a necessary investment in myself, my future. I walked up to the big man behind the check-in counter.

"Hi," I said. "I am here for Carbon."

WHEN I VISITED the offices as a guest, I had entered and turned left. Today, I entered and turned right. Each step felt like achieving a new level of clearance at some top-secret government agency because no one external was allowed in the front office. Erin led me to my cubicle outside Boone's office so that when I sat down, he saw me and I saw him. She had filled the gap between his last assistant and me, a stint of about four months.

"This is the internal contact sheet," Erin said as she pointed to a piece of paper pinned behind two monitors. A list of each employee, their first and last names, along with their work and cell numbers. Absent from this sheet were job titles. Yet on this sheet were AIM screen names. I was surprised that a firm making billions by investing in disruptive technologies was using an AOL program as the official method of internal communications. I had not sent an IM since the mid-aughts when I was still funshine208. (A friend of mine and Yuna's used to call me Care Bear; Funshine was the bear, with a smiling sun on her belly, whose magical power was her ability to use solar beams to help solve problems.)

"Here's your welcome bag." Erin held up a navy canvas tote emblazoned with *CARBON* in pure white. It contained a water bottle stamped with the same logo as the tote; a folder with an employee handbook noting that *Individuals should refrain from using vulgarities, obscenities, jokes, sarcasm*; and the sable fur of the investor class: a Patagonia fleece jacket with yet another Carbon logo embroidered on the left arm.

Erin showed me a couple of other items—a drawer of blank checks, a cabinet of supplements—then she walked a few feet out of the cubicle to the far side of the aisle. "And here's the shredder," she said, gesturing toward an industrial-size bin with a lock on it. "Someone comes by every week or two and empties it out to be shredded later. If you can't wait"—she motioned toward a nook about twenty feet away—"there's one in the printing room."

Minutes later, Courtney came over to say hello and welcome. Carbon did not have anyone in human resources, so she and Jay handled the onboarding of new employees. "Ready to go on a tour of the office?" she asked. I followed her onto the highway that circled the floor.

THE FRONT OFFICE. Doors slid open and shut—no squeaking, no slamming. Walkways were carpeted—no tap dances from loafers or clicking from heels. "Boone likes it quiet," Courtney said. A modern-art installation (what looked like a hailstorm of graphite defying gravity) clung to the walls. The dress code was business formal, which was, per the handbook, appearing in a way *worthy of the respect, and is respectful, of our investors*: men were expected to wear a *suit and tie*; women were *guided by a comparable standard*, the soft specificity here telling me the order of things. The floor plan was open. Walls and doors were transparent. Computer screens and interprandial decisions were on full display. Boone's office was nestled in the middle of a row of four. I would venture to guess that it was not the largest office. It was, however, situated on the Downing Street of Carbon: Ethan, Boone, Michael, and Neil. They were the PMs. They spent their days researching and implementing investment ideas and deciding on overall fund strategies. They had the only offices with sweeping views of Central Park. What Boone could see from his office: On one side, he had high windows, the nothingness of open air over the everythingness of a pulsing, bustling Manhattan. On the other side, when he stood up, he had a complete view of this part of the floor, as those without an office had a cubicle, the walls of which were no taller than the height of a monitor. The front office felt like a panopticon.

The library. Two velvet couches gave off marshmallow vibes. They were surrounded by walls of books and heavy, luxurious, blackout drapes, which were drawn open. This room was sun-soaked and inviting. Books stood, mostly upright; some lay horizontal, some leaned. Everything was staged and tasteful. Amid coffee-table books on art and design, biographies and histories, my eyes zoomed in on one: *Pain, Parties, Work.*

The IT bunker.

The on-site consultants' den.

The nap/break/lactation room.

The middle office. A team of traders plus one or two people each in compliance, operations, and legal, all of whom sat surrounding a double-sided wall of monitors. The traders were responsible for executing the strategies, together with generating profitable trade ideas. Compliance's job was to keep up with rules and regulations and design processes to ensure that Carbon's day-to-day would be free of violation, akin to an in-house watchdog. Legal's job was to not only know the law and advocate for the interests of the Firm but also provide advice, weighing business objectives against legal and other risks while suggesting the best paths forward. Head of legal was a tall, alert man. Head of compliance was a former lawyer who had been a senior counsel at a government agency. There were two head traders: one had played football at an Ivy League college; the other played the game of "How low can my body-fat percentage go" (and spoke with the poshest of British accents). Courtney gestured toward a corner and said, "That's me. And over there's Jay."

The elevator bank, which bisected the floor.

The back-office kitchen.

The back office. Two small televisions played CNBC. Being active in public and private equities made the accounting situation at

Carbon rather complicated. This area was huge. The valuations team, whose job it was to calculate fair values of less-liquid assets for reporting purposes, sat there. At the dead end of the hall was a conference room named Vinson, the most private room on the floor. Next to that was a dedicated row for auditors.

Courtney led me down a hallway and into a corner. She stood still, looked at me, and said, "This is the *best* part of the whole office." She pushed open a frosted-glass door to reveal the gym: A wall with built-in shelves of Lululemon and Nike workout apparel in all sizes for men and women waiting to be worn. Treadmills, ellipticals, weights, a rowing machine, TRX, balls, blocks, and bands. A yoga and barre room for stretching and floor exercise. A Peloton. All the activity areas faced the park—that view again!—the amount of prime real estate dedicated to fitness telling me so much about this firm's values. The women's locker room had a shower with MALIN+GOETZ shampoos and conditioners, a beauty line found at Barneys. Towels from Restoration Hardware were as thick as blankets. Razors. Tampons. Blow-dryers and curling irons. After you were done, you tossed your workout gear into a hamper. Carbon laundered them for you, then placed the clean, folded clothes back onto the shelves. "I come in here," Courtney said, "to freshen up before going out after work. Or sometimes"—she tittered—"before work . . . if I've had a late night." She pulled open the door to a cubby. "You can store your gym shoes in here. They're all taken, so you'll have to wait until someone leaves. It's first come, first served." I asked if we needed to lock our stuff. "No, it's totally safe." I looked at the garment rack on which designer dresses hung. "That's Sloane's dry cleaning." I looked at the floor and noticed Valentino flats, the frayed inner label and nicks on the outer leather telling me that these were someone's everyday, outside, possibly commuting shoes.

The external conference rooms. Paget, Etna, Meru.

The lobby. A gray couch, white pillows. A jar of gray and white M&M's. A gray rug tessellated with stones, rocks, and pebbles. A wall with a single work of art: a mountain peak.

"And this is Everest," Courtney said, stopping in front of double glass doors that led to the fourth and largest external conference room. Twenty-four seats circling a pond of a table, announcing that you have arrived. "Team Lunch is here every week for the front office."

The (hidden) kitchen. Three staff members sat in this dark, windowless alley. They spoke to one another in Spanish, washed dishes, prepared catering. We could call them at any time. They would have to drop whatever they were doing and change course—help us, for instance, overnight packages, order office supplies, or clean up messy accidents. They never said no to us. "You'll never have to go downstairs," Courtney said. "They'll run up your lunch delivery from the ground floor and bring it straight to your desk—automatically."

The (hidden) bathrooms. Hidden, because the door to this area looked like every other panel of the slate-gray wall that stretched across the length of the floor. The facilities were single-stall and unisex, with sinks made of swirled marble. Walls were made of stones in shades of sand and shell. Stall doors extended all the way down. Sounds, smells—nothing escaped. The lavatories were connected by a hall of mirrors with warm lighting that flowed delicately from the room's corners and edges. I tended to avoid mirrors, incidental ones like shop windows too, but, catching a glimpse of my reflection today, I did not hate the way I looked.

"And here," Courtney said, "we have the front-office kitchen." She opened a fridge stocked with an assortment of cold-pressed juices, which I recognized as being ten dollars a bottle; multiple flavors of multiple brands of yogurts and yogurt substitutes; smoothies; Chia Pods; kombucha rainbows; and fancy waters like coconut, maple, and watermelon. The cabinets teemed with peanut, almond, and cashew butters; kale, coconut, and seaweed chips; protein powders, protein bars; and cereals—the variety here could stock an entire aisle at a health-food store. I wondered if Boone was the stealth consumer of the Cinnamon Toast Crunch, which felt grossly out of place. Or was he of the Cap'n Crunch persuasion? That was here too. Espresso machine. Coffee machine. Blenders. Even a Juicero. Every kind of milk and milk alternative. "Mondays we have catered lunch for the front office," Courtney said. "Fridays we have catered lunch for the entire office. Friday mornings we have bagels. Most afternoons we have cakes or cookies or doughnuts for someone's birthday or leftover cheese plates from someone's meeting. You also get a stipend for lunch every day." Even on catered days? I asked. Courtney nodded.

When Courtney opened and shut the drawers of the kitchen, I noticed that they were soft closing. Then I remembered the hidden doors were too. In fact, the entire floor was designed so that the workhorse parts of the office—like the power outlets for the conference-room tables, placed inside wells with polished-metal covers, flush at the center of the marble slabs—were not only soundless but also invisible. Any dirty work was out of sight, out of mind.

———

SOMETIME IN THE MORNING, Jay came over to tell me that he would be sending a note to Carbon-NewYork-All to welcome me to the Firm. "But we don't want to make people feel weird about you," he said. He wanted to trim my background in the email. It was a statement, not a question. "This is for *your* benefit." I nodded as I shrank, then said sure.

LATER THAT MORNING I had a sit with Boone in his office. Winning best-performing hedge fund in the world by stock picking was like winning *Iron Chef* by boiling chicken breasts: there were much fancier cuts, much more engineered and quantitative methods for investing, especially with the rise of machine learning. But Boone wanted to win by analyzing companies well; I respected him enormously for this. I wanted to learn everything from him and came prepared with my white Moleskine, which already contained copious notes on the books he had sent.

Boone came prepared too. He gave me a sheet of paper titled *Orientation for Carrie Sun*. As he spoke, I took notes. The first three words I jotted down were *straightforward, integrity, honesty*. He explained what my mentality should be: *Not to promote BRP. No quote. No press. Not canceling mtg last min. Not too big or important. Political—no*. He described how I should interact with others: *Super nice. Helpful. Resourceful. Get back to people. Super nice*. (Again.) There was a whole section on food preferences: *Protein—not heavy. Salad/soup. Clean. Not spicy, salty. Not mayo. No caffeine / red wine*.

Anti-cancer. There was another section on important people, including business contacts, which he said we would go over soon, as well as a section on live investments and deals, four of which we went over then. The last one was the company he and a colleague had visited yesterday and now said that they had "killed." Less than a day later he had decided: no deal. He mentioned how I was the one person he gave permission to "annoy" him and what I was wearing for Family Day was "perfect." He mentioned Carbon was a "flat" organization and that I needed to understand its "cadence." He mentioned "little things," "leaders eat last," and "letting people know we care."

"We're a give-first culture," he said. "You should read Adam Grant's *Give and Take*."

I was not sure how long orientation lasted.

There was more.

Boone gave me five sheets of paper titled *CS Responsibilities and Expectations* that listed ninety-six responsibilities (from *Calendar* to *Research* to *Finances* to *Communication* to *Other projects* and *Other personal*) followed by thirteen general expectations. We went over each line; there were no duplicate items. Not all of the ninety-six required the same attention, of course, but what was required was an extreme flexibility—the aptitude to thrive under sustained and elevated uncertainty—since each bullet could dilate from hours to years of ongoing work. In particular, ones like *Willing to help firm as needed.*

As needed showed up eleven times. *Proactive*, nine. Humor, once, tucked inside a bullet under the category *Maintain to-do list*. This was my favorite because it was the easiest: *Deletion when items com-*

plete. Then the addendum: *List* can *be short sometimes.* (Emphasis mine.) Meanwhile, stitched into the responsibilities was this notion of feeling good, as in *making people feel good about calling* and *ensuring vendors feel good about doing business with us.* He explained his people philosophy, which he wanted me to emulate: always interact with others in such a way as to induce a "good feeling" in *them.*

"The key for you," said Boone, "is to watch closely and learn from others. Don't step on anyone's toes. Don't act like you know everything. Defer to others."

Then he went over the expectations. *Maximize efficiency. Positive, "can do" attitude. No ego, productive, high return on time.* When he was explaining the fourth expectation—*kindness, professionalism, going the extra mile*—I found myself diving headlong into the rapids. He said he cared deeply about doing the right thing. About morality. Before Carbon I had told myself I would never get emotionally involved with work or school again. I had been burned before by loving institutions that did not love me back; by believing that goodness and equity and justice were possible at places with elite reputations and capitalist interests to protect. Since middle school, I had valued maximizing my day (defined primarily by the quantity and quality of work completed) alongside, and equally with, being a good person. In no way did I flawlessly achieve these goals, but I tried. I cared. And Boone—he appeared to be those two values incarnate.

It was then, toward the end of my first sit with Boone on my first day of work, I became a believer again. I believed in the possibility of good billionaires. I believed in good returns and good performance and that you and I and anyone who wanted to could be a good person at a hedge fund. I also believed that the game was about more than just money. Believing in him meant that I could luxuriate in my innocence, hold on to ideals. I did not have to restructure my understanding of the world.

The final expectation was *There are no "dumb" questions in the first 18 months (or really ever)!* He put his finger on the line and said, "You can ask me anything you want at any time." I nodded. "And don't say *hedge fund*," he instructed. "We're not a hedge fund." He paused to make sure I knew he was not kidding. "We are an investment firm."

TIME MOVED. HOURS PASSED. I went with our facilities manager, Luis, to take a photo for building security; my eyelids drooped from the weight of faux mink lashes I had worn (for the first time) in an attempt to look more alert, more perfect, at the office. I tried to overcome my newfound telephobia; so many buttons on the machine meant so many ways to drop or forward or barge in on a call in error. One of the responsibilities was *No unanswered phones.* My phone rang every few minutes. I would grab Erin, who was sitting nearby, and whisper-shout, "Sorry to interrupt! Quick! Help! What do I press?" I also attended a couple of training sessions: one on compliance, where I was reminded about insider-trading laws and advised never to come close to putting myself in a problematic position, and one on technology, where I was told to behave as if all my communications would be read in public. For a late lunch, I ordered a lobster maki with my Seamless credit. I had the time and appetite to eat two pieces of it. Boone, on our walk, had implied I would face resistance—that getting others to like me and want to help me was going to be the obstacle. But everyone had been so kind and patient with me today. Was he wrong?

After market close, it was Family Day.

"Not every day is like this," Boone said as we walked over to Victorian Gardens, the amusement park inside Central Park that Carbon had bought out for the evening. He let out a chuckle and so I laughed, but I knew he was dead serious.

The gardens held up to three thousand people. Carbon's New York headquarters had fewer than a hundred employees. The venue appeared to have more staff serving burgers and operating rides than it did guests. The first image I saw as I entered the grounds has been etched into my mind: the children of Carbon employees stepping into teacups, jumping onto swings, having fun, all alone, entire rides operating for the entertainment of a few little ones. I saw happy, shrieking kids blissfully ignorant of their privileges, and wheels and planes and roller coasters—a world—that spun exclusively for them. The whole operation struck me as sad. Kids want to be near other kids. But the space between them—and the public—was too much.

I went on no rides. I hung out with the assistants. Val, the youngest of us, had joined Carbon six months earlier. She wore designer espadrilles, and something about her screamed the bold type. All the assistants, I was learning, covered at least two people. Val welcomed me into her circle with Erin, who, like her, was relatively new; Ethan's assistant, Kelly, was about to go on maternity leave, so Erin was learning the ropes and preparing to take over.

Boone found me. "Let's go meet some people," he said.

Earlier, Boone had taken me around and introduced me to the heads of each department. Now I was to meet Boone's family and friends and anyone else from work I hadn't already met. Boone ambled as though he had all the time in the world. In the moments between intros he said not a single word to me. I was accustomed to people speeding to fill silences. He slowed to observe. I did too. I observed clusters of people in the same groupings they had been in at work, with no cross-pollination. I observed white people, each person more beautiful and brilliant than the next. Boone's cousin was singled out by the assistants. Who's that? they asked me as they admired her impossible waist in a crop top. She'd been a fashion editor and cofounder of a luxury denim brand, now married to a fund manager who was one of Boone's best friends.

Standing next to Boone, I felt drops of gratitude and something like pride, but mostly I felt blank. When I accepted Carbon's offer, a recruiter (not Peter) with whom I had worked, who knew of this job but did not tell me about it, said to me, "You're no more than a Prada bag Boone wants to show off." He's wrong, I thought as I watched Boone looking at his kids.

At the end of Family Day, Carbon provided chauffeured cars to take each of us wherever we wanted to go. I returned to the office to pick up some reading and found my own way home in a cab. I took off my heels, massaged my twitching toes, and slipped back into flip-flops. Friends had messaged me asking me how my day went, but I had not sent a single text since before work. At 7:36 p.m. I replied to my recruiter. *Peter loooong day,* I wrote. *BUT I F'ing LOVE MY JOB.* I had escaped a suffocating relationship and was now living in a new city with a new job, new life: I was free. I was sure I was going to be with Carbon for the rest of time.

I told Peter I was *born to do this*.

I told a friend from high school, the one who called me Care Bear, *no time to even pee*.

September 4–30

The goalposts moved the next day.

At home, after my first day of work, I had heard my phone chime once around eight or nine p.m. Ever since push notifications were introduced, I had almost always turned them off. I had also kept my phone on silent with no sounds, vibrations, or flashes of light. Hours earlier I had added Boone to my Favorites and dragged him up top—above Mom and Dad and Yuna—and changed the settings so that Boone's contact would bypass everything and ding once for email, twice for text; everyone else was on mute. I went to check my phone. The email was sent to me and Jen and included a photo of his kids at Family Day. How cute! Later in the night I checked my phone again—at Carbon, we were able to directly add our work accounts to the Mail app, which made emails comparable to texts—and saw that Jen had replied-all.

The next morning, Boone and I had a sit. I was ready to tackle

Carbon with my *positive, "can do" attitude* when he, first thing, asked me, "Did you get my email last night?"

"Yes," I said. "Your kids are adorable." I made the same sloped brows and tilted head I make at seals and sloths and corgis.

"Can you reply to all my emails when you see them?"

"Well, I— Yes. I will. I'm sorry. I was going to respond today in person as I didn't want to clog up your inbox."

"I want to know that you read everything I send."

"I thought . . ." The email was after hours, it was on a personal topic, it did not have a question. "Got it. Going forward, I will respond to all your emails instantly."

LATER THAT SAME DAY, I was charged with my least favorite task in the world: interrupting a meeting to pass Boone a note. Elisabeth, I think, had called. "Can this wait an hour?" I'd asked.

"No," she said.

In the cube next to mine sat Lena, who had been on vacation when I came in for my interviews. She and Sloane were the two most senior assistants in tenure. In age, Lena was the most senior of us, and evidently lived with her cat in a two-bed co-op on the Upper West Side. I liked her right away: she held, in her hand, a book of literary true crime, which she would slam shut every time I popped out from behind the monitors I had positioned so I would not have to see her in my peripheral vision. She supported Michael, a PM with responsibilities closest to that of Boone.

"Hey, Lena?" I asked. "How do you pass a note?"

"I take a Post-it"—she picked up a pad—"and I take a marker"—she looked around her desk and seized the nearest pen—"and I write a note like this." She scribbled some words. "Then I fold it in half so others can't see and I walk it over."

"Do you knock?"

"No. You barge in."

I sighed loudly.

"No one likes to do it," she added, "but you just learn to do it."

I took a pen and wrote a note but miscalculated how much space I'd need; the letters smashed into each other like a Scrabble accident. If I could not plan the spacing of a message, how was I going to plan Boone's life? It took me three tries in my neatest handwriting, but I got it. I put my heels back on and walked the corridor from the front office to the external conference rooms. Boone was in Paget, the door to which was made of thick, clear, unetched glass. He saw me from afar. I pushed open the door—someone was in the middle of a sentence and stopped for a few infinite seconds before continuing to speak—circumnavigated the guests, handed Boone the note, which he read but did not acknowledge, and then I fled calmly.

After the meeting adjourned, Boone called me into his office. "Carrie," he said. "So. Your energy."

Oh, God.

"You're too hesitant," he said. "I need you to walk with more confidence and just come in, and then get out, but also be more easygoing, relaxed, and chill." On our walk in Central Park, Boone had asked me to dial down the moxie, telling me to try hard not to be so intimidating; apparently I had overshot it. I asked him to clarify his Möbius strip of a sentence, which he did, although all I heard was that he wanted me to walk like a Victoria's Secret Angel. He wanted me to be like him: breezy. I observed *his* energy: Immovable. No tics. No part of his unconscious would he let manifest in reality. "Most important," he added, "don't be weird."

BOONE WASN'T THE ONLY PERSON giving me instant feedback.

Boone's mother called. I was responsible for Boone's line; I picked up. We chatted for a bit before she told me that I was an aptronym. "Did you know that your last name is so fitting for your personality?" she asked. Later, Boone said, "Anne told me you have the perfect phone voice." I hated my voice. "She said it's strong but soothing."

Boone's father, Cooper, who looked just like Boone, came in for a lunch. Boone asked me to join at the last minute in Paget. He ate; Cooper asked me questions. After I said I was born in China, Cooper asked, "How did you come to America?" I began to explain how my parents were part of the first college classes in China after the Cultural Revolution when Boone, still chewing, stood up and said, "I've heard all this before." He took his lunch and left. I finished my immigrant story, to which Cooper replied, "Wow." We talked about my life, my goals, my hopes, and my dreams. Then he asked, "Are you married?" I saw him peek at my left hand. No, I replied. Without pause he said, "Some guy's gonna be a lucky guy one day."

I had no time to dwell.

Boone and I sat to go over his business contacts, over a hundred of them from an Excel spreadsheet that had clearly been compiled by his former assistant who had been with him for the better part of a decade. We went down the list. I said a name, Boone gave me color on the relationship. Name, "Friend . . . also an investor in Carbon." Name, "Investor . . . but also a good friend." Then I got to Adam Hoffman. As Boone was explaining how Carbon and Helium, the venture capital firm Hoffman founded in the aughts, would invest in the same start-ups, I was busy reading the details—*boone is investor in helium, adam came in, he dates models*—while thinking how Hoffman's Angel girlfriend would pass a note with perfect energy. Boone wrote down five names to add to the spreadsheet, all CEOs of companies in which Carbon had invested.

I spent the rest of the week watching closely and learning from others.

From Boone, I learned not to lie, not even in situations in which he and I would be the only ones who would know. Weeks ago, Erin had said yes to a meeting that Boone had not wanted to take; he knew the guests were about to make an ask. Now it was too late to cancel. Boone went. After the meeting, he told me that if people in this organization reached out again, then I should, without spilling the truth, slow-roll it and provide them with a "legitimate excuse" for why he could not see them. "But do not lie," he said as he stared at me. "Ever."

From Lena, I learned that rules were rules—sometimes. "We're getting Bergdorf's," she said, handing me a menu over our shared cubicle wall. "Want anything?" BG Restaurant was an iconic destination for ladies who lunch. I asked her what she liked to get. "I usually order the Gotham Salad." I glanced at the prices. Is it okay it's over the stipend? I asked. Do we put the overage on our personal card or something? I might have stared at her for a beat too long, wondering how she had time to read her book-club picks at the office; Michael seemed to be just as busy as Boone. Lena waved her hand and said, "Don't worry about it."

MOM ARRIVED OVER THE WEEKEND to help me set up my studio. Between unpacking and assembling the furniture I had ordered from CB2, I kept thinking about Fidelity.

The second time in my life I thought it possible my parents did not view me as a failure was when I was working at the mutual-fund giant in Boston. Mom would call with updates of so-and-so's son or daughter working "in finance" because she had informed what felt like the entire Chinese community of mid-Michigan that I was working "in finance." She seemed proud of me; I felt content, relief. Since I had never told her (or my dad) how much I was making except that my signing bonus was enough to buy a new car, her pride must have come from the fact that I was holding down a job at a company that she and her friends recognized and understood; they talked of 401(k)s, the Contrafund. Then, still on the phone, after sharing some good news (it was always good news) about her friend's kid in finance, she would ask me if I knew this person.

"No, Mom," I'd answer, reminding myself to be patient. "Why would I know this person? Fidelity and Morgan Stanley are huge companies in very different areas of finance."

It took me a long time to get the lay of the land. Much of finance had been designed to obfuscate and complicate to the point of exclusion—of this, I was certain, because of one incident when I was a sophomore in college.

I was interviewing for a summer internship at Citigroup in a sales and trading role and led into a room with dim windows overlooking Midtown. I was given a sheet of paper with some equations on it. This was 2005. A white middle-aged man across the table leaned back in his chair and asked, "What can you tell me about what you see?" I looked down. In a year, I'd be graduating with a math degree, a finance degree, and an econ minor, and yet I could not begin to tell him anything intelligible about the Greek letters and symbols in front of me. "Honestly," I said, feeling dumb and humiliated, "I have no idea." The interview did not go well for me, but things went worse for Citi. The man explained that the equations were variations on one of their main lines of business: collateralized debt obligations. In particular: mortgage-backed securities. I failed to decipher what Steve Carell's character in *The Big Short* would describe as "dog shit wrapped in cat shit" after the proliferation of CDOs became a primary cause of the 2008 global financial meltdown. Citi would become insolvent and need a government bailout.

I was determined not to let this experience ruin my goal of working in finance—specifically, quant finance: I was obsessed with the controlling of chaos. With order, logic, form, structure, reason, rationality, and sense. I believed if I tried hard enough I could discover a pattern within any system, and even if I couldn't explain the why of an event, that I could predict if, or when. By the fall of junior year, I had at least three full-time job offers: one for quant research at a prop trading firm (a firm trading not on behalf of clients but for its own account for profit); one for quant modeling at a large asset manager; and one, maybe, for a generalist role with a quant bent at a hedge fund. I withdrew myself from consideration as soon as I received Fidelity's offer for quant equity research. (The hedge fund would implode within two years.)

Fidelity was by far my first choice. Nicknamed "Fido," it was the world's largest mutual fund company with managed assets then of around $1.2 trillion; the storied place I'd read about in high school when I picked up Peter Lynch's books from the library; the place of canonical financial wisdom, like investing in "things you know about" and finding "tenbaggers" (a stock appreciating ten times or more); and the place where employees might build their careers, spend their lives, and retire fulfilled after helping the rest of America achieve their financial dreams.

That was what I believed, anyway, and not without reason: My first day included an orientation with the rest of the investment associate (post-college) and analyst (post-MBA) class who were hired to do equity research. There were maybe thirty of us: half associates, half analysts; a few women. During one of the sessions, a senior portfolio manager gave us a pep talk about our collective purpose. He retrieved a letter from his pocket and began reading it aloud; it was from someone who'd invested in his fund, thanking him for his good performance over the years that had enabled the letter writer's children to go to college. To make possible the education of future generations—what could be more meaningful than this?

In 2006 Fidelity employed around forty thousand people worldwide, with, as I recall, a couple hundred or so doing investment research and portfolio management. I was on the quant equity research team on the institutional side and the only woman in the group when I joined. The other person who started at the same time and in the same role as me had a bachelor's and master's from MIT. At twenty-six, he was the closest in age to me on my team. My boss, John, also had a master's from MIT and reputedly did not take a single sick day in his sixteen-year tenure. I could barely legally drink when I started, but he gave me immense responsibilities early and fast. The optimizer I built was supposed to take a year; I finished it in six months and moved on to additional projects. I loved my work, my team, my boss. I heard people who had been there a while joke about how I had missed the "good ol' days." But it seemed unlikely to me that John and other members of my team would have participated in the activities to which those days referred: a $160,000 bachelor party, thrown by a few brokers for a star Fidelity trader, aboard a yacht with female escorts, ecstasy pills, and a dwarf-tossing competition. I was glad to have missed this. Soon, though, I began to see how the good old days were very much still here.

One afternoon, after getting lunch at Faneuil Hall Marketplace, I returned to my desk and a coworker—older, white, and married—was waiting for me in my cube. He wanted us to watch a video together about, in his words, "yellow fever." I did not know how to say no. After the ten-minute clip during which he chortled, I thought he would leave, but he stayed. I know John saw, because he walked past us again and again while eyeing my coworker. An hour later, I said I had to get back to work. After he left my desk, I remembered my interview with this same man, who, in the middle of our thirty-minute meeting, asked me, "Are you Chinese?" Um, yes. . . . "My wife's Chinese too." But he wasn't the only one making inappropriate comments. Quant teams frequently have a support staff of programmers and tech specialists to help with data and computer issues. The person John had tasked with helping me learn Java said to me one day, not long after I joined, "You're only here because you're a woman and you're pretty." You're only saying that because you haven't seen my work or résumé, I shot back at him.

The one woman in our group who helped with recruiting and noninvestment tasks had been the assistant to our team before she married a PM at Fido, one of John's best friends. True love— beautiful. Then there were two female associates on the fundamental (as opposed to quant) side who started around the same time as me and whom I was friends with. One told me, reluctantly, yet somehow in a tone betraying her desperation to share the secret, that she had been sleeping with a research analyst eight years her senior. Eventually they would marry; he would be promoted to PM. Was there no other path for women at Fidelity except to marry a male PM? The other female associate had a boyfriend she'd met in college back home in Miami. I also had a boyfriend I'd met in college; he was in Boston. She and I would meet up for cheap eats and talk about growing up in immigrant families and how impossible it seemed to be a female PM with a happy family and kids. She also told me that some men in her cohort, white and barely out of Greek life, talked of sleeping with multiple women on their department's floor.

The institutional arm of Fidelity moved from downtown Boston to the outskirts of Providence, Rhode Island, after the firm had successfully lobbied the state's lawmakers for a tax break benefiting its highest-earning employees. We had an open office. I would go make tea in the kitchen and get back to my computer and there'd be messages: *You look hot today. Nice skirt.* The trading area had a desk lamp. Every time a woman walked by, I was told, someone would adjust the light to face up for hot, down for not. Someone else told me the men talked of the chief investment officer's assistant's "rack." During the holiday party of my last year with the firm, one of the traders came up to me and whispered in my ear, "I'd like to lick your cunt." So far, I had not reported anything. Not because of fear, but because of discipline. I was determined not to let any man distract me from my goals. I did not want to waste more time trying to seek justice for sexual harassment or, from earlier in my life, assault. My biggest fear was not being believed. I wanted to be left alone to do my work well—and I did: year after year I received more than 100 percent of my bonus target for completing more projects than I was assigned—but it was getting harder and harder to maintain focus. I asked a coworker, who was white and male and had never made any unprofessional remarks to me, what I should do about the trader. "Think about his family," he said. "Think about his kids. You don't want to ruin his family, do you?"

(When I told my mom about this in broad strokes and how I was so unhappy at my job, she said, in one of the great shocks of my life, "Quit. Come home. I'll take care of you.")

I had tried to leave Fido before because of its culture. One day, after a year or so at my job, I walked into a recruiter's office—I remember the early sun straining to warm up the dark, wooden room—and he looked at me across the table and said, "You have two strikes against you already: you're a woman, *and* you're Asian." I never saw this recruiter (who himself was of Asian descent) again. Through other avenues, I interviewed at a few places, though nothing panned out. Then, in 2008, the economy collapsed. I stayed put.

Fidelity whittled its workforce. My two associate friends weren't given promotions and had to leave. I was promoted, and a year later promoted again, to a co–portfolio manager, but I was not sure I deserved any of this: workers around the world were losing their jobs, homes, and retirement savings as I watched my base and bonus and profit sharing go up and up and up with, honestly, very little effort on my part—and this felt cosmically *wrong*. I did not feel like I was adding value to the world. I felt insulated from harm, disconnected from humanity. I had to get out. I did not report the sexual harassment because there was, I thought then, no point. The people to whom I would report it—HR and my higher-ups, about whom I had heard rumors of extramarital affairs with people they had either met at or through work—I saw as part of the problem.

I was only three days in at Carbon but could not imagine Boone allowing a culture like that here. I remember specifically thinking that Boone would never cheat on Elisabeth because, one, he loved her so much, he had already mentioned their wedding anniversary months in advance to me, and two, if he did—well, he would *not*. An affair would be so inefficient.

My mother left for the airport before sunrise on Wednesday. I almost cried, which startled me. I was transported to this time of year eleven years ago when I stood on the sidewalk outside my dorm, watching my parents' car get smaller and smaller as they drove down Amherst Alley and left me. This was the moment I had been waiting for my entire life. I waved at them. Dad drove; Mom sat in the passenger seat and did not look back. I could feel silly tears falling out of my eyes. Dad later told me that Mom had cried the whole way back to Michigan starting when she shut the car door. Now I looked around my five-hundred-square-foot studio. Mom waited for my furniture deliveries. She set up my internet. She took out all the trash and the moving boxes and bought me clothes, shoes, a floor mirror. Anything to help me do my job. The one thing Mom and Dad wanted from me was for me to settle down—to *decide* already; Mom would ask me again and again why I couldn't be more like Julie, Tina, Mary, Linda—but this was the very thing I could not give them. I was inching closer, perhaps. At least in career. Which may be why for three days and three nights, neither Mom nor I had raised our voices.

I TEXTED YUNA on Sunday.

> Wanna come visit?
>
> > Yay!! Carrieeeee. Wassap.
> >
> > I would love to go visit. Just need to find a weekend where im not working.
>
> Let's do it!
>
> > I work til like 1am twice this week and Saturdays. I slept all day today . . .
>
> I miss you a lot
>
> > God me too, its been so stressful

I had never lived full-time in New York before and felt lonely. Being an only child had mostly inured me to this feeling, although at times I had wished for a sister. My best friend from college lived eight blocks away, in Times Square. Kristi and I were close because she was incredible; she was kind to me no matter what others whispered about me. We were also close because we were secret die-hard introverts, lugging our bodies to frats and clubs in Boston even though we much preferred to stay in; now she stayed in with her husband, who was going to med school at Columbia. At night, after a long day at Carbon, I would think of Kristi and Yuna, both women of Korean ancestry who had grown up in the Great Lakes Basin. Kristi started out premed, discovered she hated premed, changed to consulting and later big law. Yuna started out nursing, discovered she hated nursing, changed to waiting tables after dropping out of college and searched for signs of what she might want to do next. Yuna and Kristi had chosen their initial paths because, they had said, that was what their parents wanted for them. Whenever they or anyone else asked me why I chose my path, I denied my parents had any influence.

THE ASSISTANTS ORGANIZED a welcome dinner for me at the Mark Hotel on the Upper East Side. We left the office at six. We walked through the hotel lobby, which was tiled like a zebra, and over to the booming restaurant, where we sat down, ten of us, at a round table under a skylight. We ate. We drank. We talked about Botox, about which I could contribute no stories. Whenever there was a lull in the conversation, everyone's eyes seemed to skip back over to Sloane. I thought of my first week of work, when Sloane and her entourage had stopped me in the aisle next to my cube. Smiling, she had said, "So! Tell us! Are you married? Single? In a relationship?" It was unsurprising, then, that Sloane was the person who looked at me midway through dinner, across a white tablecloth sea, and said, "So! Tell us! How do you like Carbon?"

"I love it, I love it, I *love* it." I was explaining what about "it" I was loving so much when my phone, which I had set on the table, face down and on silent mode, went off. I had set my ringtone to be the intro to "Rather Be" by Clean Bandit, a song I had heard over the summer in spin class as I dug deep into my soul and committed to the climb that was Carbon's insane interview process. A violin melody started playing. "I'm so sorry," I said. "I have to take this."

"Boone?" Sloane asked.

I scooched back my chair, nodded, and stood up. Since I was looking at my feet, trying to make sure that I did not trip in my high heels in front of a dining room full of beautiful people, it was not clear to me who made these comments: "Yep, this is your life now!" and "God, you're so skinny." This was the second time someone here had remarked on my weight. The first time I was returning from the kitchen to my desk and an assistant walking toward me saw my outfit and said, "You're such a skinny bitch!" I was wearing a vegan-leather skirt and had been worried whether bare knees were permissible on business-casual Fridays. At this dinner, my tweed skirt would not stay up, even though I had fastened a belt using the innermost notch. I had sensed my body, inside and out, being observed at work, which only made me want to eat (and be) less.

The restaurant noise was deafening, so I hurried to the lobby to answer Boone's call. He was playing golf and wanted me to get him a car back to the city. I called our go-to limo service, requesting a luxury SUV to be dispatched at once. Then I returned to the table. My colleagues ordered rounds and rounds of drinks as I nursed my one glass of champagne. After another couple of hours, we finished, paid, and walked out through the hotel bar, at which point Sloane whispered loudly to someone, "I think that's Big Ang!" I expected one of the others to ask, Who's that? No one did. "Oh, my God!" someone else squealed. I googled *Big Ang* in a yellow cab home.

THE NEXT DAY, during a morning sit, I asked Boone, "Did you get home okay last night?"

"No."

"*No?*"

"The car didn't come."

"*What?* Why didn't you call me? I'm so sor—"

"All good." Boone shrugged. His buddy with whom he'd golfed, also a hedge fund manager, gave him a ride. BOONE IS SO NICE, I thought. SO NICE. He moved on to other items on our to-do list. I watched his mouth move up and down and down and up, but my mind would not budge from my mistake. There was only one Deepdale Golf Club. But maybe there was more than one entrance, and I didn't ask him where he was, although . . . Hmm. He did not specify either. But maybe he did not specify because *he* wanted *me* to get in the habit of asking the right questions. "When in doubt," Boone said, "ask. There are *no* dumb questions."

AT SEVEN P.M. the same day, Val and I left work to go to Soul-Cycle on the Upper West Side (the same location Boone went to but at seven in the morning, when he would ride front row only and only ever with this one instructor known for having super-high energy as she played battle anthems of rock and dance). After pounding in place for forty-five minutes, we stopped by a juice bar, then walked down Broadway en route to our apartments. Between sips of a peanut butter smoothie for her and a watermelon one for me, I asked, "How do you like your boss?"

"Ari's good. He's probably the most, like, not Carbon, you know?"

"What do you mean?"

"He goes out and parties. He comes in late. And, uh . . . he liked some of my photos on Insta at like midnight on a Saturday." She took another sip of her smoothie. I thought of her social media; one recent post was of a new Chanel bag. "They were previous posts too."

"That's inappropriate."

"Honestly?" Val took one more sip. "Your boss is the best."

IT BECAME CLEAR to me that everything was a test. During a sit in late September, Boone said, "I want to do a surf trip." He had been watching Edouard, the strongest tropical storm originating in the Atlantic Ocean since Hurricane Sandy had destroyed much of the Caribbean and eastern United States, but he was disappointed when Edouard lost intensity.

"Got it," I said. "When?"

"That's for you to figure out."

"What's your ideal time?"

"Sometime in the next couple weeks before things get too busy."

"How long?"

"Two nights. At least two full surfing days."

"Where are you thinking?"

"Malibu."

"How many people?"

"Plan for up to eight."

"Minimum number of bedrooms?"

"Let's say six."

"Do you want direct beach access?"

"Yes, definitely. Carbon Beach." Malibu has over twenty miles of coastline along the Pacific Ocean. Carbon Beach, otherwise known as Billionaires' Beach, is a mere mile of it, where Larry Ellison of Oracle had spent an estimated quarter billion dollars on nine homes. Because the houses there are properties of the 1 percent of the 1 percent of the 1 percent, Carbon Beach homeowners have no need or desire to rent out their abodes.

After I spoke to Jen and Maya, who consulted Elisabeth as well as the kids' schedules, I settled on a Friday afternoon to Sunday evening starting in eleven days. I had to check, of course: Airbnb, Vrbo, Villaway—nothing. I checked Zillow's satellite view and counted maybe fifty to sixty houses on Carbon Beach. Slim pickings. Jen gave me the name of a luxury-home rental broker she had used before. I contacted them, as well as a concierge service that Jen and Maya used for the Prescotts' personal needs. Both companies sent me options; none of them were on the right beach, some looked like cozy little cottages up on Cape Cod. I remembered item six of general expectations: *Effective leveraging of external resources.*

I found Max through the *New York Times* and the BBC. I was leveraging Max's service, for which Boone would pay a surcharge, but more important I was leveraging two respected news departments, their brands, their fact-checking; I was under pressure with no time to do proper due diligence. The *Times*, in an article a year after the financial crisis, wrote that Max had rented a villa in Saint-Tropez to the owner of a Russian telecom company for a quarter million euros per month for three months. The BBC, in an article mere months ago (the date of which assured me Max was still operating at world-class levels), reported that he'd often send clients to Calivigny Island, a private islet just south of Grenada. Price tag: over fifty thousand dollars a night. So, I called. Max picked up. He got right to work. He was not able to source one of those fifty-odd mansions, but he did find a modern six-bed on the water, a few beaches over. I told Boone while this house was not on Carbon Beach, it was closer to the spots the local surf expert had recommended. A week after he gave me the assignment, Boone signed the contract.

There were more details: Reservation at Nobu Malibu. Breakfast catering at the house. Different breakfast catering the second morning for variety. Alcohol at the house, on the plane. Chartering a plane. Catering on the plane. Cash, for payment of surf guides and tips. Surfboards. Rental cars. As I went over the final itinerary with Boone, he okayed each line by making a dot or check mark with his pen. When he saw the line for vehicles, he struck through the text.

"Carrie," he said. "No. You think I'm gonna show up to the beach driving a Cadillac Escalade?" He wrote down *truck*, something *low-key*.

One of Boone's refrains was "How you spend your days is how you live your life." How you practiced was how you'd perform in the championship game. There was no task too small. No task too minor so as not to warrant maximum rigor, focus, and care. I treated each task he gave me like an optimization puzzle, by breaking it down into components: Objectives. Decision variables. Constraints. In case I had not assumed correctly what Boone's constraints were and were not, he had told me several times: "Carrie, remember, money can solve nearly everything."

The biggest insult at Carbon was to call someone inefficient, so I solved each task he gave me with a supreme attention to time, not dollars. And, as I solved each task, Boone was himself solving for the answers to a different set of questions: Could my judgment be trusted? Could I be trusted? Did I understand that Boone, as Emma had said, cared about every detail of everything? How much of the world not in my control would I be able to anticipate and control?

ON ONE OF THE LAST days of September, Boone and I sat to review month- and quarter-end items. As he signed reams of paper, he said, without looking up, "Things are going to get busy next month with the two firm events and the raise. I want you involved."

Fourth Quarter

Any second now, the elevator would ding, the doors would open, and Jamie Dimon would step out onto the thirty-sixth floor of the Mandarin Oriental, a five-star hotel where Carbon was hosting a two-day, private event for its portfolio companies: the Carbon Investment Conference. Boone was kicking off the sessions, which he had told me were held every other year so the start-ups in Carbon's portfolio could meet and learn from one another.

I had been contacted by Jamie's security detail earlier in the morning and, minutes ago, finished giving them a walk-through of the area. I had also been in nonstop communication with one of our brokers at J.P. Morgan, a managing director whose job today appeared to be, like mine, a matter of pure tracking: "He's still at home." "He's on his way." "He's downstairs and coming up"—at which point I ran over to the elevators in muted steps, my gray fitted dress restricting my range of motion.

Jamie was the president, CEO, and chairman of the board of JPMorgan Chase, the financial services company extolled by many as the white knight of the 2008 financial crisis. J.P. Morgan was one of our prime brokers, which meant that it acted as a one-stop shop, providing us with a menu of services in support of complex and large-scale trading. Days ago, Boone had tasked me with scripting his and Jamie's fireside chat onstage. I had asked Boone, What theme? "The future of finance." Okay, not broad. What else? "Fintech." He paused for a second and added, "Jamie's doing us a huge favor, so don't be weird." I assured him that I would be normal. I watched hours and hours of Jamie's interviews on YouTube. I read research reports on J.P. Morgan published by others on the sell side. Most important, I called our broker, who had a direct line to those who were a constant presence in Jamie's life. Anything we should know? Mood, et cetera? "He's feeling good," she said. "He's joking around. He doesn't like it when people tiptoe around him and avoid the elephant in the room." Months before, Jamie had revealed his cancer diagnosis. This would be his first extended speaking engagement since undergoing eight weeks of chemotherapy and radiation treatment. The morning after talking to us, he would speak to the public via J.P. Morgan's third-quarter earnings call.

Ding.

Jamie walked out. He looked past me. I said hello, introduced myself, and he continued looking past me. I delivered him to a boardroom, where I passed him off to Boone's partners; next, I shuffled back to the ballroom, grabbed Boone after he gave his opening remarks, handed him the sheets of paper with my notes for his and Jamie's chat, then delivered him to Jamie. I felt like a UPS guy whose packages were rich white men.

As Boone and Jamie made themselves comfortable onstage, I snuck to a seat in the back. The conference was a must-have ticket (one that could not be bought and was nontransferable) for entrepreneurs because it gave them access to a golden faucet of Wall Street capital: Carbon, Argon, and a few related funds. After the first session with Jamie, Ethan, the co-chief of our private equity unit, would introduce the co-CEOs of one of the world's hottest direct-to-consumer brands, whom he would surprise onstage with a calendar featuring their heads photoshopped onto police officers, gymnasts, and superheroes. After that, more panels, more talks, including one on online finance (for which I wrote Boone's introduction) and another with the CEO of the world's largest brewer. All sessions operated under a cone of silence. But irrespective of whatever deals might happen here, it seemed to me like the whole point of the game was to get oneself inside this room.

I wish I remembered more from Jamie's talk, but I don't, probably because I had heard it before. My mind wandered to his address to the Harvard Business School Class of 2009, which I had used as a model for today. Jamie had lectured for forty minutes and sounded wise and sincere and authentic while saying nothing that any person who cared about ethics and morality would ever disagree with. At least five times he said "Do the right thing." "It's not what you say . . . it's actually what you do." "Treat [people] all the same, whether they're clerks or CEOs." (I forgave him for not noticing me earlier.) Jamie said he valued, in order of importance, family, humanity, country, *then* his company. J.P. Morgan—last. I did not, for a second, doubt that he believed he held those values. I believed he believed every syllable he spoke, including what he said about self-deception: "I do it all the time. It's one of my favorite things to do." But there are the values we say we have, and the values we strive to have. There are also the values we believe we have in order to live, not to die of the horror of seeing a stranger in the mirror.

From the hour, I remember only one moment: when Boone asked Jamie, verbatim, a question of mine. Jamie had previously spoken about the idea that everyone has a book about them that's already being written. He had claimed he would not need to talk to you to get to know you; he could talk to your bosses, colleagues, subordinates, friends, teachers, parents, and then be able to craft a fairly accurate story of you. I was curious: If he thought so much could be gleaned from others, what suggestions did he have on how to be the author of your own book?

"I tell people," Jamie said as he gestured with his finger, "that you actually have to *behave* in the way you want the book to be written. If you're going to be a jerk, don't be surprised if someone ends up writing about how you've been a jerk."

THE FINAL EVENT of the conference was Casino Night at the American Museum of Natural History. It was held in the iconic Hall of Ocean Life, where a full-size model of a blue whale dangled over tables of craps, blackjack, roulette, and poker. Votive candles and pink uplighting sparkled. Cobalt lights cast a deep-sea spell across this handsomely dark room, which made all the men look like James

Bond. Carbon had paid celebrity poker players like Jennifer Tilly to come hang. I entered the poker tournament, the grand prize for which, if I recall correctly, was a week's stay at any Aman resort, a chain of ultra-luxurious properties noted for their historical locations: inside a national park on the coast of Vietnam; amid the UNESCO-protected ruins of ancient Greece; at a summer palace where a secret door led you to an imperial garden of the Qing dynasty. I did not make it past the first table. I called someone's all-in with a high pocket pair and was rivered—I made the best decision with the information available to me and lost.

CARBON'S INVESTOR DAY was held the day after the conference. The location moved from a luxury hotel to Jazz at Lincoln Center for a change of scenery (although, technically, it was in the same building). After I got home from Casino Night, I had spent hours foraging for a quote for Boone's presentation the next day.

At the time, Carbon had a stable of public and private equity funds that invested in a variety of companies across the globe. "What they're the best in the world at," said a cofounder of the Michigan-based fund of funds when I had lunch with him before I moved to New York, "is taking a business model that's been proven to work and identifying similar companies in different geographies." Carbon was about to start raising capital for Venture Fund IV.

I needed an ending note to Boone's presentation, a state-of-the-funds address. It had to encapsulate his current sentiment on investing while ringing true but not cheesy, smart but not boastful. He had told me he wanted to say something about time, about how each moment is but one point in time on a specific path of history. Using this and variations on this theme (a moment in time, a spot of time, awareness of a point in time), I searched and searched—Google Books, Goodreads, Genius, IMDb, TED Talks, Wikiquote, and Bartleby.com—and I had found nothing. Mainly because, in addition to the specific idea he had asked me to help him verbalize, the unspoken assumption was that the author of the quote had to be more of a big deal than Boone himself. I'd offered up options, a few of which he did not instantly reject. "And who said that?" he'd ask. I'd say a name. He'd give me a silence and shoot me a stare, and then a ghost of me would duck.

At Investor Day, I met Penelope, Boone's former assistant, the one who everyone from Jay to Lena told me had done everything for the Firm. She wore a jet-black suit with sharp lines. She was an LP in Carbon and, as far as I knew, the only ex-employee in attendance. "I tell everyone," she said to me during a break, "that your job is"—she leaned in, whispering—"the *best* job in New York." I wondered under what circumstances she had left.

I saw someone who'd been in the same year as Josh at the Stanford Graduate School of Business. "Carrie!" he shouted when he checked in. "What're you doing here?"

"I work for Boone!" I shouted back.

"No shit!" He was attending this event with his mother, who was the founder of one of the world's largest marketing agencies. They were a big deal in their home country in Europe, the same country as Boone's mentor, Martin, the founder of Argon.

I saw Martin. Then I saw a man who looked a lot like Martin but decades younger. Then, at 1:22 p.m., I texted Peter: *Just saw Elias*

Cohn. Cohn, whose name was on Boone's spreadsheet of business contacts, was the billionaire founder of another brand-name hedge fund. Peter had placed someone in a position similar to mine with Cohn. But seeing Cohn today gave me pause. From the outside I had perceived Boone and Cohn to be in some sort of competition; they both ran large hedge funds that showed up on best-of lists year after year. It occurred to me then that I had been wrong: Cohn was an investor *in* Carbon's funds; he and Boone were on the same team. The real enemy for hedge fund managers was not Another Hedge Fund.

All the seats in the amphitheater were taken. I asked the event planner for extra chairs and sat in one of them in the back. Boone's presentation was going well, I thought, but there was no way to know how well until the close of the new fund, when all the subscription documents were due. Then we'd have a number—hopefully around the target raise north of a billion—telling us the confidence in our investment abilities and brand. Boone paused at center stage. Behind him was a four-story glass wall overlooking the Columbus Monument, Central Park, and Billionaires' Row. Since I had not been able to find a famous saying to Boone's liking, he had made one up. I aspired toward his sense of self-worth, his belief that his words not only mattered but mattered enough that he was able to quote himself. He breathed, then read, slowly, off the screen: "It is imperative that we be here now, in the present moment, and take note of all that which time—years and years—will make obvious."

THINGS DID GET BUSY. If by *busy* Boone meant *crazy*. It was his habit to outline and let you saturate his statements with color.

Elisabeth had hinted to me that Boone was not great at expressing emotion. "That's why," she had said, "he needs someone like you." She could not have known that I had grown up in a house with emotions as wide-ranging and unpredictable as his were corseted and (more or less) stable. I was always watching and observing, observing and watching, attuned to the smallest signs of yet another winter and when it might thaw. Because of this, I was not terrible at coloring. I felt useful, worthy—I loved it.

But irrespective of how hard I pushed and how disciplined I was with my routines at the office and at home, work was so busy and so crazy that I was becoming a stranger to myself. One Saturday, I fell asleep before eight p.m. and stood up a good friend, the first friend I had made in America when I was five. Another day, I canceled a welcome dinner Jen and Maya had planned for me hours before we were supposed to meet; I was too tired. Most concerningly, though, I was forgoing commitments I had made to myself.

The first item I had packed upon receiving Boone's offer call was the journal Yuna had given me one Christmas. I had told myself I was going to write in my free time after my day job at Carbon. What better, lower-stakes way to start than with a journal? I had kept diaries off and on but stopped sometime toward the end of eighth grade when my mother said something to me that made me suspect she had read them, asking, "Is there something wrong with you?" *Máobìng* was the term she'd used. Instantly I felt guilty for having a *fault, defect, shortcoming.* For having wants and admitting them on the page where I wrote *I'm depressed* and *seriously thinking about running away*; that *I really love mom, but I really REALLY dislike it when she comes home & has a frown on her face* or when she *shouts (gets angry) for no or small reasons*; that *I'm afraid to talk to mom. Afraid at whatever I might say, she might yell back.* I stopped writing. Thirteen years later I started up again after Yuna sent me this present from Goop. Its cover was custom engraved with *cara*—her matching one with *anam; anam cara* means "soul friend" in Irish—and I designated it as the diary for my inmost thoughts. I had only ever made one entry in it. Seven weeks after moving to New York, I had yet to open it. It was true, I had no time. But I also could not bring myself to open it. I could not stand my own voice, on the phone or on the page.

Yuna came to visit the weekend after the two Firm events. She slept on my red sofa, next to the two framed photos I had put up in my studio: Mom and Dad at home, to remind me of the happy, easy, and normal childhood I was certain I had had; and me and Yuna at dinner in Ann Arbor, after we had had the conversation we have yearly around the holidays about how we wished we could stop time.

Saturday morning, as we were lying in silence, scrolling on our phones and recovering from our weeks, I asked Yuna, "Do you want to go to MoMA this afternoon?" Yuna's aunt was an independent curator based in New York City and Seoul, married to a London-born artist who had painted public murals in Covent Garden and Brixton. Yuna would always gush to me about the exhibitions she saw at MoMA. I lived an eight-minute walk away.

"Not really," she said. "I'm too tired."

Yuna spent the afternoon getting her eyelashes done. I went into the office. I had been going into the office every weekend, mostly on Sundays, when I could prepare for the week without interruption.

On occasion, Sloane was there, as were a few analysts. Every other Sunday I would see Felipe, one of the kitchen staff, who, if he happened to be near a phone when I called, would pick up before the end of the first ring. I asked him once how he had come to work at Carbon. "When we moved buildings this year," Felipe said, "Boone asked me if I wanted to go with him. I've been with Martin a long time. But here, I can try something new. Boone is so nice to me, always. So I come in to straighten up. It's easier to make everything look good when no one is around." I had never seen any other kitchen staff members there on the weekends, so I asked him, Does your boss know you come in? "Maybe," he said. "I don't know. I told him once. But it's okay; I just want the office to look nice, how Boone likes it."

Sunday morning, over French toast and eggs, Yuna asked me the question she asks me every time we see each other. "How're your parents, Carrie?"

"They're good," I said. "They were very upset when I broke up with Josh. I told them I was not happy because he tried to control me; they didn't care. My dad was like, 'Who cares about happiness?'" When I'd told my parents back in August that I'd decided to end my relationship and move to New York, they'd screamed at me at the top of their lungs. I did not flinch, did not speak, did not step away from them even though I thought I might get hit in the face. Dad said I was "messing up big-time." Mom said I had "nothing" going for me. She repeated her favorite phrase for whenever I did something she did not like: Nǐ bushì wǒ de nǚér le. They made me send emails to their friends to explain my decision-making. I had no reaction except to make myself hollow. If I did not resist or fight them, then the storm might blow over faster. As I typed an apologia describing my "need to work, a lot," and how I had come to discover Josh wanted something more "traditional" in terms of "homemaking," I shrugged off my mother's go-to line: *You are no longer my daughter.* Being Chinese meant you never dwelled. Instead you leaped forward. My parents appeared to—and expected me to—move on in a matter of minutes, hours, a maximum of a few days. Where there was rupture there was never repair. Only forgetting. "Anyway," I said. "They're great." Neither Yuna nor I expressed any emotion. "How're yours?"

Yuna sighed. "They're fine. They're getting older." Every month Yuna sent money back to her parents. Her dad, who had emigrated from Korea, had been a microbiology researcher at Michigan State University, but he had difficulty adjusting to the immigrant life and later stopped working. Her mom waited tables at a Japanese steakhouse. Yuna lived with her boyfriend, Jason, in the city in which he had a job and drove an hour each way, every day, to *her* job, the one that was allowing her to help pay off his student debt. "It's hard, Carrie. It's so hard. All I do is work, work, work, and I don't know what the fuck I'm doing with my life."

DAILY, IT SEEMED, people pressured Boone to do an interview or be on a panel or speak publicly somewhere. In case his preferences had changed, I once passed an inquiry to him and asked, "Do you want to participate?" To which he replied, "Why would I want to participate in something public when I spend all my time trying to stay private?" It reminded me of a time not long ago when the new iPhone came out, and, as I was handing it to him after IT had finished setting it up, I asked, "Do you want a case with that?" To which he replied, "Why would I want a case with that when the whole point of a phone is for it to be thin?" I guess there *were* dumb questions.

Boone's advice to me was to "stay above the fray." Put your head down, do good work. Don't get caught up in office politics or gossip and you'll be rewarded. He wanted me to reduce the aperture of my consciousness. To be aware was to add risk. Control inputs to control outputs. But, me being me, I had set up Google alerts to monitor our firm as a way to stay tethered to the outside world. "Just don't let it get to you," Boone said when I told him about the alerts.

In November there were two stories of interest.

The first was about how Carbon had sought special tax rulings for some of its international investments by using a hybrid financial instrument designed to be treated as debt in one country and equity in another, allowing it to reduce its tax liabilities.

The second was about how Carbon had made a spate of trades via pseudonymous shell companies (like many other hedge funds), allowing it to avoid certain regulations.

When I read the stories, and the comments, I labeled Carbon's activities as "ingenious, legal, although not in the spirit." Yes, they kissed the line between right and wrong and the laws were morally problematic because the only people able to navigate this legal labyrinth were those with deep pockets. But they did not make these rules. As far as I could tell, they did not lobby for them either. What was wrong with following the rules and trying to gain an edge?

I ARRIVED AT CARBON when fundraising was as easy as showing up. Bridget and Emma would schedule and prep meetings with
existing and potential LPs, then text me exactly when I should send
in Boone for five minutes. Boone said he wanted me involved; there
was nothing for me to do. He asked me to proofread two things. The
first was an investor letter, the drafting of which was one of the
main responsibilities of IR. By the time Boone sent me the draft,
there were no errors, it was perfect. (Save for the two spaces after a
period Boone required of us.) The second was the deck for the new
fund. I cannot remember anything about this except for one time
when Boone and I sat to go over the pages. I flipped through the
printout and stopped on a slide containing past-performance numbers so high—near and over triple-digit percentages, yes, *that* high—
that I fought hard not to drop my jaw while looking at him with
knowing eyes. He looked right back at me and said, "Do not mention those numbers out loud. Ever."

Fund IV ended up with commitments well above the anticipated
amount. It was one of the largest VC funds to close that year. I saw
the result of Carbon's cumulative advantage, the path-dependent nature of its success: Carbon's past returns, that slide on which I had
stopped, allowed it to attract a better network—better talent and
human capital, better advisers and consultants, better founders and
portfolio companies, better VCs with whom to exchange ideas, also
better LPs who were patient with their money and could cut bigger checks—which allowed it, in turn, to generate better returns.
The venture industry would have a banner year: money raised would

total over thirty billion, with 12 percent of it coming from a single firm—ours.

"IT GETS VERY busy at year end," Boone had warned. It was December. "Do as much as you can in advance." So, I tried to do as much as I could in advance, but no matter how fast and efficiently I worked, it was as Boone had said it would be: things always changed at the last second.

Boone moved in tandem with the public markets, which meant that at any time during the week, some market, somewhere, was open. News happens; markets absorb the news; Boone and his colleagues monitor the news, the markets, seeing what's priced in and what's not, revising up or down their best- and worst-case scenarios across multiple time horizons—years out—to determine whether the risk/reward opportunities were getting more or less attractive; then trade accordingly. Carbon felt like an international newsroom stationed inside a think tank. There was no hour we weren't on call. I had learned not to plan too much or far in advance. I would prep materials for a meeting that would get moved, usually postponed, sometimes canceled. By the time the same meeting happened, even if days later, I would have to reread the news, refresh the data, reprint the pages and the models—redo the work. Carbon was known for being aggressive, for having strong convictions and packaging them into concentrated bets. Every day that Boone was in, I would look at him, a person with a stomach of steel, in awe.

When not reacting to Boone reacting to the world, I did my other work. Gabe and I sat maybe once a week or two. He knew how exacting Boone could be and wanted to give me space to ramp up on his boss's work before I got to his. He explained his five-step research process and wanted me to help with steps one and two, only if I had time. He also asked me to keep him apprised of Boone's mood, Boone's thinking, and where Boone wanted Carbon, as a firm, to go. Even though Gabe sat in a cube on the other side of me, mere steps away from Boone, he and Boone spent scarcely half an hour together one-on-one each week. Boone did not chitchat. If you went into Boone's office, you had to deliver news. News that might affect Carbon. As such, the only people in frequent rotation on Boone's calendar were the three other PMs, Jay, and me.

Work could sprout from nothing. Weeks ago, Elisabeth had flown commercial for a mother-daughter trip to London. Boone joined them at the last minute. I was surprised that he had consented to flying first class. On the way back they encountered the great leveler that was the border and for hours they waited in line. "*Never again*," Boone groaned upon his return. "But I need Global Entry just in case." Global Entry is a US government program giving preapproved travelers front-of-line privileges for customs and immigration. To become a Trusted Traveler, you submit an application, pay a hundred dollars, agree to a background check, wait for conditional approval, and, finally, schedule an interview at an enrollment center, often at an airport, where your photograph and fingerprints are taken for official records. The wait for an appointment could be months. Boone could not be burdened to go to the government; he wanted the government to come to him—and to come soon, before the holidays. "I think Maya might have worked on some of this before," he said. "Check with the family office."

Maya gave me a name and number. "Call this guy," she said. I prepared a quick speech on how we were an office of international travelers, how getting Global Entry would mean the world to us by saving us so much time. I did not know how friendly a federal law enforcement agency would be to a hedge fund. (Recently, Boone had to remind me, for the second—though last—time, "Stop saying we're a hedge fund. They have a bad rap these days.")

Answer was: super friendly. I was seconds into pleading my case with Maya's contact when he said, "Sure, we'll come to you." We needed a minimum number of applicants, which I was confident we would clear. Boone and Elisabeth and their kids signed up. I did too. Then Boone asked me to extend the privilege to the rest of Carbon and his family.

When the two officers from US Customs and Border Protection arrived, I put them in Vinson. People came, people went. Dozens of Carbon employees enrolled with no more of a detour to their day than going to the bathroom. I offered the officers lunch; they said no. Boone and Elisabeth might have intended the commercial flight to be a teaching moment for their daughter but it turned out to be one for me. The border moves. For free. All I had to do was ask.

A THURSDAY around lunchtime, at work, on Gchat:

> ME: i'm feeling very odd lately

> YUNA: i don't know if its the weather, sickness, work, or just the end of the year

> YUNA: but ive been feeling very moody

YUNA: then at one point i'm very mellow

ME: if i'm honest

ME: i've been feeling really depressed

ME: then sometimes i'll be okay

ME: then back to being really depressed

YUNA: really? i mean i've been moody, not so much depressed

YUNA: hang in there carrie, your job is pretty intense and when you come home it's like you're by yourself

ME: then i start to think

ME: what's wrong w/me

ME: why am i so weird?

ME: i want TRUE connections w/people

IN MID-DECEMBER I had my year-end review in Boone's office. He looked down at a printout of my self-evaluation and asked, "Gabe's only twenty-five percent? I'm surprised."

The first question of the self-review had asked us to deconstruct our jobs and include an allocation of time and effort by person. I had given Boone 100 percent, Gabe 40. Then I second-guessed myself and lowered Boone down to 75. Boone tried to understand my job, but he had no idea how much went into supporting him because he only ever saw the finished products—like the two Power-Points for an offsite earlier this month wherein he presented one new investment idea and one best practice, both decks of which I made with mere notes and highlights from a messy stack of papers he'd handed me the evening before; or the Firm's holiday card, for which our designer and her letterpress team had to work overtime because he'd requested last-minute changes, all of which I supervised, working those night and weekend hours as well. The work I completed in advance made room for caprice. I sat three feet from him and felt worlds away.

Boone pushed a piece of paper across the table. "You're not supposed to see this," he said. "Jay doesn't want us showing you guys the supervisor-feedback form." Below his scores for me was a scale from 1 to 5 reminding supervisors of Carbon's definition of grades. 3 was bolded and elucidated with *consistently and fully meets the high standards of Carbon*. It did not mean average—3 meant world-class, 3 meant going above and beyond while being *mature, respectful, courteous, positive*. I saw almost all 5s, a few 4s, no 3s. Communication—specifically, speaking up, clearly and succinctly—needed work. On this, though, I felt like a 1; there was so much I wanted to say. But a few times during sits, when Boone asked me a question and I took an extra second or two (never more than two) to contemplate an answer, or when I interrupted myself because I remembered a new piece of information of higher import than whatever I was in the middle of sharing, he'd cut me off and say, "Speak faster."

"I have to shred this," said Boone, taking back the sheet. Next he retrieved a document, which he had typed in Calibri. Boone mentioned one point for positives—*Mostly just being a highly-capable, professional, team-oriented, attentive to detail, upbeat, extremely bright, pleasant person to work with!*—and beelined to the negatives, over a page of *Things to work on.* I took notes. He wanted me to learn the order of things, learn to put the team over the self, the collective over the individual, and, above all, maintain world-class standards. He wanted me to understand his world, go to the *next level on research*, and become more of *a leader through hard work.* One of the top goals for next year was to gain a *deepening knowledge of what we are doing.* He was giving me permission to see—and tasking me with understanding—Carbon's game.

At the end of my review, Boone asked me if I had any feedback for him. I mentioned one item: If he could please be clearer about expectations, then I might be able to do my work even better. I wanted to know what was and was not within the scope of my job.

Boone nodded, then handed me the document from which he had been reading. He had handwritten and underlined CS *feedback* during our chat. Under that, an arrow, traced over with doodles. Beside the arrow, blank space.

DAYS LATER, BOONE AND JAY called me into Paget. My offer letter stated that I would be eligible for a discretionary bonus after one year. I took them at their word and did not expect anything.

Jay pulled a sheet of paper out of a manila folder and slipped it across the table.

"Don't annualize it," Boone said, half a second after I already had; my various bonuses would add up to about 90 percent of my base. "You're doing great. We want to get you on the same cycle as everyone else, so we're giving you a bonus and a raise." My life would be so easy if I could just accept fully and without question whenever people gave me things. I was grateful, so grateful, but also confused, wondering if everyone was on the same cycle, since presumably employees started at different points throughout the year, then why would Carbon have written mere months ago that my bonus eligibility would begin after twelve months?

They were telling me: *Look at how we can change the rules for you.*

THE WEEK OF HOLIDAY parties arrived. Carbon received wine, candy, cookies, chocolates, sake from Nobu, and a Johnnie Walker Blue Label I rescued from the trash after someone had tossed the bottle away. We installed a tree shimmering with silver and blue ornaments. We lit a menorah. The Firm took great care to respect all religions; I remembered a notable absence at the office during the High Holy Days.

Every year, early in the week before Christmas, Martin's investment firm, Argon, held its party at a Cipriani in Midtown. The venue, formerly the headquarters of a bank, was a designated New York City landmark, noted for its old-world opulence in an Italian Romanesque style: soaring columns, cast-metal chandeliers, marble floors inlaid with complex geometrics, and a nave-like ballroom with sixty-five-foot-high ceilings. As I walked into the party I felt like I had stepped onto the set of *Elf*: glittering lights, bouncy castles, a real-life Santa, a flurry of fake snow falling on a garden full of gnomes. All employees under the Argon umbrella and their partners and kids were invited. Hundreds of people. I was there alone.

A crowd trailed Martin wherever he went. He had been deemed

a wizard of Wall Street and a godfather of hedge funds. He was often credited with popularizing the modern hedge fund industry, all because of a profile in a prominent financial magazine detailing Argon's stunning performance out of the gate: forty-some percent compounded annual returns for the first several years, after fees. Toward the end of two decades of great returns was when Boone got his start; years later, Martin would cut a check for Boone to branch out on his own.

What amazed me about Boone's origin story—and what permeated Martin's holiday party—was the importance of family and the apparent ease with which bosses and subordinates socialized like one. I also noticed how Carbon and Argon differed, how we all sought to distinguish ourselves from the generation above: Martin was gregarious; Boone was not. Martin endeavored to expand his work family; Boone did not. I thought of how moving work relations onto the register of kinship, invoking concepts like lineage and fatherhood, normalized the way power and wealth flowed and compounded through patrimonial structures. Moreover: The language of family acted as a subliminal defense against charges of favoritism. Most people consider it natural to favor one's own offspring over those of a stranger. Even Jamie Dimon had said his number one value, above humanity and country and J.P. Morgan, was *family*. But this kind of positive, helpful bias toward a subset of people (as opposed to a negative, harmful bias toward those not in the set) nevertheless results in social hierarchy and tiered societies.

The Martin family was in the business of ensuring its own kind remained the fittest for survival. In case I wasn't sure who was in and who was out, at the start of my job, in addition to the Carbon contact sheet, I was given another sheet listing every leaf of Argon's ancestry tree.

LATER IN THE WEEK, it was Carbon's turn. The location of the Holiday Party changed each year. In the ladies' locker room at the office I slipped into a white silk shell and black velvet trousers. I put on scarlet-red lipstick and walked out in shiny peep-toe booties.

Before we took a party bus to Gramercy, we held an employees-only wrap party in our largest conference room, Everest, which had been transformed into one of Santa's workshops. Several people joked to me that this was not a rap party. Don't expect Jay-Z or Eminem. The benches and counters and center table were piled high with toys for various ages and genders. I had volunteered to purchase thousands of dollars of books on the corporate card. Never before had I been so click-happy, ordering hardcover sets of Harry Potter, Percy Jackson, and the Hunger Games. All of us—front and middle and back offices—drank Veuve Clicquot in glass flutes as we wrapped the books, trikes, Legos, and Monopoly sets with rolls and rolls of paper studded with rainbow lights and festive bears. I could not help but observe other people's wrap jobs. We were efficient, until we were wasteful; we were world-class until we weren't. Without inflation I'd have to give Boone the same grade as I would give his microwaving skills: B.

Ninety minutes later we headed downtown. (Sloane, who had planned this whole evening, had scheduled a crew to clean up the office and truck the toys to charity.) The party was adults only, held at an upscale Italian restaurant trying very hard to be casual. I spent the cocktail hour talking to an analyst who had gotten his job by cold-emailing one of the PMs. At dinner, I sat at a round table with Boone, Elisabeth, Jay, Jay's wife, Mina, and a data analyst who had started the same week as me. Midway through my malfatti with suckling pig and arugula, Boone rose to give a mini-speech I had written for him that afternoon. He had wanted humor, but I had not been at the Firm long enough to be fluent in its brand of comedy. Hours before, Boone and I had sat in his office staring at each other, trying to come up with jokes. I did not know how transgressive he wanted to be, so I let him lead. We agreed on a few bits, one of which I vaguely remember, something about one of the head trader's buttons popping off his too-tight shirts. Boone was in good but not great spirits. Employees who weren't on the investment side were not allowed to invest in the funds—SEC rules, we were told—hence, we did not necessarily have up-to-date information on how the funds were doing. I had asked a friend in accounting about the numbers. "It's looking like the main fund will finish the year in the teens, mid-teens," she said. Isn't that good? I wondered. "Not for Carbon," she answered. "We're used to double that."

Compared to the rest of the hedge fund industry—the asset-weighted return of which would be around 4 percent that year—Carbon's returns were stellar. The main fund would finish up in the mid-to-high teens. The US economy, after a few sluggish years following the Great Recession, began picking up speed: the number of working Americans finally exceeded its precrisis high; the unemployment rate dropped below 6 percent for the first time since 2008; the S&P 500 had fifty-three record closes, finishing the year up 13.7 percent, a number that included dividend reinvestment.

Globally, a Chinese tech company raised $25 billion in the biggest IPO in history; the MSCI World Index, an index of mid- and large-cap companies across twenty-three developed markets, returned 5.5 percent. There were approximately forty new unicorns, or start-ups worth more than $1 billion, and Carbon had invested in an array of them. This year was also the best year on record for US VC exits, liquidity events whereby VCs and their LPs get their invested monies and then some back, usually through an IPO or an acquisition.

But for all the successes in public and private equities, the financial situation for the average American had not been improving. For the past several years, incomes adjusted for inflation rose for only the top 10 percent of earners; for every other group it was flat, or lower. What was beginning to alarm me was not so much Boone's net worth relative to an average American's as much as it was his net worth relative to itself. If the rate at which a billionaire's net worth increased was more than an average person's rate of increase, then inequality would widen and widen until infinity, bound only by his generosity, *his* choices—or a new world order.

THE NEXT DAY, Friday, in the evening, Boone and I were alone in the front office. "Carrie," he called out, then motioned for me to come in. I grabbed a small bag from under my desk. I got up and walked over. I knew that Boone was a gift giver because Erin had received a large green monogrammed Goyard tote for supporting Boone for a few months.

I sat down.

He got right to it. "Don't make a scene," he said as he handed me two large bags. "Open them later. And Merry Christmas."

I took the bags from him and put them next to my chair. I retrieved the little bag on the floor next to me. "I got you something too," I said, passing it to him.

One, two, three seconds went by.

"Open it."

He fiddled with the tissue paper and pulled out a frame.

"You know how you wanted a quote for your Investor Day presentation? And how I couldn't find one?" I paused. "Well . . . I found one." It had taken me six weeks of ambient searching. "It's your concept of an exact point in time—to pay attention to the most important things happening today because they will determine the future." He pulled out one more item from the bag: a DVD. "That's the source. If you have seventy minutes, it's a great watch."

I had asked a friend who loved graphic design to make a print of the quote using Carbon's official Pantone colors. She gave me sixteen options. I ordered a white frame and inserted the cleanest-looking one into it:

> *Of all the inventions of humans,*
> *the computer is going to rank near, if not at,*
> *the top as history unfolds and we look back.*
>
> *And it is the most awesome tool that we've ever invented.*
>
> *I feel incredibly lucky to be at exactly the right place,*
> *in Silicon Valley, at exactly the right time, historically,*
> *where this invention has taken form.*

As you know, when you set a vector off in space . . .
we are still at the beginning of that vector.

Steve Jobs, 1995

When you set a vector off in space, it continues without end. It keeps going and going until some external force compels it to change direction or stop. Boone got up, turned around, and placed the frame on his trophy shelf.

WHEN I GOT HOME that evening, I did not open the presents from Boone right away. I did not have a tree, so I put them on the floor next to some large windows, in the pile of gifts I had already received from work: A Beats Pill XL from Carbon. An engraved Tiffany key chain from Jen. (Nothing from Gabe.) A five-hundred-dollar gift card to Bergdorf's from Michael, Ultimate Ears portable speakers from Neil, also Powerbeats2 from Ethan, I think—but I had lost track.

For weeks I had been getting home from work and collapsing, unable to bring myself to do anything. I would not turn on the lights. I would not eat. I'd sit in the dark and scroll through Seamless for upward of an hour, unable to decide on a cuisine, restaurant, or dish. I could easily decide on Boone's lunch and sometimes dinner and every minor and major aspect of his life: whom to meet and when, what to read or say. One evening, fed up with my inertia, I looked at the Carbon tote sitting next to me on my couch and reached for what was inside. The cookies, each of which weighed more than a third of a pound, were Carbon's corporate gifts to our business partners that year. (There had been boxfuls of leftovers.) I continued reaching and reaching and reaching, and it was after eating four giant cookies—a pound and a half of dense dessert—that a sharp fear of losing control pierced my stomach and thrust its contents toward my throat. I ran to the bathroom. An urge to push two fingers into the soft palate of my mouth came back. I lifted the seat. I looked into the water. The only time I had felt this urge before was one night during my first semester of college. Since then, I had not come close to feeling the urge again, never mind giving in to it. I did not give in now. I got up and brushed my teeth.

For some reason I had been unable to do the most basic tasks for myself. Write. Eat well. Achieve any semblance of self-regulation. I questioned my reality and doubted my doubt, unsure if I felt nothing or something or perhaps everything. Without fail I would end up in the same dumb self-awareness paradox: Suppose I did not know myself. How am I to *know* that I did not know myself? I could not name, much less describe, any of my internal states. But no matter what I called the issue affecting me—a weakness of will or akrasia, a lack of self-control or discipline, or, um, idiocy—I was scared of it. It was new and of unknown origin and in clear revolt against something I did not understand. I was nervous it would unravel my life. With whom lay the *máobìng*: Boone or me? I had agreed to give him five to ten years. I could not—and had not ever—let my life affect my work. And so I cleared the deck: all work, only work; no other goals, including writing, until I could get a handle on this job. I needed to get a handle on the part of myself that knew, after the binge, how intoxicating it felt to let loose and be free.

LATER THAT NIGHT, as I sat on the floor, blinds up, lights off, with ambition shining all around—the pale glow of tall office buildings, the faint neon of giant screens and marquees—I unwrapped the presents. A $2,500 gift certificate to SoulCycle. A large Balenciaga tote. A winter coat from Derek Lam I discovered cost over six thousand dollars when I went to the Madison Avenue store to exchange it for a smaller size. I opened his card last. The words, in his handwriting, were simple, kind, and positive. He believed in me, in my *extraordinary capabilities*.

Carbon was everything I had ever wanted in a job.

It was me. The problem was all me.

PART TWO

You are at work on yourself, though
there is, as yet, no real you;
your wants are themselves
a work in progress.

—AGNES CALLARD,
Aspiration: The Agency of Becoming

First Quarter

Carbon played a different game.

One of the first things I took notice of in the new year was Carbon's crossover status. Most private funds can be classified as a hedge fund, private equity fund, or venture capital fund. Within hedge funds, the strategies varied from long/short equity to macro to event driven, among others. Within equities, funds had historically specialized in either public or private and then, within that divide, perhaps in a few stages of a company's life cycle. Venture funds might focus on early- or late-stage start-ups; public equity funds might focus on stages segmented by market capitalization (as measured by a company's total outstanding shares times its stock price), which very roughly correlates to maturity. Carbon made investments from Series A to pre-IPO; on the public side, from small to mega cap. It deployed capital across the entire life cycle of a company through separate public and private equity vehicles. Wall Street started to categorize funds investing in both public and private equities as crossovers.

Although Boone founded Carbon as a hedge fund, the Firm launched its first PE fund within a few years. But a decade and a series of private equity funds later, Carbon was still trying to shed its reputation as a public equity–first investor. Every few months, Boone would make a trip to the West Coast. During the planning stage of one such trip at the beginning of the year, he said to me, after telling me to be extra-nice to those in the Pacific time zone, "Hedge funds aren't so welcome over there." I asked why; Boone responded with something about being seen as clueless. As the *Wall Street Journal* had reported, venture capitalists viewed hedge funds as "the antichrist of patient, supportive early-stage investing." Start-up founders were "suspicious of money that comes from outside the Valley." Tech was booming again with frothy valuations; the public markets had more recently suffered a crash; the hottest jobs for college graduates and industry veterans alike were increasingly located in the Bay Area rather than in Manhattan. In the war of the moneyed coasts, between Wall Street and Silicon Valley, the latter was pulling ahead.

But the fact that Carbon invested in public and private equities was not unique. What I believe made Carbon sui generis was its investment team and, in particular, how it was organized. Even at crossover funds, many analysts covered their own special universe: a set of companies in a certain sector, at a certain stage or market cap. At Carbon, Ethan was the only PM focused exclusively on venture and he had one person working directly under him. Most everyone else—partners, analysts—covered some mix of public and private companies, from start-ups in stealth mode to large companies in the S&P 500. A good business is a good business, and an IPO did not change that. When the rest of the world was becoming more specialized, Carbon was, in a way, turning more generalist. In doing so, it could better identify themes and synthesize data from disparate networks: it could bring its stock-selection skills and deep industry expertise into the start-up space; it could bring its venture knowledge—of where the disruptions might be—into the hedge fund side. There seemed to be material learning and information spillover between the public and private markets. Plus, one idea might yield returns on the public equity short side *and* the venture capital (long) side by betting on the rise of the disruptors in addition to the fall of the mature players, doubling the return on time.

Another distinguishing note was Carbon's obsession with time. A fair number of people care about maximizing efficiency and increasing their returns on time. It was not believing in these corporate values that made Carbon distinct but, rather, its instantiation of them. I played piano, so the first definition I knew for *cadence* was how a musical phrase resolved itself and provided a sense of conclusion, completion. I was also a runner, so I knew other definitions: rate, rhythm, and the regularity of beats. My piano teacher used to tell me I was absurdly bad at keeping an even tempo; she said I was always rushing. (Which made sense: I had always had the feeling of running out of time.) A decade later, I felt utterly at home working for Boone, whose cadence was not fast but fast*er*. Not velocity but acceleration. Not process but process improvement. Speak faster, do faster, decide faster. During countless sits, after we had completed every item on the agenda, Boone would ask me, "What else?" As in: What else can we do and decide on today? The rhythm of work was a constant drive to shorten the distance to decision. If you can decide on something now, do it. Don't wait.

At the end of each month, there was a scramble to get Boone to sign documents, the most important one being the Carbon redemption form. It was the do-or-die nature of these signatures that taught me everything. I hadn't realized how much Boone was invested in Carbon until half a year in: He had bet the farm. This was, financially, a good thing for him. In terms of optics it was a spectacular thing for him. It aligned his interests with those of Carbon's LPs by showing them how much he believed in himself, so much that he was risking his everything—reputation, livelihood, nearly all of his net worth—on his own funds. Boone held such conviction in Carbon that he lived, in a way, month to month. Boone's life and investing philosophies seemed to revolve around never letting time or money sit idle. If you have it, invest it. Deploy capital fast.

The pinch point for deploying capital fast was whether you could obtain good information quickly enough to reach a conviction that would be strong enough. Speed and quality are, in many cases, inversely related. The faster you move, the more likely you are to break things and make sacrifices in the quality of your product or the depth of your insight. Here, I thought, Carbon was quite clever. Before a meeting, Boone and his colleagues would do as much homework as possible—maybe call around and check on a company's management, its distribution channels, what its customers and

suppliers were saying. This enabled them to get into a ready-set position to ask the best questions so that, after the meeting, whatever
information obtained would be actionable immediately. If you were
a founder, who would you prefer: the investor who shows up knowing everything about you, or the investor to whom you must explain
yourself and prove your worth? Furthermore: Deploying capital in
the venture space gave Carbon access to an even higher quality and
quantity of information, which it could then use to make better decisions on where to invest *next*. Start-ups often shared sensitive information with their investors. Carbon was able to get this, get on
the cap table (a breakdown of a company's ownership), and get
on the inside track for future rounds. Everything was about the assist, the setup, the option, making the decision today that would il-
luminate paths for higher returns *tomorrow*—what Boone called
forward-looking decision-making, what I understood as extreme future orientation. The result, I became convinced, was that Carbon
was able to paint one of the most complete pictures of what was
happening in a given industry at any one point in time.

I began viewing Carbon as a decision factory, the main input of
which was information—specifically, objective, and not subjective.
Boone did not care about hunches, gut feelings, or intuition; he concentrated explicitly on fact-based decision-making. Your output was
as good as your input, which was why Carbon paid an army of people to amass information, and why it focused on getting on the inside, on gaining access to data of all types. Boone invested in a slew
of private funds. He sat on the board of an acclaimed hospital in
the city, co-leading its investment committee, deciding on matters
related to the hospital's portfolios. Carbon also received the best

corporate access, those private meetings between investors and companies. This was an enormous advantage because the CFO of, for example, Microsoft could not spend thirty minutes with every person who had a question for him. Here was a feedback loop: higher quantity and quality of information allowed Carbon to make better, quicker decisions, which allowed it to generate greater, quicker profits, enabling it to spend more and more on information. Asymmetric knowledge is asymmetric power. Carbon wanted to know everything about you while you knew nothing about them.

MLK WEEKEND WAS COMING UP. I had been working so much that when Boone decided to take two rare vacation days while traveling in the Bay Area, he told me to go and relax, forget about work, have fun with my friends. One of my friends had planned a group vacation in the Caribbean; I had booked a flight to join her. Soon, I would turn thirty, and yet I was still trying to convince myself that I was an extrovert, flinging myself into drinking and partying even though I had done that enough times by then to know that I hated it. It had nothing to do with the others involved (who, for the most part, were smart, kind, and interesting) and everything to do with me. I kept getting into situations I reasoned I should want to be in, only to discover days, weeks, months, sometimes years later that I did not want to be in them at all.

At 6:21 a.m. on Thursday I took an Uber to the airport and hopped on a plane to Saint Martin. I touched down on the island and began texting and calling people—from 11:49 a.m. to 9:53 p.m.—for work. I have no memories of being with my friends on day one.

Day two, the rest of the group arrived. The organizer of the trip, Kira, and I had met through another classmate of Josh's at Stanford GSB. She put me in the largest suite with two other women from New York: Lucy, the founder of a jewelry line that had been spotlighted in *New York* magazine and *People StyleWatch*, and Parmita, one of Kira's longtime friends.

In the evening, eighteen of us—nine men, nine women, all in our twenties and thirties and single except for two couples—sat on the veranda, drank, and introduced ourselves. I was finishing up a run and joined the party late. (When I was not texting to confirm whether the *cristal is chilling in ice bucket stand*—for work—I was on the phone again and again, pausing my run, with more of Carbon's vendors, business partners, and staff.) On wrought-iron chairs overlooking the cerulean sea sat a plastic surgeon, a biotech investor, an HBS professor, a private equity investor, and a stem-cell-transplant pediatrician with an MD/PhD, among others. Stanford, Harvard, Penn, Duke. I hated these situations that felt like an elitist season of *Bachelor in Paradise*. I went last, hoping not to go at all, introducing myself as "in finance, also an aspiring writer." I did not mention MIT, Carbon, Fidelity, or that I had dropped out of Penn.

The plastic surgeon was cute in the way Leonardo DiCaprio was cute: an objectively handsome person for whom I could never summon an attraction. As soon as the conversation broke, he came to talk to me. "I found you instantly so intriguing because of your discipline," he said. "You were working out on vacation when everyone else was drinking." Parmita later told me that the surgeon followed me around like a puppy; the surgeon told me, on the beach the next day, that he needed a break from Parmita because the motor on her mouth never stopped running. I, too, noticed how Parmita filled silences as if she were filibustering herself, repeating her points of pride, including how she had gotten a perfect score on the SATs and had been the youngest ever VP at a middle market bank. But the more the surgeon spoke ill of Parmita and the more Parmita spoke nonstop about everything else, the more I found myself feeling for her.

In her self-introduction, Parmita had, like me, said only that she worked "in finance." Later in the night, when we were alone in our bedroom, I asked her, leading with notes of curiosity rather than judgment, "What did you say you do in finance again?"

"I work at Insight," she said. Oh, I work at Carbon, I explained. "So I just say that I work 'in finance,'" she added, looking down as she unpacked her toiletries, "because most people won't know the difference." I wanted to hug her. Maybe it was how she hesitated when naming her company or how she said so few words about her job that I sensed an anxiety in her I understood all too well. How many times had people told her that she could—or should, or ought to—do more? She used to do investment banking at Goldman and J.P. Morgan and, before that, had studied rhetoric at a top university in Chicago. Now she worked in sales, pitching her firm, Insight—an expert network, a company providing access to leading experts from academia and industry on every topic imaginable—to some of the biggest names in the hedge fund world. Carbon was a major client of Insight, one of the market leaders with a network, at the time, of nearly half a million experts. To some, Parmita's transition might have seemed like a step backward because it was moving away from the money, away from buy-side investing, but I saw it as a leap toward doing something closer to what she loved (speaking, socializing) and could absolutely, if she wanted to, be the best in the world at (selling, business development).

On Monday, a market holiday, Parmita and I flew back on the same flight. We shared a cab to Manhattan. Her apartment in the East Village was up first. "Let's do happy hour sometime?" I asked as she stepped out of the car.

"A hundred and ten percent," she said.

IN LATE FEBRUARY, Carbon held its annual Investment Team Retreat. Sloane, who was perennially speed-walking in and out of her cube in front of Neil's office, never sat with Boone unless it was about the retreat. Courtney joined them too.

Sloane's life appeared to be what several of Carbon's assistants aspired to have. They commented on her "massive" wedding ring, her Net-a-Porter deliveries to the office, her cookouts with celebrity chefs in the Cayman Islands, and her loving and devoted husband who worked at a bulge bracket bank. Every time I saw Courtney in Sloane's cube, which was multiple times a day, Boone's words popped into my head. *Stay above the fray.*

Getting Ethan, Boone, Michael, and Neil in the same room for more than a day was like getting the subways in New York to all run on schedule: it happened at most once a year—so the retreat overflowed with team-building activities. Snowmobiling. Dog sledding. Inner-tubing. This year it was held at Amangani in Jackson, Wyoming. To prepare for the outdoor sessions, Sloane and Courtney asked each attendee for their clothing and shoe sizes, then ordered them complete outfits from boots to ski jackets capable of surviving

the most severe conditions. The couple dozen people—all men except three, the two heads of IR and one new hire who was helping
an analyst with data and research—dressed uniformly in the cult
brand Arc'teryx.

If you weren't outside competing physically, you were inside
competing mentally. To prepare for the indoor sessions, each attendee had to make two PowerPoint presentations. These caused
everyone, including Boone (and me, as I made both of his), a lot of
stress. Carbon was preoccupied with tenbaggers. The pressure to
find companies in which you might make ten times your investment
was not unlike the pressure to produce box-office hits: the time
from initial conception to your thesis playing out could take years, if
it played out at all; but in the financial markets there was no memory of past hits—you were as good as your most recent bet.

The prior year's retreat was held at Amangiri in Canyon Point,
Utah. When I saw photos of Carbon at the resort, I felt myself split
into a self who was present and another imaginary self who fled to
one of the four corners of the earth. Josh and I had gotten engaged
at Amangiri. I had no negative memories of the place. No positive
ones either. When my parents saw photos from that evening, they
asked me, "Why do you look so sad?" Josh had proposed with a ring
in a navy box from the same jeweler where Boone had purchased
Elisabeth's latest anniversary ring. When I joined Carbon, I saw, on
Boone's calendar, that Boone had not long ago been to Tiburón, the
golf course attached to a gated community of million-dollar properties in Naples, Florida, where Josh and his parents owned a home
and where I had spent many winter weekends. When I began dating
again, the first person I liked—someone I had met on an app, who

was doing his own start-up in the fine arts space—hung out with many of the same people as Josh did because they had both gone to Harvard for undergrad. He asked me out again; I said I couldn't.

With Boone away at the retreat, I thought I would finally catch up on some of the admin work I had been putting off. Between time-sensitive tasks like "find me Mitt Romney's number" and non-time-sensitive ones like expense reports, I had no choice but to prioritize the former. Jay and other assistants had told me that our two receptionists could provide extra bandwidth and help on an interim basis. These were the rules: as needed, one-offs. The entire investment team plus the heads of each department were out of the office. There were no meetings requiring the receptionists' attention for days. I asked one of them to assist me with Boone's expenses by calling hotels and other vendors and requesting emailed invoices. Not for all of the line items—I planned on doing most of the task myself—but for some. Anything would be a big help. She said sure. Within half an hour my phone rang.

"Hi, Sloane," I said. She never called me. "How's the retreat?"

"Good!"

"That's great—"

"So I heard you asked reception to help you with expense reports."

"Yes. I did."

"Yeah, that's not how we do things around here."

I kept silent.

"We all have to do our own. That means you too."

"Okay, I didn't know. I thought we could ask for help with one-off things."

"It's okay," she replied. "You're new. But now you know."

I did not tell Boone about this call. He had told me that Carbon was a low-politics culture and I had believed him. My performance was judged on how much *I* exemplified Carbon's values, one of which was to "give first." At least two people here did not want to give first, not to me. It was fine. All good. I would do it myself. So I put on headphones and started calling vendors and filing reports month by month, including expenses going back years that I had inherited from Boone's former assistants. At least one month still had Penelope's name attached.

THE FOLLOWING WEEK, on an almost-spring day, with the whole team back in New York, I stepped onto a treadmill. It was early evening. Boone had left. For years I had run for an hour five or six days a week. I had mostly kept up the running at Carbon but in the gym, because it was more convenient than doing a loop around the park. The hour was frequently sewn together from smaller pieces because I'd receive a text or an email to which I had to respond.

Ding.

I looked down.

I was halfway through my run. I was going at a faster pace—an 8.5-minute mile instead of my usual 9.2—and my phone was resting on the ledge, so I did not have to pick it up to see that the email was not time-sensitive. I can't remember what it was about, if it was sent to me or merely one on which I was copied; I let it sit. Then I ruminated over whether I should let it sit, and, after an excruciating several minutes, decided no, I could not. I feared that Boone would say something to me again like he had after my delayed response to his Family Day email with his kids' photo—and yet, then and there, I refused to stop. For months I had been letting work intrude on my life and now felt that for the sake of my sanity I needed to complete this *one* personal goal, to run for *one* whole hour, or else—I'm not sure how long I agonized in debate as I ran, ran, ran, putting one foot ahead of another, until finally I resolved to answer the email while running. I picked up the phone and began typing a reply.

I looked down.

Black.

I felt my chin slam the belt as I was thrown off the end. "I'm fine!" I yelled, before I heard gasps and an "Oh, my God." I calmly checked my body. I was wearing a pair of Carbon-provided Lulu-lemon pants. They were intact; I had hope. As I rolled up my tights from my ankles, all I could think about was not letting my dumb decisions affect my ability to do work. Starting midway up my shin, I saw that my skin was no longer whole. The friction of the rubber, looping at over ten feet per second, burned my epidermis, past the red, outer layers into the glistening white. A streak of burns on each leg from the kneecap down, as if a craggy stone had skipped across the water that was my skin. My palms, my chin—they burned too. My head, hips, back, joints—everywhere I was in pain. Emma from IR and May from accounting were there. So was José from the kitchen staff. He ran to the ice machine and returned with double Ziploc bags carrying relief. He helped me up. I leaned on him. He walked me back to my desk.

A few colleagues told me I should go to the hospital. "I'm fine," I said. But I wasn't. I couldn't walk. Quilts of skin were missing from my knees. I took an Uber home at 6:48 p.m.

The next day I took an Uber back to work at 7:42 a.m. In the late morning I recounted what had happened to me to Boone. "Carrie," he said. "Go to the hospital. *Now.*" He called the assistant to the president of the hospital, who got me in that same day, in the early afternoon, to see a doctor specializing in women's sports medicine. (The doctor was also a team physician to the WNBA's New York Liberty.) Boone told me to tell his driver, Ed, to take me. Elisabeth called to offer support. "Try Boiron arnica and calendula creams," she said. "My friends and I—our kids get bruises all the time. Boiron helps the body heal faster." I did not tell Boone it was maybe his email that had tripped me up. That detail was beside the point. The point was that it was my fault. When would I learn that I couldn't do two things at once? That perhaps I should just stop the tread-mill? And so I cleared the deck, again: I doubled down on work and only work. No more personal goals of any kind.

I ordered Elisabeth's creams. They did not help. For weeks, new skin would grow over the wounds and I would take a step, bend my knee, and tear the scabs right back open.

AT MY YEAR-END REVIEW, Boone had told me I would be re-ceiving quarterly reviews until we were fully in sync. I had my next one in his office in mid-March. I was hitting all of his goals for me. There wasn't much to discuss. "How're your knees?" Boone asked.

"Not great," I said. "To let them heal, I need to not walk. Obvi-ously I can't do that."

"Show me your scars."

I got up, walked around the desk separating us, and stopped a couple of feet in front of him. I stuck out my right leg and hiked up my skirt. He leaned in. I pointed to my right and left knees. After almost two weeks, the wounds were still red, open, and unprotected. Then I felt my spirit leave my body. I saw myself from Boone's point of view: clinical, not sexual. He held a deep curiosity about endurance. Prisons, hockey, heli-skiing, big-wave surfing. Any arena where a loss of focus might spell death. There's this phrase in Mandarin: *chīkǔ*. I grew up in a house where *eat bitterness* was a badge of honor. My parents' ability to *chīkǔ* was what had allowed them to survive coercive rustication—to not let the work-point system of their youth break their spirit, a system in which they were given daily reviews in the form of points for how well they had labored, monitored on output and attitude, and anything less than perfect would mean being docked, they told me, sometimes half a day to a full day's worth of points, points that were then exchanged for poverty wages at the end of a harvest depending on their team's production. My only option, I believed then, was to *chīkǔ*, not complain, and keep on walking.

After inspecting my knees, Boone leaned back, said nothing. He seemed unimpressed.

"To make matters worse," I went on, "I can't work out. So, to keep healthy, I just completed a six-day juice cleanse."

"Really?"

"Yeah."

"Good," he said, cocking his head as if to say, That's all you've got? "Now see if you can do another week."

Boone ended the review with pointers on how to succeed at Carbon. He mentioned Sloane. I took notes. He wanted me *not to over-step* Sloane's boundaries. He also wanted me to be understated and modest but not too much. *Not to get bossed around. Not play politics.*

LATE MORNING. I was rushing again. I was in an Uber on an errand for Boone—one that made me feel like I was in the middle of a heist, carrying more cash than I would ever carry again in my life— when the driver and I hit gridlock in the Fifties going down Park Avenue. I could not tell what the holdup was. Traffic lights turned green, red, green, red. Standstill. I was antsy, dreading the moment that my phone, which had been fused to my palm since the start of my job, would ding with a message telling me my presence was required back at the office.

Suddenly three people stood in front of my Uber in the middle of the street.

A man was holding up a sign: an image of red hedge clippers.

A woman was holding up a placard: *BAD KARMA BAD BE-HAVIOR BAD POLITICS* beneath a photo of someone I had seen at Investor Day.

Another man was holding up a poster naming that investor and his hedge fund.

I realized we must be stopped in front of Elias Cohn's building.

Cohn, as far as I knew, had not done anything illegal. He had a reputation for rankling people since his style of investing was more public than Boone's. I turned my head, and saw about a dozen more demonstrators holding up signs. *CUOMO: NUMBER ONE*

RECIPENT OF HEDGE FUND CASH. NY NEEDS JOBS &
HOUSING. MAKE WALL STREET PAY!

I looked back at the woman. Her face was one not of anger or
hate but of resignation. She appeared tired, and yet here she was.
Something disturbed me about this whole setup. I couldn't then
pinpoint what, but I recognized her kind eyes and stiff upper lip,
which seemed to be saying, *I'm not asking for much. I only want things
to be fair.* I wondered if she saw me, and if she would know that she
was also, in effect, targeting me, because the injustices she and her
fellow travelers were fighting against were perpetuated by not only
Cohn but also Boone.

Then I felt the car start to move (the protesters had stepped
aside), and so I raised my phone. I snapped three photos. I did not
want to forget the world.

An errand that was supposed to take fifteen minutes ended up
taking over twice as long. Down in the streets the city was noisy,
hot, chaotic. Up in the skyscraper our office was silent and cool,
doing business as usual. I can't remember if Boone said something to me (he probably made some comment about how I should
be *in*creasing my efficiency—I felt I was on a leash of efficiency),
but I do remember having this thought: We can, in fact, afford to
slow down.

A FRIDAY AFTERNOON, at work, on Gchat:

> **ME:** JOSH IS STALKING ME
>
> **ME:** he is sending me so many linkedin messages

ME: he sent me one today that was like

ME: "please can we talk"

ME: LEAVE ME THE F ALONE

YUNA: that is the worst and it's freaking annoying

YUNA: we need to get him on a restraining order or something

ME: i've blocked him on phone

ME: gmail

ME: all google (hangouts, etc.)

ME: facebook

ME: and linkedin

ME: all avenues he's tried to msg me

ME: if he continues

ME: i will consider getting a restraining order

REG FD, THE DECADE-PLUS SEC rule, had been designed to even the playing field by weeding out selective disclosure. In reality, though, large institutional players got highly preferential treatment when it came to corporate access. Carbon's employees were able to get on the calendars of CEOs and CFOs of major corporations and ask smart questions, gather insights, and even if they did not receive a straight answer (or any answer) they could observe body language and other nonverbal communications. While it is illegal to trade upon nonpublic information that would materially impact the price of a security if disclosed—the definition of *insider trading*—it is not illegal to discuss general trends, ideas, even strategy.

Boone went to many of these meetings. Recently, he and his consumer staples analyst, Matt, traveled to a town in the Midwest that was the world headquarters of a packaged-food brand. Boone and Matt were set to meet with the company's CEO to do a tour of the facilities.

When Boone traveled, he frequently offered his friends and colleagues a ride. The catch was that you had to arrive at the meetup spot (usually an FBO, or fixed-base operator, the small terminals for private aviation adjacent to the runways) before him because he did not, under any circumstances, wait. For most people the calculus more than made sense because flying private saved hours upon hours: not only were there no security or boarding lines, but a passenger could, in theory, arrive at the FBO one minute before takeoff and leave on time with Boone.

The outbound flight was set for circa seven thirty a.m. out of Teterboro, New Jersey, the closest FBO to Midtown. When Boone and Matt were supposed to be wheels up and eating a breakfast of fruit and eggs and toast, I got a call. "Where's Matt?" Boone asked.

The soft belly of my stomach turned into stone. "Let me find out and call you back."

NetJets is an on-demand private jet company, so details like specific aircraft and FBO can change at the eleventh hour. An airport can have multiple FBOs. Teterboro had five, one of which, Signature Flight Support, had two terminals: East and West. I had updated the calendar invite within the last day or so with new information, a change of meeting location from one Signature FBO to the other so that Matt and his assistant, Sloane, would know precisely where Matt's driver should drop him off. But I had not sent a separate email to Sloane or Matt to alert them to the change. I thought the "Send Update" option in Outlook would suffice.

I called Matt. He picked up a split second into the first ring. He had gotten to the FBO early and was waiting for Boone at the wrong place.

SOMETIME NEAR THE END of March, Boone summoned me into his office.

"Remember that flight with Matt?" he asked.

Oh no. "I am *really* sorry that you had to wait like ten to fifteen minutes." I was being earnest. To be anything else never crossed my mind. "Going forward, I will absolutely send a separate—"

"Did Sloane apologize to you?"

I had to think about it. I shook my head.

"She did not apologize to me either."

I kept silent.

"She did not say one word to me about it."

I tried to imagine a scenario in which, by accident, I missed a piece of information and wasted ten or so minutes of Neil's time; I felt certain I would chase him down in the halls, say sorry, tell him how I had already taken the steps to ensure that it would never happen again. But maybe Sloane never got the email from Outlook. Maybe it went to spam. Maybe there was a glitch with Outlook and it did not actually "Send Update." I clenched my teeth and looked to the side and gave Boone my best *I'm trying not to play politics like you told me to* smile.

Boone looked at me with unmoving eyes and said, "I know what to do."

Second Quarter

The more I worked, the more I felt a burgeoning resistance to overwork and the need to pack my weekends come spring with high-intensity doing nothing. The person I talked to daily and saw at least once a week was Parmita. She spent her days at Insight listening to her clients, mostly large hedge funds in the same league as Carbon. She understood exactly what I needed: to make plans so I would have something to look forward to, but also be able to cancel them at any time, for any reason. I had stopped going into work every weekend, preferring to do my Sunday-evening emails from home, but I had been going in enough—to log all of Boone's meetings into a custom tracking application, to catch up on Boone's expenses so I would no longer be carrying the debt of others—that when Parmita emailed me on St. Patrick's Day at 11:23 a.m. with a surprise ticket in my name to Stockholm for Easter weekend, I thought, *Yes.*

In the Venice of the north, Parmita dragged me to the Moderna Museet. I had cast a vote for "stay in / do nothing" but was outvoted; Parmita had invited another friend, an analyst at a different hedge fund giant, to come. I was glad they made me leave our Airbnb. They were meandering through the exhibitions when I, several rooms ahead of them and trying to complete this viewing with economy, saw something and froze. I had not known I could feel so seen by an oval. A small black oval by what appeared to be the world's finest pen, traced over and over in concentric ovals that lightened gradually but furiously with each inward curve until the ink, unable to escape the pull of the two loci, evaporated into the abyss—and yet something remained: the center was off-white. The artist's pen at any one point in time had an infinite number of choices—a mathematical truth—but what had compelled this artist to choose a point and the next point and the point after that, to form a literal string of choices that coiled into a tapestry so full of sense and order? My gaze swept from the drawing to the handwriting on the left side of the page, small and childlike: "it was the controlling of chaos by one of us."

I zoomed out. The oval was one of fifteen such pages of text and drawing that together, in succession on a wall, made what I understood—for the first time—as the story of my life. A child in an environment that was supposed to be healthy. Woman, man, voices, fighting. Terror. The "terror of perceiving chaos" on the child's face. But the child "did not die" and "did not scream." Did not shatter, splinter, or fall to pieces. The child retrieved a broom from a closet and started cleaning. Moving and doing. Doing and moving. A symbolic act that can take an abundance of forms: painting, sculpting, writing, running, working.

The title of the piece was *Sublimation*. The artist, Louise Bourgeois. An artist whose oeuvre had been, as I'd read before, animated by childhood trauma.

I sped through the rest of the museum and returned to the lobby, wandering outside to wait for Parmita and her friend. A spider, a large sculpture that I had failed to notice on the way in, towered over me.

WHEN I GOT BACK from Europe I knew changes were coming. In Boone-speak, "I know what to do" meant war. I arrived at the office after taking an early flight and missed a few hours when the market was open. Boone told me never to miss a Monday morning at Carbon ever again.

Boone would involve me when he was ready. I did not need to pry; I never pried. From my view into his office I could see that the icy pond in the park was half thawed by March, fully by April. Patches of grass popped up like squirts of lime. My knees had scabbed over. I did not want to disturb the growth of the new skin, so I refrained from working out. That did not stop Boone from gifting me—randomly, because there were no market holidays aside from Good Friday in April—five private lessons at Elisabeth's favorite fitness studio on the Upper West Side. Maybe he had noticed. I *had* gained weight. But I did not think too hard about it, instead shuffling my feelings toward gratitude, thankful that my boss appreciated me. In January, he'd given me a three-thousand-dollar credit at the Ritz-Carlton, Lake Tahoe. In February, for my birthday, he'd given me a five-thousand-dollar shopping spree at Barneys and five private lessons at SLT, a fitness studio its founder had called "Pilates on crack." In contrast, Val's boss, Ari, had not given her anything since she started—not a gift certificate, not an extra cash bonus, not a thank-you card, not even prepared notes for her year-end review (which he kept rescheduling).

As I was waiting for the other shoe to drop, Boone called me into his office. Martin was on his way over for a coffee. "I want you to meet him," Boone said. "But I don't want to make it into a thing." We agreed: sometime during their coffee, I would wander past the kitchen with a real business need, and Boone would wave me in for a drive-by.

I went to the bathroom to freshen up. What I was wearing that day: a white silk blouse with a black trim (and the top button firmly buttoned), a black pencil skirt patterned with blush-pink roses, and a pair of walkable heels with black suede straps. After giving Boone and Martin a good twenty minutes, I left my desk holding a large envelope I needed to drop off at reception. As I turned the corner, I saw the television on the wall. The Masters—golf, a sport that was as much about the control of the mind as it was about the body—playing without sound. I turned my head farther to the right, saw Boone and Martin, then caught Boone's eye and heard a "Carrie!" with such genuine surprise that it made me, for a second, question my everything. He, an architect of the illusion of choice, motioned for me to come in.

They were sitting. I was standing. They did not get up. "I'd like you to meet Martin," Boone said to me, then turned to address his mentor. "Carrie's my new assistant."

I had been aware of Martin since my late teens. The summer after my junior year of high school, I attended a program at MIT for the world's top students in science, technology, engineering, and mathematics, many of whom ended up with Wikipedia pages that included the term *child prodigy*. Around seventy of us spent six weeks conducting original scientific research and attending lectures given by Nobel- and other prizewinning scientists. I was paired with a mentor at what's now known as the MIT Kavli Institute for Astrophysics and Space Research, analyzing data from one of NASA's flagship telescopes for the project "High Energy Spectroscopy of X-ray Bursts using Chandra HETG." One of my goals in life then, as I wrote in my application essay, was to discover a theory of everything.

Shortly after this, I heard that a participant in the program a few years ahead of me—winner of the most prestigious math competitions in high school and in college, who was then at Harvard—was interning at a hedge fund. What was so special about a hedge fund that he—who I had expected to father a new branch of mathematics or at a minimum prove the Riemann hypothesis—would give up his goal of advancing science? This was the early aughts. I googled *hedge funds*. Martin's name was everywhere.

I looked down at Martin, eighty-some years old, and felt in the presence of financial history. "It's so nice to meet you," I said.

"It's so nice to meet you too." Reports of his strong accent were true.

It was my turn. I had nothing to say. I did not want to blather about the weather or golf, so I smiled wider and wider without showing my teeth.

"What's that?" he asked, pointing to my chest.

"Oh?" An envelope, my hands, my blouse, and my breasts, which could not have been asking for attention since I had checked my outfit before I went on this drive-by—there were no loose buttons, no gapes at the bust. "This?" I held out the papers.

"No." He squinted. His finger inched closer, and closer, and almost touched me. "That."

Still no idea what he was referring to.

"Your fingernails."

"Oh!" Of all the things to notice first about me, he pounced on those ten square centimeters. Everything was illuminated; I understood his genius. "I love nail art," I said. "It's a fun little way for creative expression." I looked at my nails, which I had designed and hired a technician to paint: Words. Water. Two tiny turquoise rhinestones. "Here I have a line from a writer whose nonfiction I love." I talked about the writer, mentioned his name, and explained, "His essays remind me to pay attention, to notice more. To keep my eyes and ears and mind open. The world is so rich with stories and information—you just have to know where to look." From the edge of my vision I saw Boone smile in a way I had never before seen. Then I added, "Just like investing."

"David who?" Martin asked.

I enunciated louder. "Foster Wallace."

"Never heard of him."

"CAN YOU GET ME the operating agreement?" Boone asked.

"For—?" I asked in reply.

We were in a sit. I cannot remember the day. Whenever Boone heard a question he thought was dumb, he either did not answer or answered by asking you another question that made you doubt your judgment. But here, I was sure, the stakes were too high for him not to be explicit. He was a member of many LLCs I knew about, probably more of which I had no knowledge. He shot me a look he reserved for questions like *Do you want to talk to the press?* before slowly, reluctantly, parting his lips and telling me what he wanted.

"I NEED YOU to do something important," Boone said to me one morning. He explained. I nodded, then walked back to my desk. My row went Erin, me, Lena, Sloane sitting outside the offices of Ethan, Boone, Michael, Neil. Erin had moved into Kelly's spot while she was on maternity leave. Everything I had to do I had to do without catching the attention of Sloane, whose body sat mere yards from me but whose ears seemed to detect activity multiple states away.

Hey, I typed to Lena on AIM. *Can Michael meet with Boone for lunch today? Off the cal.*

I typed the same to Erin asking about Ethan. The default information protocol at our firm was need-to-know. I did not tell them what was happening; they did not ask.

Sure, they replied.

I'll IM you when and where, I typed. *But around noon.*

There were two conference rooms for those without an office to make private calls. My go-to one, Townsend, was in front of Sloane. I worried that she might be able to read my lips, so I walked over to the other one, Logan, and dialed Nobu, the restaurant a stone's throw away from us where on any given weekday it was more likely than not that at least one Carbon partner was there. I asked to make a reservation for three for somewhere "way in the back" and "at least semiprivate." It was impossible for most people to get reservations, especially for the same day, but we were on a list. Nobu said they would put a table behind a screen.

When the sun was high and bright, Boone walked out and over to the restaurant. Minutes later, I messaged Erin and Lena to send Ethan and Michael down.

An hour went by.

Then a half hour.

It was a day like any other day. Sloane had gone out. Neil was at a lunch somewhere I do not remember. Then Boone came back. Ethan and Michael followed in behind him. I went down and walked up the street to close out the bill and tip an extra few hundred dollars.

DAYS LATER, I pinged Sloane. *Boone wants to know*, I typed, *if Neil is free for lunch today?* I made another reservation at Nobu. Boone and Neil left. An hour or so later they came back. Not right after but within the hour Neil called Sloane into his office. It could have been a normal sit for them. I was not sure; I did not gawk. When she came out, I saw no signs of a buccal flush.

THE CHERRY BLOSSOMS were blooming. Lena and I took a walk around the park at an hour when the orange sun shone only on the tallest trees. She had been supporting Michael long enough that, at the most recent year-end shakeout, when people around me whispered guesses, she was the one person to predict the two partners who would, sure enough, leave in January—but even she could not guess these next departures. I looked up at the clear sky and felt small.

"Something big is happening, right?" Lena asked me.

I continued staring at the sky. "I think so."

"Who do you think it is?"

I had given Boone my word that I would never lie. Back when I still believed in the tooth fairy, my mother found out that my father was actively pursuing other women because some woman in China had written Dad a letter, which Mom discovered by accident. Mom shared details with me, leaned on me, told me to pretend that I knew nothing. I have kept this secret—and my word to her—all this time. But we lived in a small apartment in graduate-student housing and I would hear her yelling through the doors that didn't quite go down to the floor. One night, her wails pierced my dream. I woke up and rushed to the other bedroom. Mom had drunk a bottle of tequila (or maybe it was Moutai). She did not drink; she was allergic. I thought the world was ending. Dad sat next to her on their bed, rubbing her back. I went back to my room and stayed up staring at the moonlight, telling myself I would try extremely hard never to lie.

I let my gaze fall to my feet and said, "I have no idea."

MONDAY MORNING IT made the news: Neil had worked along-side Boone for over a decade; Isaac, another partner, was set to depart as well.

The source for the stories was a letter Boone had written that had gone out that morning to LPs. He had labored over each word. We had had sit after sit in which he would read the letter, point to a word, and ask me, for instance, "What's another word for *integral?*" I would tap the thesaurus app in my brain and offer up suggestions: *Vital? Fundamental? Essential?* "What's another word for *stellar?*" *Outstanding? Exceptional? Astounding?* He shunned all of my synonyms. He worried about the phrasing, the tone. He did not want to seem oleaginous in his appreciation of Neil, nor did he want to seem like he was wounded or hurt or on his way to winding down. He wanted to project confidence, consistency, endurance. He wanted to signal that he was winding *up*. But I received many emails and calls from people asking, "Is everything okay?" "Is Carbon shutting down?" "Is Boone about to retire?" Boone hated these questions.

As a result of Neil's departure, Michael would be the sole head of Carbon's public equity and Ethan the sole head of Carbon's private equity. Boone wanted to simplify operations and get rid of internal conflicts, so he and Michael decided to roll two of the funds into one. It might appear from the outside that Boone would have no official role in managing the Firm's portfolios. To assuage concerns, Boone wrote that he would be closely involved in investment re-search and fund management. This was classic Boone-speak. If you did your homework, you would decode this as Boone asserting how he would not be stepping away. Carbon would now see the depar-tures of four partners in six months. Boone felt like he was asking a lot from his LPs to stay the course (that is, not pull their money) while the Firm reorganized itself.

"This is the right thing to do," Boone said to me before the letter went out. Typically, when you put money in a hedge fund, the fund held your money for a period after your initial investment during which you could not cash out. Carbon's lockup period was long, and, even after the hold, the ongoing redemption rules were byzan-tine. "We're going to let people take their money out." In Boone's eyes, I was certain, I saw a pinch of fear. My mind flashed to Marina Abramović's *Rhythm 0*, a performance-art piece in which she abdi-cated all will and invited the audience to do to her as they wished with seventy-two objects, including a bullet and a gun. The crowd started off gently, then escalated into violence by cutting up her clothes and her neck, drinking her blood, bringing her closer and closer to death. Boone gave his LPs the option to redeem as they wished from the public equity side; to destroy him; to kill Carbon.

And now we would wait.

IN JUNE I wanted to do something special for Boone's birthday. Months ago, days before my thirtieth, I had walked into Boone's of-fice to ask for time off during a busy period, and before I could push the ask out of my mouth, he said, "Whatever you want, the answer is yes."

The gift that Boone would have wanted more than anything was to fast-forward time. Every few days he told me how he could not wait for the Firm's changes to be over—when those who would be leaving had left; when Carbon could regroup, refocus, and reset after knowing the total amount of redemptions. Lacking chrono-kinesis skills, I settled on a surprise guest speaker to boost company morale. I brainstormed with Parmita. This was, in her words, what was *SO in vogue right now amongst the hf set*: meditation speakers, FBI crisis negotiators, *cool* authors like the sociologist who wrote that book on privilege *everyone* was talking about. Parmita offered to have Insight source someone. She passed me off to her colleague who covered our account. I asked him to give me a few names of speakers available to come to our offices on the afternoon of June 18. I had put in this request on a Thursday. By Monday afternoon, an eternity in hedge fund years—time was measured by the split second, something I learned when right-handed Boone refused to sign papers prepared by his accountant with *Sign here* Post-it flags stuck on the left-hand side because inefficiency—I still did not have a list from Insight.

But I was not waiting on them. I had already called the president of one of the world's top speakers' bureaus with a roster that included Michael Lewis and Alex Rodriguez. Within twenty-four hours, Todd had given me a handful of people with whom he had confirmed availability. One was a retired Navy SEAL who had fought the Taliban and written a bestselling book about it. I had also asked Todd to check on a few others. Mike Krzyzewski, who had just coached Duke University's men's basketball team to another national championship, turned us down due to prior commitments. As did Roger Federer, citing his tournament schedule. I stared at the list. No one felt right. Many of the people who had first come to mind, like Bill Belichick, I was told, had already spoken at Carbon. I started over. What did Boone like?

THE SPEAKER DID not say yes at first. He gave us the answer many men give when asked to volunteer family time: "Let me ask my wife."

His name came to me when I was thinking about revealed preferences. As Nobel Prize–winning economist Paul Samuelson wrote: "The individual guinea-pig, by his market behaviour, reveals his preference pattern." Boone loved games. He especially loved people who changed the game on others. He hated waiting for anyone, wasting time, traffic, lines, and crowds. And yet, at least once a week for about half the year, he drove to and from a hamlet on Long Island during evening rush hour to play in a hockey league. (Or, rather, Ed drove him.) Boone had played hockey in prep school. He held rink-side tickets to the New York Rangers that he would use a few times a season. He cringed whenever I said *ice hockey*. He corrected me every single time: "Carrie. Stop saying *ice*. It's just hockey." But what about *field*? I would think.

There was only one possible name.

THE WEEK OF THE SURPRISE, Boone seemed testy. Team Lunch was when analysts, partners, and traders could present and debate the ideas they had been working on. "Why has Neil been going to Team Lunch?" Boone asked me. He noticed and read into everything. I did not think he was always right in how his game would play out, but he was right enough that fate seemed to be doing his bidding. I had wondered what would happen to Sloane. During a recent sit, Boone, sensing a question I had not verbalized, said, "Sloane came to me earlier and resigned."

WITH ONE DAY TO GO, Val whispered to me in the kitchen, "I think Boone is grumpy because he thinks we forgot his birthday!"

ON THE MORNING of the surprise, Boone was in Montreal. He had had enough of NetJets. "Can't someone pick it up for me?" he'd asked. No, I said, I already called Bombardier and they told me you should go pick it up yourself. "Do I have to do the delivery ceremony?" No, I said, but I think it would be a nice gesture and take ten minutes—tops—for you to shake hands with and thank, in person, the mechanics and engineers who literally built your plane.

4:14 P.M.: I HURRIED to the ground floor. Boone's favorite hockey player was with two men in black. I had told Todd to tell the Center's manager that neither of them could sit in on this event because of company policy; they said that they would come back around six. I shook hands with the sports legend; in his other hand, he held a bag. We walked to the elevators and went up.

Boone had gotten back from Montreal around noon. I had scheduled a session for him with his yoga instructor in the gym in the
hour before the surprise so that we could set up in peace. The Center and I arrived in Everest. We stood motionless to soak in the view.
Against the wall of windows, Mylar balloons, each the size of a tod-
dler, spelled *HAPPY BIRTHDAY BRP.* On the main table: party
hats, noisemakers, streamers; at least five kinds of beer; red velvet
cookies stuffed with Nutella, chocolate chip cookies stuffed with
cheesecake, chocolate chip cookies studded with four kinds of Bel-
gian chocolate and French sea salt; Levain cookies, the ones on
which I had once binged; a three-tier cupcake tower, some flavors
studded with chocolate chips; a German chocolate cake, which was
Boone's alleged favorite, although I had never seen him eat cake;
and, the zenith of the table, a three-dimensional layered cake
sculpted in the shape of a hockey puck in the Rangers team colors
with a fondant player in full uniform. On the dry bar: handles of
Tito's and Fireball and Patrón; a bucket of bottles of Cloudy Bay;
another bucket of pink and gold bottles of Veuve Clicquot, all of
which surrounded an ice sculpture of Mount Everest, through which
a vendor had carved two luges for shots.

"Here," said the Center, handing me his bag. "I brought jerseys." I
counted two and knew that they were worth at least a thousand
each. I thanked him and handed him to Michael, who had just come
in. Then I went to get the puck. I had bought an official Rangers
puck and convinced the Center to write a personalized autograph
on it as my birthday present to Boone.

I walked through the kitchen. On the island was an ocean of
Nobu: the dark burgundy of bluefin tuna, the rosy pearl of fresh

yellowtail, the fierce tangerine of king salmon, surrounded by sashi-
mis of yellowtail jalapeño bathed in a yuzu sauce, buttery salmon
topped with a twirl of microgreens, tuna tataki dressed in a soy
and sesame vinaigrette, plus mounds of miso black cod—marinated,
browned, dusted with kataifi and wrapped in butter lettuce—and
also crispy tacos stuffed with king crab and salmon and lobster. All
of these were plated by a Nobu chef who had been hiding in our
secret kitchen, tweezing and sculpting each bite onto nests made
of bamboo. On the side table, more desserts: Tubs of Häagen-Dazs,
which people had told me was Boone's alleged favorite, although I
had never, ever seen him eat ice cream. Pints of Tipsy Scoops. Sprinkles. Fudge. Caramel. Cherries. Dominique Ansel, the progenitor of
cult pastries who had invented the Cronut, had come out with his
next big thing, the Cookie Shot: a chocolate chip cookie shaped like
a shot glass, lined with melt-resistant chocolate so you could pour
the vanilla-bean milk into the cup and chew/sip at the same time.
Ah, *efficiency*.

"Carrie," said Erin as I made my way back to my cube, "Martin's
on his way up." I tucked the jerseys under my desk and ran back to
reception.

4:32 P.M.: I TEXTED Boone's yoga instructor, *Tell him he needs to
go NOW.*

People had piled into Everest. The lights were on; I turned them
off. Through the glass doors of the conference room, I saw Boone in
a white dress shirt, black pants, and a light blue tie, an ensemble he
wore so often that the assistants asked me if Boone owned more

than one outfit. He sauntered over looking down, thinking and deciding, barely turning his head to see what was happening in his office. He almost walked past us before he glanced up and caught
my eye.

He came in.

We yelled, "Surprise!"

The lights turned back on.

Boone's cheeks turned red. He spun to his left and saw the Center and jumped back a foot. I watched the two men shake hands
and thought about the strange distance between you and your he-
roes, as if you were inside one of Zeno's paradoxes, wherein all
motion and change appear as illusions and it seems impossible
for Achilles to catch up with the tortoise, the tortoise with a head
start, until one day, against all logic, he does: Achilles overtakes the
tortoise.

People talked and grabbed beverages. Boone, a Heineken. I asked
him if he wanted the prep sheet I had made of the Center's stats and
accomplishments. He said no, he'd be fine.

The Center, Boone, and Michael sat down on three barstools the
kitchen staff had helped me deposit at the front of the room. The
crowd settled in. The Center began speaking. Not about how to win
(that would be way too elementary) but about how to *keep* on winning. "You need to go out there and play each day," he said, "as if it
were the championship game. There is no such thing as a slump."

The conversation turned to the importance of playing as a team.
The Center was said to have changed the sport of hockey into a true
team game. "When you win the Stanley Cup," he said, "you share
the win."

"So, after you've won a championship," Boone asked, "what was your routine or psychology right after?"

"I went right back out there. We'd celebrate a bit—you know, have dinner, drink out of the Cup." The Center's gaze traveled around the room. "But I was always the first guy back on the ice, in the rink the next day."

The three men spoke about skating to where the puck *is going* and not where the puck *is*, which was a treasured hockey quote of business leaders. "But then," Michael asked, "how do you know *where* the puck is going?"

"Practice. That's all it is. If you practice enough, you can sense things. You know where the open ice will be." Watching the three men interact I could not help but notice the banality of genius. It occurred to me that Carbon did not have any superpowers beyond the boring and total efficiency of the enterprise. People worked like machines, which was to say they made goals, they accomplished them—this was the genius of following through. The genius of training your brain through practice and more practice to encode as much as possible into procedural memory so there would be no deliberations of the "Do I feel like doing this now?" sort; no excuses of the "I'm tired" or "I'm having a bad day" sort. There was will, followed by action. Mean it, do it. There was no such thing as a slump. But I wondered if the genius here could also be the horror: Your brain might not have full control over exactly which parts of your experiences in daily practice to encode. You might, through no conscious fault of your own, encode a lack of moral sensitivity if every second of every day your attention was fixated on self-interest, winning, profits, money, crushing it, killing it, and destroying your competition.

I looked at my watch, then snuck out. I went back to my desk, picked up the jerseys, rejoined the crowd, and wiggled my way bit by bit up to the front. Boone thanked the Center for coming. The crowd thanked Boone for not delaying the imbibing part of the bash, clapping feverishly. I handed the Center his bag and a thick black Sharpie.

"I have a little something for you," said the Center as he turned toward Boone, who smiled. A cause, an effect. I was able to make someone happy; the world made sense.

Boone looked at me. "We'll give away the second one?" he said— I think. I stood a few feet away but could not hear him over the party. He asked again, "We'll raffle off the second one tomorrow?" I nodded as Boone slipped a blue jersey with a red number over his head.

People descended on the ice luge, taking turns kneeling on the carpet and doing shots.

We called out for the Center. We whooped his name. "Do a shot!" we chanted.

The Center stood to the side. His face turned dark pink.

"C'mon!" we continued. "Do a shot!"

"I will do many things," he said, smirking, "but I won't get on my knees."

"Oh, touché!" someone shouted.

"Not even," he added, still smirking, "for my wife."

"Can I get Scarlett Johansson for *my* birthday?" someone else barked at me.

Six o'clock came. I went to find the Center. He was in the kitchen with Boone. They stood by themselves next to the wall of windows, looking in the same direction over the park with the American flag atop a building flapping in the wind. The Center was speaking into Boone's left ear and pointing to something in the distance with his left hand. Boone stood still at first, then began nodding as the Center put his right hand on Boone's right shoulder in a motion that could verily be described as a pat on the back. I walked away, letting them be.

7:47 P.M.: *SO SORRY*, I texted two friends with whom I had made dinner plans that I had just canceled. *I am so sorry*. The Center had left, but Boone was still there, and, if I was at work and not otherwise injured, I never left the office before him. A group of people lingered. Boone wanted pizza. I ordered enough for everyone and gave Boone a whole pie and to my surprise he ate a majority of it. I saw Boone and Sloane talking, sitting alone on a bench against the glass wall. She had tears in her eyes. These were her last days.

Later, after Sloane had gone home, I walked over to Boone. I took her seat on the bench. "You know, Sloane . . ." said Boone, with an openness I recognized as ephemeral as the flower of a night-blooming cereus, "she's sad to be leaving. She thanked me. She said she appreciated how she had a front-row seat to some of the coolest things happening in the world."

I felt an inexplicable swell of tears rise inside of me, a chaos I contained and quelled and would never let crest at work. I thought about recent events—the new plane, the personnel changes, the reassignment of portfolio-management responsibilities—and how they had all cascaded, in a way, at least from my perspective, out of those ten minutes he had spent waiting at an FBO. Change ten minutes, you could change everything. I gathered myself and said, "Of course, Boone. Of course she's sad. She's given so much of herself and her life to Carbon."

Somehow Boone and I got on the topic of dating. I had blocked Josh everywhere, had not shared my work email with him, had not communicated with him since last fall. Days ago, Josh had sent an email to me at work with the subject: "Very Important, Please Read." I read the first sentence—"I forgive you—totally"—and marched over to IT to tell them that I had a stalker and to please block this email along with Josh's many other emails, including the burner from which he had contacted me. If he had guessed my work email, what else would he guess, or do, next? He forgave me for not being a virgin. That was his opening line. I read a bit more of the first of six long paragraphs: "Do I wish you had never slept with anyone else before I met you? Of course, most profoundly. But I hope you can understand that it was only because of my helpless love for you, so beyond any other power, that I wanted you all for myself." To write to me at work, on work servers, at an email address I had never given him and then talk about my sexual history for all of IT and Jay and Boone to potentially see—it was too much. I told Boone about this at our very next sit, assuring him he did not need to worry because my attention was on work and only work. I kept my life organized into neat little compartments: Work. Personal. Past. Present. I did not (and to this day have not) read this email in its entirety.

Boone, as we sat facing each other on the bench, told me to

ignore everything and not file a restraining order because then my laundry would have to be public. He said something about how finding the right partner was likely the most important decision you'll make in your life.

"But how do you know if someone's the right partner?" I asked.

"It takes time—years and years. Talk is cheap. Only with time will someone show you what they're truly made of."

The party wound down. Boone maneuvered around a growing field of dirty plates and torn streamers and pizza crumbs to come find me. "Let's tip the night cleaning crew five hundred each," he said, pulling out his wallet and handing me cash.

11:15 P.M.: I SURVEYED the damage. Bottle caps, filthy napkins, half-eaten cookies everywhere. Boone hadn't eaten dessert. None that I saw. The custom Rangers cake, which had cost more than a thousand dollars: untouched, into the garbage—not a single slice of it was cut. I walked past the center table and, with my index finger, swiped some frosting off a few cupcakes on my way out.

WHEN I GOT TO WORK the next morning the second jersey was missing. Boone had one; I had placed the one we were going to raffle off today underneath my desk. The theft had to have been an inside job. We kept many valuables out in the open. An original Warhol lay lightly wrapped in the consultants' room. Women's designer shoes—Gucci, Givenchy—in the locker room, unlocked. Boone's clothes—Loro Piana coats, suits—in his office, unlocked. Cameras covered every part of the floor except the bathrooms. At least one person on the internal contact sheet wanted to take from, not give to, Carbon. I asked our facilities manager, Luis, what to do. He said he would prefer not to pull the tapes because one of the cleaning people might lose his or her job.

"What do you want to do?" I asked Boone in our morning-after sit. "Do you want to pull the tapes?"

He pressed his hands down in a gesture of closure and said, "Let it be."

Third Quarter

D o you feel the difference?" Boone asked. He inhaled through his nose. We were in a sit in July. More than one person had referred to Neil's departure as a divorce.

"It's quieter," I said. "Less gossipy for sure."

Boone had just gotten back from Sun Valley, where a boutique investment bank with an outsize influence held an annual conference known as the summer camp for billionaires. Carbon had received an invite but only one, like most of the firms there except Amazon, Facebook, and a few others. As part of the regroup, Boone had asked me, weeks earlier, to ensure that the invite would return to him this year. "Ah, yes," I said, peering down at my notepad to jot down this task, "because most of the public photos of us are of Neil at Sun Valley." When I looked back up, I saw a fold of his eyes and crease of his mouth that was new to me. Maybe things were getting to him—all the people who had reached out, asking us if Boone would be okay. Maybe it was the dissonances of change, how all change is a betrayal of the way things were. Or maybe he was anxious only about redemptions. After a pause, he said, "We planted those."

Neil's office had gone to Ari, Sloane's cube to Val. Boone wanted to focus, simplify, and align, which meant that the investments not in Carbon's core areas were mostly unwound. Neil's reports, orphaned, were given new fathers. I felt for one person who had told me how he'd shown up on his first day of work ready to pitch Neil some new ideas, only to have Michael pull him into Vinson, the back-office conference room where no good news was ever delivered, and say, "You work for me now." Sean was in his twenties, an Ivy Leaguer who had grown up in the Midwest. "Everyone here," Sean said to me one day when we were working late, "is so fucking talented." He joined the periodic weekends-at-Carbon crowd of me and Felipe and, soon, one other person who worked for Ethan exclusively on VC. Sean's cube was positioned such that he had a direct line of vision to Gabe, who'd been given an office. "Everyone here," Sean said to me another day, "is a fucking beast. Gabe's monitors are never not on work, not even for a minute at lunch." I mean, I said, Gabe sends me emails at like midnight or five a.m. all the time.

I placed my running shoes inside the one free cubby in our women's locker room.

As for the reset, I worked with Boone to make his presentation for a special Team Lunch, the purpose of which was to remind everyone—and by *everyone* Boone meant the investment staff—of Carbon's culture, values, and long-term direction. "Very few hedge funds make it twenty years," Boone said to me. I nodded, slowly, thinking about reversion to the mean. How nothing exceptional lasts forever. "We have a long road ahead." I guess we *were* a hedge fund.

EVERY RETREAT FEATURED a guest speaker. This year's had been Jim Collins, a legendary management consultant who had written the business classics *Built to Last* and *Good to Great* that had introduced canonical ideas like Confront the Brutal Facts. There was one slide that made it clear to me what Boone and other people were doing at Carbon. A slide that caused me, for the first time, to truly question what I was doing there.

The title of the slide was *Our Firm's Long-Term Goals*. The page was divided into four sections, top to bottom, each a Collins concept. As I worked on this page, I felt transported to my hometown library, which served a population of twenty thousand, a bland brick building sitting across from an athletic club whose claim to fame was that its star member had been the runner-up to Andre Agassi in the '99 US Open. There, starting the summer after sixth grade, I had checked out books like *The HP Way*, lured into the business section by a curiosity about my parents, whom I would overhear talking about stocks and buying on margin; whom I would see, in the mornings when I was a little girl, perusing the stock tables of the *Lansing State Journal*. I began seventh grade with a sudden sense of direction: For an autobiography project, on the cover page, I drew a woman in a suit in front of a desk with the nameplate *CEO Sun*. On the goals page, I wrote *MIT*. Major, *don't know*. But maybe *medicine, computer science, or business*.

After reading *Good to Great* in high school, I remember thinking that another one of my goals in life was to be a Level 5 leader. Those were the leaders who, in Collins's words, built enduring greatness through "a paradoxical mix of personal humility and professional will." They were "more plow horse than show horse." I was living my dream—or, rather, an ersatz version of it. I was not, not yet, a Level 5 leader myself. But Boone was. And Boone, who would never admit that that was how he saw himself, wanted me to embody *his* values, stressing to me over and over again how he saw me as Carbon's number one cultural ambassador.

Now, then: What was this Level 5 leadership for?

The first goal was the Big Hairy Audacious Goal, what Collins describes as a goal that falls "well outside the comfort zone" and is "so clear and compelling it requires little or no explanation." Carbon's BHAG was exceptionally high returns only—for the next fifteen years. There was no talk of brand, no vision about the world, no values-driven mission statement. Nothing about passions, inspirations, or disruptions. Many funds and fund managers will try to differentiate themselves through branding of some kind, and most entrepreneurs say the brand of a VC makes a difference when deciding which fund's capital to accept. But Carbon seemed to believe that money is money is money. It was the models, the numbers, that reigned supreme.

The second goal was the Twenty-Mile March, what Collins calls an ability to "self-impose a rigorous performance mark to hit with great consistency." If the BHAG was the *what*, I thought of this as the *how*. How do you walk across a country? You don't sprint when it's downhill. You don't languish when it's uphill. You keep a steady pace. For Carbon, the march was twofold: world-class investment efforts on a set number of well-selected companies each year alongside continuous improvement of the Firm's culture and processes. The second part was not new. Emma from IR had told me about the dancing goalposts. The first part told me that Carbon was agnostic as to public and private equities as well as stage and geography; the pace was not as many as possible but a certain number, which was quantifiable and well defined; and its timescale was annual, which meant that it could win some and lose some, quarter to quarter, as long as it maintained its yearly pace. Lest anyone think Carbon was not aiming high enough, the term *world-class* reified the aim to be the best in the world and was an adjective applied to *efforts*, not companies, which showed a degree of epistemic humility.

The third goal was Distinctive Impact, what Collins believes is an output of the BHAG and the Twenty-Mile March. What do you want your unique contribution to society to be such that if you and your firm disappeared, people would miss you? For Carbon, this was performance done the right way, with a goal of building an investment platform that everyone aspired to be associated with. Two words stood out. The first was *right*, which moralized and separated Carbon—the good guys—from everybody else. The second was *everyone*. Carbon did not seek to be the end goal for only those in the know; it sought to be the platform that everyone aspired toward. The word *everyone* was important because when you aspire, you inevitably give those who could help you realize your dream some power. As Boone had said to me last month, after I told him I had joined the junior board of a nonprofit, "Carrie, why didn't you go through us? Remember, with our name, you can do anything you want in this city."

So well thought out, so carefully worded, were these three goals.

The final goal was Distinctive Impact with the clarification of Community, as in how we want to contribute to the broader community. This was the moment when Carbon would reveal itself to me, reveal how aware it was of its role in society and whether Boone's directive to "give first" included the giving of himself to the rest of the world. I knew Carbon to be fiscally generous. Every year around the holidays, each investment team member could designate a charity to which Carbon would make a sizable contribution in his or her name. Boone had his own foundation with Elisabeth (as did other PMs with their wives); he also gave personally. He was on the board of the Argon Foundation, which Martin had founded decades ago with the aim of breaking the cycle of poverty. He contributed to the philanthropic endeavors of his friends and peers, and, when he did, it was often at the highest level of support (and anonymous). It surprised me, then, on this slide of long-term goals, that Boone filled in this fourth section with *TBD*.

TBD. The slide turned into a mirror, a visual articulation of the order of things. I saw a reflection of an ethos I had thus far refused to admit existed: make money, do good, but if you only have time for one and not the other, then you will choose money, job, and work over doing any good. To me, the *D* stood for *decided*—as in to be decided *later*—which made me think of the time value of decisions. If every person decided on first things first, then those decisions (on, say, investments) would start accruing and compounding while other decisions (on doing good, making change; on reform, progress, and justice) would be punted until who knows when. But there was a price to the punt—mental, physical, soulful, financial—that would inevitably be paid by those whose decisions were deemed as not enough of a priority.

Working on this slide removed the moral wrappers, the narrative frostings, the sweet addictive stories I had been telling myself about my job, myself, Carbon, and Boone. He did not make the world a better place. Neither did Carbon. Nor I. Whatever greatness he and Carbon had achieved had not come from noble motives. At Fidelity, I could at least comfort myself by saying I was part of an organization that served the average retail investor. At Carbon, we were serving world-class returns to a list of the most prominent billionaires whose names decorated museums, pavilions, plazas, galleries, libraries, gardens, and research centers. Sure, we had university endowments as LPs and the returns Carbon provided would in theory go toward awarding grants and funding scholarships—but that was not why anyone was here.

Carbon's funds had long been oversubscribed. This meant that it could select its LPs and how many shares of its funds to ration out to each. It could choose to accept only the cleanest, classiest money. Carbon was allocating the highest returns on capital to the largest fortunes, but, more than that, it was investing in the change it wanted to see. It did this not only through its portfolios by selecting innovative start-ups but, perhaps more important, through its investors by selecting LPs whose endeavors would reinforce—rather than challenge—its worldview. A view shown thus on this slide: You can be as aggressive an investor as you want and do whatever it takes to achieve the highest returns (goal #1) so long as you give back and

give well (goal #4). People were here because they believed in this
gospel of wealth. Earn a lot first. Give a lot later. But who is to say
that the process of earning won't compromise the person doing the
giving?

AFTER I FINISHED THIS SLIDE, I knew the *TBD* meant an
opportunity—maybe. My one-year work anniversary was coming up.
At my last review in July, days ago, Boone had told me I was hitting
all of his goals for me. He told me to become more of a leader by
being more proactive and offering to do more. I wanted to pitch him
on spearheading Carbon's philanthropic efforts.

So, I dug up the notes from the retreat taken during a session on
Distinctive Impact in Community. I read the twenty-nine crowd-
sourced bullet points. There were no names attached to the bullets,
but the sheer number of them, the depth of thought in them, meant
that people truly cared. They felt a duty to give. For the first time
since I joined the Firm, I saw an acknowledgment of social issues like
education, hunger, and homelessness, with suggestions like making
internet available to more people; providing online courses for kids
in remote areas; meeting with people who are unemployed and
helping them with their résumés; wiping out *poverty*—other than
this word here, nowhere else on these pages was there a recognition
of unequal distribution of assets or anything that might suggest how
hedge funds and private equity, before they gave back, took too
much. But there was a focus on *less privileged* people and *under-
privileged* kids, vague terms for a firm obsessed with precision. Less
privileged by race? Gender? Class? All of the above? I printed these

slides and wrote down notes in thin blue ink next to this fourth Collins concept with the hope of forming, what I was calling in private,
the Carbon Initiative.

I looked down. I read my notes. I saw the four Long-Term Goals
packaged into neat little compartments—BHAG, Twenty-Mile March,
Distinctive Impact, Distinctive Impact in Community—and it was
too late. A thought trespassed into my mind. At once I understood
something upon which my salary depended on my *not* understanding: many of the social challenges mentioned in the notes for the
fourth section would be easier to solve if the first section on making billions and giving those high returns to the already wealthy
and privileged, thereby perpetuating inequality—that is, if Carbon
itself—did not exist.

I recalled a sit at the end of one of my first weeks on the job.
Boone said with pride, "We were just examined by the SEC and
came out clean. No violations." He waited for me to have an appropriate reaction. I did not, I was new; also, should this not be the base
case? He went on: "Do you know how hard that is? We had *zero* violations. Only two small warnings." What were the warnings? I asked.
"I forgot to list two things on my conflicts-of-interest disclosure
form." There it was: Carbon was the best version of a hedge/venture/
crossover fund within the global financial system. It was not perfect, but it was the epitome of performance done the right way.

BACK IN MAY, the morning after the letter had gone out to LPs
informing them of Neil's and Isaac's departures, Boone and I were
in a sit. "Carrie," he had said. "Do you know much schadenfreude

there is toward me?" His job was hard, so hard. For him, I had respect to spare.

Two months later, near the end of July, Boone gave his presentation at the special Team Lunch. We had an answer to the problem of redemption. Boone told me not only did investors not want to take money out, many asked to put more money in.

IN AUGUST, BOONE chartered a yacht and went somewhere far away with Elisabeth and their friends and family for a week. That was when I could take a week off too. I had planned to go on my first solo vacation, but Parmita and I had become rather close. We supported each other through all sorts of self-improvement projects, from changing careers (she had been interviewing to move on from her job for as long as I had known her) to losing weight (she'd eat only broth and oysters on certain days of the week; I had recently gone to an Eastern medicine wellness clinic for a crash diet) to perfecting our skin-care routines (she'd administer blue-light therapy to herself at home; I'd apply steroid creams and hydroquinone and avoid the sun). Neither of us wanted to date. Especially not me. But then she'd give me tough love. *We HAVE TO GET MARRIED*, she said on Gchat while reminding me how no guy was going to want to date me if I put MIT and Carbon on my profile. *How the F DO WE GET OURSELVES MARRIED.*

We headed to Europe to regroup, refocus, reset, and rebalance our *qi*.

We spent a couple of nights in Vienna before taking a plane, train, and bus to a wellness hotel in Adelboden, Switzerland. We checked in and received a surprise at the front desk: two tasting menus would be comped during our stay. We got to our room and found another surprise: an arrangement of white lilies, red roses, twigs, and leaves in a shiny black vase beside a note thanking me for all my hard work, signed Boone and Elisabeth.

Parmita and I were in the Alps. We spent our days apart and met up at night for dinners neither of us was in the mood to eat. My crash diet, for which I had paid nine hundred dollars at the wellness clinic, had ended on the day our vacation had started. I had gone on this diet because one day in July I stepped onto the scale and found that I had gained twenty-four pounds since the start of Carbon. The change worried me—mainly because I had to buy new clothes and did not have the time or headspace to coordinate separates for an updated wardrobe—but I was most surprised to discover that I had an appetite. For much of my twenties, I could eat a chip or a fry or a spoonful of ice cream and without any effort stop at one.

My first-ever binge was on those monster Levain cookies. Since then I had not come close to having another episode. But I did notice a hunger. My hunger. I ate and ate, more and more, though I tried to swat away the cravings I had once killed with such ease. After weighing myself that day, I immediately googled the most intense weight-loss plan in the city. The clinic gave me a choice of a ten-day, two-week, or four-week program. I opted for the middle one, spurred by Boone's casual comment months ago that I should "do another week." A comment that I had known was over the line, but I had told myself he was just trying to help me optimize my health. By the start of vacation, after four days of breakfast, lunch, and no dinner, then a six-day fast, then another four days of

breakfast, lunch, and no dinner, I had lost twelve pounds. I felt extreme mental clarity—I felt on top of the world, high on control.

The hotel was known for its spa, which had indoor and outdoor
heated pools as well as a Finnish sauna, a steam bath, and a rain
shower, all of which Parmita and I avoided because we loathed our
bodies in swimsuits. On our last night at the resort, we sat down at
the restaurant to have the tasting menu. "I don't want to eat that
much food," Parmita said. "Can I just get broth?"

"Get whatever you want," I said, eyeing an entrée of freshwater
fish from a Swiss lake. "It's on Boone anyway."

"Seriously. You have, like, *the* best boss. You have the coolest job
in the world."

"I know." I looked up from the menu and past the glass doors,
over to the green mountains, wondering if I would not be happier
living in a chalet. "I love my job so much."

Two weekends after getting back from Europe, Parmita and
I left the city again to go to WeWork Summer Camp. We liked to
cram our schedules after work with events requiring prepayment—
Glamsquad, Soul Survivor, LIVE from the NYPL—so that any sunk
costs would require us to go out when we would much rather cancel, stay in, sleep. We went to these events to keep busy, to avoid
realizing things we weren't ready to realize yet. So we each bought
a $550 ticket to leave on a bus at seven a.m. for the Adirondacks. I
regretted this decision the second we stepped onto the party loco-
motive. I continued regretting it after we arrived at Girls Camp,
where I saw a far too high ratio of bunk beds to toilets and showers.

WeWork billed itself as a hot tech company, one that a firm like Carbon would surely invest in. But I found only mess and disorganization. Events did not start on time, the wi-fi barely worked, the Korilla food truck promptly ran out of food. I remember thinking that Boone would never invest in WeWork. He was unmoved by temptation, manias, fads; pinned behind his monitor was a quote from Steve Jobs: "I'm actually as proud of many of the things we haven't done as the things we have done." Parmita and I studied the weekend's itinerary. We were unimpressed by the offerings. We decided to forgo all events.

But around eight the next morning I pulled Parmita out of bed after I decided I wanted to make it to one event. Eleven of us stood on the banks of a lake: four women, seven men, including a professional wingman known as the real-life Hitch. I looked at the spirited WeWork lady who was telling us, "This is your tribe—you're the Inspired Tribe!" The rest of the camp attendees were asleep. For the icebreaker we went around in a circle introducing ourselves, saying why we were looking for inspiration. Most people mentioned career ambivalence. I glanced to my left, wondering what Parmita would say. She had started the summer with three job prospects but, despite making it to the final rounds, did not get any offers. I had been receiving messages like *my friends aren't even going to be friends with me soon* and *I'll be the charity case* and *I have a middle class job that barely pays my bills and is like embarrassing.* (She was making, she had told me, over three hundred thousand.) I was pulled from my reverie when the person to my right, a tall Asian man who said for work he was helping modernize his family's real estate company, shared this about himself: "I have no idea what my passion is, but

I'm here this morning to find it." I looked at Parmita and battled an urge to roll my eyes, thinking that you don't find your passion like you do your socks. But then I wondered if he was, in fact, phenomenally wise to know just how much he did not know himself. I went next.

"I'm Carrie," I said. "I'm here because I'm always looking for inspiration. Also, I *love* my job. I'm living my best life right now."

In late August I met up with Jen.

For our first hang outside of work the previous fall, Jen and I had gone to hot yoga (so fitting a suggestion from the woman who ran the Prescotts' personal life), after which we got brunch and bonded over a dislike of social media. Jen told me she had once worked for one of the most powerful women in tech in a similar capacity as she did now for Boone. She also told me she had never had a Facebook account. I remembered going to an event in Brookline, Massachusetts, when *Lean In* was published. I was dating Josh then while trying to forge my own path, feeling judged by those around me for leaning out. Nearly all of my life I had been labeled an overachiever; two years after walking off the b-school track, I perceived people labeling me an underachiever. I also remembered thinking about the book's critics, about what it would take to work like her, wondering what kinds of hidden help Sandberg and other top female executives were receiving. As I got to know Jen, I knew the answer.

Jen had graduated from an elite university. Not only was she book-smart—she remembered every minute detail I had ever told her, including those not germane to our work—but she was insanely people-smart. One of the first questions she asked me when we sat down to brunch was "How are you getting along with Sloane?" She never pushed, only observed, and asked me question after question while listening with the heartfelt thrill of a perfect first date. She was the only person at Carbon who never, not once, made me feel like I was wasting my potential. She was also the only person who knew the full extent and intensity of my job.

It was summer in the city. Jen and I decided to take a walk after work. As we circled the reservoir in the park, I reflected on a year in my job and, for the first time, took the risk of sharing a thought with someone from work, about work, that was not 100 percent positive.

"The volume is maybe too much," I said. "I feel maybe burned out."

"I don't know how you do it," Jen said. "When he goes sixty, you go sixty. When he goes a hundred, you go a hundred." Jen had used this car metaphor before to describe my and Boone's working relationship. She had repeatedly made it known that I was doing much more in scope than previous assistants. But to match Boone step for step—to work like him—what were the costs to me? I did not have a staffer to pack my suitcases or to sort and clean and hang up my wardrobes. I did not have a runner to deliver my gloves to the office when I forgot them so I could later text as I walked home because I wanted fresh air (while my driver stood by in front of the building, should I change my mind). "Are you able to handle your workload for Gabe?"

Imploding with shame, I confessed, "No." Gabe had gotten the okay to hire someone to help him, but he was so busy he did not have time to complete the recruiting process. He had asked me to pitch in more and more, and I did, volunteering my time because I found doing deep dives on enterprise software names much more stimulating than filing expenses. I explained to Jen that Gabe's calendar was just as busy as Boone's; no one's calendar had any slack. Boone, Gabe, the three other PMs—they were all the hardest-working people I knew. "Plus, Gabe's so understanding that I just end up feeling awful," I said. "He's always coming in second; that's not fair to him. But managing Boone's life is already *more* than one full-time job." I breathed, slowly, in and out. "Boone is so nice. Honestly, I like him so much. But I think . . ."

The name of the game at Carbon, at least with Boone, was modesty, downplaying, understatement. Acting like a start-up when you're the clear incumbent because concealing your position—being underestimated—lets you have a much bigger playbook. I had been trying to calibrate my philosophy to fully match Boone's, which seemed eminently reasonable and empirically so successful, but lately I could not shake the feeling that I had been taken advantage of. For instance: Boone once told me to ask IT to do a task, and, when I asked the staff, they said no. I asked if they could please try to figure it out. They quoted me a time frame of over a day and a price tag of over three thousand dollars for new software they would have to download. I said nothing to IT (or to Boone). I thanked them for their time, hung up, and did the task myself in about a minute using a free app on my phone. It was not about this one minute I had spent doing someone else's work; it was that this was a pattern occurring day after day. Boone could underplay himself and remain highly effective because everyone knew that he was the founder of Carbon. When I—a woman, an Asian American immigrant, an employee and not an owner—underplayed myself, I sensed people viewing me as a pushover.

I did not share any of this with Jen. I went on: "I love working with Boone. I don't need credit, I don't need power; I just need someone to recognize the work behind the work and notice when it might be too much."

"Carrie," Jen said. "You are doing *way* too much. Talk to Boone. You should offload some responsibility. At a minimum, you should not support Gabe. Other people like Boone have a *team* of assistants. You are just one person, *and* you split your time."

"I'm sure it'll be better the second year," I said. "I'll be fine."

BOONE SPENT THE TWO WEEKS before Labor Day at his house in the Hamptons. As a thank-you for planning his surprise birthday celebration at work, he had given me a three-night vacation to the Surf Lodge, the sceniest hotel in Montauk, along with private surf and yoga lessons for two. I had never been to the end of the world. I invited Yuna to join me.

Yuna and I picked up a rental car around noon on the Monday of the last week of summer. I sensed a chill between us. She sat in the passenger seat and did not initiate any conversations or ask me any questions. I talked; sometimes she gave me a "Wow" or a "Cool."

Our early lives were similar: we were born in Asia; we were only children; we grew up in the Midwest and lived in cramped apartments when most of our classmates lived in houses with yards. Then our lives branched apart. She had never gone back to college. She had bootstrapped herself and did not think it was worth it anymore;

she wanted to make money. I left MIT without paying a dime. Through scholarships and my parents covering the rest, I started my first job after college with zero debt. I would often look at Yuna and think not about how I could be her but that I was her: I attributed the majority of the differences in our lives to luck, my luck of financial security, made possible not by my own hard work but by immense gifts from my parents and other favors from God. I would look at Yuna and see the precarity of the American dream.

An hour passed. "Carrie," Yuna said, "do you mind if I smoke?" I said I would prefer it if she did not, citing my previous pneumonias. Yuna had smoked on and off and was always trying to quit. She had lost considerable weight since I had last seen her. I stopped our drive around the midpoint, at a nature reserve; I wanted to stretch my legs, but mostly I wanted to give her a break. The second we got out of the car, she pulled out a cigarette. "Carrie," she said as we stepped onto a trail, "I don't want you to have to breathe smoke, so I'm going to keep away from you, okay?"

Hours later, we arrived at the Surf Lodge and checked into our suite. Yuna dropped her bag next to one of the two queen beds. She smiled at me, walked out to the deck, and nestled herself into a yellow chair. She took out a cigarette and her phone, began scrolling and smoking, occasionally looking up and out over the rippled pond reflecting the hazy afternoon sun.

At eight the next morning we drove to the beach. Neither of us had surfed before. We changed into wet suits and waded into the ocean. Our instructor led us to an area away from most people in case we lost control of our boards and bodies. When the instructor yelled "Go!" we would swim to catch a break, jump onto our boards, and try to land on our two feet. Our instructor had told us that standing up in any way would be considered a success. Yuna and I each managed to pop up once or twice. After that, we called it, short of our full lesson time. I could feel the distant pain hurtling toward me, about to set in. At some point while trying to make my way back to land, I had no more energy to swim half against the current. I was tired, worn, I let the waves wash over me. "Carrie!" the instructor yelled. "Come back now! You're going to crash into the rocks!" And then I did, I crashed. It hurt like a million tiny punches. I tried to rise up, leaning on the slippery stones for balance. I made it back. "That was dangerous," said the instructor, running over to help me out of the water. I was not aware of the danger, nor had I been warned of it before I got in, but now that I had crashed, the experience was not so bad. My legs and arms and torso were beginning to wobble, but I was able to stand up.

At eight on the second morning we took a yoga lesson in our room. The teacher who came to our suite was tall, tan, thin, and blond with perfectly tousled windblown hair. When I told her we were at the Surf Lodge courtesy of a gift from my boss, she asked who. I said Boone. "I know Carbon." She placed her mat on the floor. Of course the gorgeous sylphic yogi in Montauk would be best friends with the wife of a former partner at Carbon. Yuna and I told her we couldn't move. The three of us stretched (lightly) for an hour.

The third and final morning, Yuna and I woke up at seven thirty to get dressed for our second surf lesson. As we were about to leave, I looked at her, moving like a slow loris. Then I looked at myself, unable to raise my arms. "Yuna?" I asked. "Do you want to surf?"

"Do *you* want to surf?"

"I'll go if you want to go."

"I'm fine either way."

"Let's cancel."

"Okay." She laughed, the first genuine emotion I'd seen from her all week. "Thank God!"

A couple of hours later, we packed up, checked out of the Lodge, and headed back to the city. As I drove I could not hold it in any longer. "Yuna," I said. "What's wrong?"

"What?"

"You haven't said anything to me all week. You're disengaged. What's wrong?"

Yuna let out a sigh. After a long moment, she said, "I dunno, Carrie. I honestly don't know." She stared out her window. I kept silent and stole sidelong glances at her. We were the daughters of immigrants before we were ourselves immigrants. Perhaps that impulse to live as characters inside our parents' stories first had led us to where we were now, feeling as though we had never really experienced a coming-of-age. Yuna had told me before, in conflict situations with current and previous boyfriends, that she'd freeze and shut down despite having an earnest wish to show just how much she cared and how deeply she felt; her boyfriend would press her, accuse of her underreacting or being cold; she would retreat more. I did not press. Eventually she said, "Our lives are so different. You live this glamorous life in New York and I—"

"But I don't."

"But you do, Carrie."

"But I don't. I didn't ask for any of it."

"You've changed, or—I don't know if *you* changed, but like, your *life* has changed."

"Where's all this coming from?"

"You know, my friends in Kansas—I tell everyone about you. They ask me, 'Aren't you jealous of a friend like Carrie?' I'm like, No. Never. I tell them never. But now I come here and I feel so out of place. I would never go to the Hamptons by myself or—"

"This was my first time too! And I wasn't going to invite anyone but you. I don't like it here either."

"But this is your life now. And, like, you love your job. My job . . ." Her job, which she had gotten through her previous boyfriend, was testing new models of Galaxy phones on various cellular networks to find bugs so that Samsung could troubleshoot them before their release dates.

"What's wrong with your job?"

Yuna let out another sigh. Quietly, she said, "I think I hate my job."

"Okay. Well. That's okay. You loved it before, so what do you think is the problem?"

"Actually, yeah, no, I freaking *hate* my job. I work all the time, for what?"

"Are you getting paid well?"

"Yeah. That's the problem."

"How much?"

"Eighty. But my boss is a butthead. I go in basically every weekend. We're so short-staffed, Carrie, it's nuts. We're a Korean company and, you know, actually I don't know if you know, but in Korean culture everything is based on hierarchy, so I have to address everyone by their rank and title—we don't even call each other by our *names*. What the freakin' hell! We're in America!" I thought of how the staff in Boone and Elisabeth's family office called them Mr. and Mrs. Prescott, sometimes Mr. and Mrs. P. "And since I'm the newest member of my team, all the shit gets dumped on me and I just have to smile and nod and stuff. It's so stupid. But, you know," she said, her voice soft again, "I help out my parents. And, like, there's Jason with his student loans, and I also take care of a lot of our bills. I feel like I'm stuck."

"Yuna." I breathed in, breathed out. "I can't tell you what you should do, but you should know you're not alone. I love my job, but—honestly? I've been starting to have some doubts too. I'm on edge *all* the time; it's twenty-four-seven intensity. Even if I have time off, I'm always on call, so at any second I might need to go and completely change my plans. You know the journal you gave me? The place for me to be brutally honest with myself? Well, my *one* personal goal when I moved here was to start writing in it, and I've written nothing. NOT ONE WORD. I haven't even opened it. Okay, so, yeah, my bank account has gone up a bit and I get to wear some fancy clothes and go on fancy vacations, but you know as well as I do how empty that is. I want to be a writer. I thought Carbon was everything I could've ever wanted in a job, in a day job, at least, but . . ." I sighed. "I don't know why the more I succeed at Carbon, the more I feel like I'm going crazy. Literally. I feel like total fucking chaos. Then I start down a spiral of hating myself for not having my shit together. Also, side comment, Yuna: Some people may think my job has status, but *so* many other people look down on me, actually. Because I'm an assistant. They think I should be doing more with my life. But why? Says who? What if I don't want to?"

"Oh, my God, Carrie, I know!"

"Why can't people trust I'm doing the process that works *for me*?"

"All I want is to make enough money so I can take care of my parents and Jason and also"—Yuna chuckled—"me, obviously. Like, maybe buy a house one day? That'd be nice."

"Those are great goals. Don't let anyone tell you otherwise or that you need to do more."

With my eyes on the highway, I saw that Yuna looked over at me. "What're we gonna do?" she asked. I shrugged, said nothing. She looked ahead, through the windshield, and together we stared at the road.

THE DAY AFTER LABOR DAY, Boone called me in early for a sit. I hadn't seen him in weeks. "How was Montauk?" he asked.

"Great. Surfing's difficult. But we did okay."

"Who did you go with?"

"My best friend, Yuna. You spoke to her for my last reference call."

Boone nodded.

"How was your end of summer?"

"Good," he said. "Ready to get back to work. It's going to get really busy." He paused and studied me, so I paused and studied myself too. My knees showed permanent scars over which I had caked on concealer. I had gotten back on the treadmill; I felt better, healthier, more like my old self, and managed to keep off ten of those twelve costly pounds. "Happy one-year," he said. "I notice your hard work. As a thank-you, we're going to get you invested in the fund."

I did not expect this.

"We want you to commit to the long-term success of Carbon." But I could not add to the investment; I needed to keep it on the DL. "The fund can only have a small number of investors like you, and now we're giving one of those spots"—he looked deep into my eyes—"to you."

I felt cleaved in two. One part of me, the experiencing self, was tremendously grateful for receiving money—of course I was, it was *money*—while the other part of me, the observing, thinking, and judging self, always the stronger self, could not ignore the fact that I would not be able to add to the investment. I was beginning to see inequity and could not unsee it. Here, I saw the stratification of LPs in Carbon's funds; my bottom layer meant I was at the mercy of Boone's munificence. Even with this stroke of luck, I had no agency, no freedom. Also, we were not a flat organization as Boone had described to me before. If he was asking me to keep quiet about this, what privileges was he extending to or taking away from others?

He went on to explain the tax-free gift limit, then said, "Lis and I will each transfer that amount to you. I still have to talk to her about it, but I'm sure she'll agree." This made the pre-tax total of their gift just under 20 percent of my annualized comp last year. "Anything else?"

Jen's words buzzed in my ear. *Talk to Boone.* I inhaled and held my breath and thought about her words for one, two, three, four seconds before I decided no, I could not. I feared if I spoke up and he said no or did nothing or TBD'd me and my concerns—or, worse, blamed me for my burnout—then I would have no choice but to leave. I was not yet ready to blow up my life. "No, nothing. Thank you so much, Boone. I really appreciate it. I understand that this is a big gift." I could not pitch him on spearheading our philanthropic efforts either. I needed to do less, not more; he just told me things were about to get crazy. "Everything's great."

"Good. The second year will be much better, I promise."

FAMILY DAY THIS YEAR STARTED off at Carbon. "Who's that?" an assistant whispered as we huddled in the front office, wondering about a woman I had never once seen. She pushed a stroller with one arm while holding an infant with the other. "I think that's Nate's wife," another assistant responded. Nate was the controller. "If I didn't work," a third one said, "I'd be that skinny too."

After an hour, we made our way to the Central Park Zoo, which Carbon had bought out for the evening. I took extra notice of my surroundings on the walk over. How the smells of trash, urine, and manure permeated the air beneath the bright lights of Billionaires' Row. I was about to move from my studio in Midtown to a one-bedroom in Flatiron; my commute would increase from six minutes by foot to twenty minutes by train. Carbon's offices, Boone's apartment, and his family office were all within a short walk of one another—I was leaving the nest.

To the zoo, I had invited Parmita and a colleague of hers she had described to me as "the world's most awesome human." At nineteen,

Katherine had dropped out of college and founded her first company. She was now an entrepreneur-in-residence at Insight. I wanted to introduce her to Boone. Parmita missed the event with the excuse that she was dressed inappropriately for viewing animals. Katherine got to the venue minutes before me. I found her near the monkey section. Together we circled over to the heart of the zoo, where Boone was standing alone.

"Hey, Boone," I said. "I want you to meet my brilliant friend Katherine."

"Carrie says great things about you," he said to her. "You're doing a start-up?"

I looked over at the sea lions swimming in a pond that surrounded a tiny island made of rock—not fish in a fish tank, but mammals in a glass pool. In nature, they had adapted to survive being underwater by closing their nostrils. Sooner or later, though, they had to come up for air.

Fourth Quarter

B oone had told me at my review in July to ask for help on temporary things. When Maya from the family office and I were texting about how we had both been feeling *so bad* that work was so *busy* and *messy* and *frantic* and *hectic for everyone*—this was after a few times I'd be on the phone with her or someone from her office and the call would drop dead mid-sentence; whomever was speaking could not spare the one or two or five seconds to inform me that she had to go, it was an emergency, she'd call me back later—I wrote: *I used to joke I didn't have time to go the bathroom. Yesterday, it was like I didn't have time to breathe.*

It was sometime around the beginning of October. Back office had been sending me emails asking me to submit my overdue expense reports. Months had passed since I had asked for help and Sloane had intervened. At reception sat two new women who were both young and so nice. One had gone to Tufts, the other to Yale.

They helped me with small tasks, like printing. In the late afternoon when much of the front office was away at conferences or meetings off-site, I walked over to their area. I prefaced this ask—calling hotels and other vendors and requesting emailed invoices—with the same disclaimer I gave them every time. "If you're too busy," I said in my gentlest tone, "just let me know, okay?" All good, they said. "Anything you can get to in these expense reports is fine," I added. Within a half hour my phone rang.

"Hey, Courtney," I said. "How's it going?"

"Good!"

"Great."

"So reception told me that you asked them to help you with expense reports."

"Yes, I did."

"They're feeling really overwhelmed right now and won't have time to do them."

"That's not what they said to me."

"Unfortunately, they won't be able to do it."

"What about next week?"

"They can't, no."

I knew how hard it was to say no to someone more senior than you, so I was not upset, not at all, at the women at reception. I called them right after I got off the phone with Courtney. Dawn, the one who went to Tufts, answered. "Hey, so," I said, "I know you're overwhelmed. Do not worry about a thing, okay?"

"I am so, *so* sorry," Dawn said, her voice soaked in apology, so much so I almost volunteered to help her with whatever work she had to complete. "It's just that, this week, we already have a ton of expense reports to do for Courtney that's due in a couple days."

I hung up. I looked over at Boone—he had returned to his office and was at his computer typing—drew a deep breath in and rose up from my chair. Several people had said to me early on—a throw-away comment I had indeed thrown away, choosing to believe Boone over my peers—"The secret to success at Carbon is getting other people to do your work for you."

I walked into Boone's office. "Hey, Boone?" I said. "You know I never bother you with politics and I never ask you for help."

He gestured toward himself with both of his hands. "Out with it."

I slid the door shut, sat down, started telling the story. "So then Courtney—"

"What'd she do?"

"She calls me and tells me that reception can't help me. But then I find out from reception that they can't help me because they are doing *her* expense reports."

Boone reached for the phone and pressed the speaker button. A dial tone, a look. "I'm calling her in right now and firing—"

"No!"

"No?"

My heart rate doubled. The dial tone hung in the air. I sighed and shook my head. "No."

ALL I WANTED WAS HELP with the work. Now the same work would be there plus even more work as I had to spend more time, more emotional energy, resolving interpersonal issues. We still did not have anyone in HR. Boone and Jay told me and Courtney to get to "a good understanding." We had to "clear the air." I was on my own. I sat across from her in Meru, the same room in which she had interviewed me fourteen months earlier. She walked in wearing her black Givenchy Shark Lock boots, as energetic as she was blond.

"I think it was a misunderstanding," she said, smiling. "That's just how I communicate."

I was less mad at her, more mad at the futility of this theater of resolution. I smiled sincerely, wanting this to be over ASAP so I could get back to work; I regretted speaking up.

"My communication style is very direct and can come off as blunt and abrasive."

I nodded.

"Jay's expense reports had *so* many items because of all the Firm's events"—yes, but so did Boone's; besides, why was it on me to adjust to someone else's communication style, why was it on me to be more understanding?—"and he told me that I could get help from reception."

The storm of indignation I had felt had by then moved on, but its dust had fallen and settled on the shape of a person, a name, one that I had not dared to let myself see: Boone. He'd meant well. He'd meant to side with me, to protect me, to make my life easier. I had only wanted him to make things fair—to give me the same access to receptionists' time, or to hire more help for me. But no: Boone would much prefer to fire someone—to make a *onetime* change—than to make a process change and set a precedent. I looked at Courtney and said, "All good."

BOONE TOLD ME, "If you know anyone you think is smart and I'd like, send them my way." I believed in Katherine. She wanted to develop new ways of assessing human potential. The current US education system was stale and unfair, she thought; it primarily taught students how to test well and gain admissions into colleges, which ends up being a process favoring middle- and high-income families with the means for test prep. She was trying to raise two million for a seed round and close by Thanksgiving. She wanted to pitch Boone. I had informed her that we were in the middle of another raise and Boone had given us a mandate, for the foreseeable future, of "nothing non-mission-critical." As soon as Fund V wrapped up, I would pass along her deck and put her materials in Boone's "To read" pile along with the highest recommendation.

ON THE THURSDAY before the last week of October, the fundraising deck for Fund V went out.

"YOU NEED TO get it checked out," Boone instructed me the second he heard I was on crutches. I could not put any weight on my right ankle; I could not walk. "Call the hospital. *Now.*"

Nothing non-mission-critical. This was the busiest week of the year. The offsite for which I had to finish Boone's presentations, one of which was *Our Standardized Investment Methodology*, was on Thursday. Also by Thursday I had to write a script for Boone's fireside chat with Derek Jeter. There were fundraising meetings, earnings calls, webcasts; Boone dialed into as many as he could, but he was getting so busy he missed a lot of them; I would join as his proxy and take notes. Boone was in the process of building a new billion-dollar long position. He also wanted to initiate a short on a company going public soon, for which he had asked me to do preliminary research. No, I could not leave work.

But Boone forced me to leave at three to go see a doctor specializing in foot and ankle surgery. When the doctor walked into the exam room, I explained how I had stepped on a pebble on an uneven sidewalk while running outside. He did not look at me or ask me any questions. He must be curt and cranky, I thought, because it was the end of the day. He tried bending my toes, rotating my ankle, and pressing down on my foot—pure, sharp pain, no degrees of freedom. "You need to be in a boot for at least four to six weeks," he said. "You should get an MRI." The next day I took an Uber to work at 6:24 a.m. and left at 7:45 p.m., ignoring the doctor's orders.

The offsite at a golf course in New Jersey went well and Boone and Jeter, I was told, had a fun, inspiring chat guided by insightful questions. I did not get to go. Someone else told me that in Boone's presentations, he gave me credit. "Carrie pulled this," he had said. Boone called me in between sessions to tell me I was "the master puppeteer." The next day Boone told Jen (who told me): "This week could not have gone smoothly without Carrie. I walked onstage cold without reviewing the questions or presentations and she just gets it." To all this, I felt numb.

I would like to think three days later, when I booked the MRI, it was because I realized I should not put my work above my health, but it was only when Boone demanded that I get one that I called the hospital back. I was given an appointment the next day.

JOSH CALLED CARBON. Reception picked up. They called me and asked me what to say. I told them to provide the caller with something neutral like "Carrie's unavailable."

Nothing non-mission-critical.

Parmita offered to write an email telling Josh to leave me alone. Back in September, Josh had sent a 500-word email to my parents talking about how he had been angry at the world—angry that I had gone through, as he phrased it, a "rough time" in college, and not knowing how to deal with all that anger he redirected much of it back on me. He signed off: "As a serious smarty pants, I'm sure she is doing very well in New York. Interestingly enough, I decided to move there part time." *He moved to New York.* My dad had no emotional reaction. His non-reaction made me feel like he was on Josh's side. My mom feared for my physical safety, since I had told her, whenever I tried to end things with Josh, he would say things like "I will kill myself if I am not with you" and "If you get a restraining order against me, I guess I will go to jail." But my mom had no solutions except for me to acquiesce. I was afraid Josh might accost me outside the building, so I took Parmita up on her offer. She wrote a draft, I okayed it, she sent it.

A memory returned: I can't remember the year. It was one of the many times I had tried to separate from him. We were in Michigan. Josh would not accept the breakup, so I had asked to accompany him to his next therapy appointment. I began, "Thank you, Dr. Wright, for letting me join. I am here because Josh won't acknowledge or respect my wishes. I am stating for the record, in front of a witness, I do not wish to be in a relationship with him. I do not love him. I wish to be single." His therapist, a leader in the field of mental health, turned to him and asked, "Josh, what do you have to say to that?" Josh looked down, to the side, at neither of us, and said, "I do not believe Carrie." His therapist calmly asked him, "So you do not recognize Carrie has needs and wants and a reality that is separate from yours?" Josh, equally as calm, said, "No. I do not believe her." I, calmer than either of them, thanked his therapist and walked out of the room.

Six days after Parmita sent her email, Josh responded with a 748-word reply, beginning by stating that he was "surrounded by a bevy of lawyers day in and day out" and knew "where the legal lines" were and how he had "crossed none." Then he asked: "So why is it that Carrie cannot respond herself?" He reasoned: "It can only be that she still has deep feelings for me."

Nineteen minutes later I wrote to Josh: "I have zero feelings for you—positive or negative. Please leave me alone."

Twelve days later he replied: "I don't believe you at all."

I WENT BACK to the same orthopedic doctor after several weeks in a boot. He came in, looking down, reading my chart. "How's your ankle?" he asked.

"It's fine, I think."

"Oh." The doctor pointed to something on my chart. "I see here

Dr. Marshall called you." Dr. Marshall was the chairperson of the department of radiology for the hospital.

"Yes, she did."

"You must be someone if Dr. Marshall called you."

"No."

"No?"

"No." I was annoyed at the slight upward pull of his lips. "Well, I mean, my boss . . . he supports her research. And he's on the board of this hospital."

"Ah." The doctor asked me how I was feeling and what I could and could not do with my ankle. He went over the results of my MRI—two torn ligaments on the outside, one partial tear on the inside, one bone fracture—and gave me a prescription for months of physical therapy. He asked me what I did for work. I help my boss with his life, I said. Mostly business, some personal. I hid my offense at his reversal of bedside manner and never saw this doctor again.

Boone donated money to medical research. This act in isolation has to be classified as doing way more good than not. But placed inside the system of health care, it also meant that some people—Boone and I—got to walk ahead of others.

FUND V CLOSED on the Monday of the week of Thanksgiving. As partner no. 557 with an interest of 0.000812 percent in the main fund, I had received a copy of the deck. I flipped through the pages and thought about what made Carbon, from where I was sitting, different.

Owning Market Leading Assets Globally. Boone did not travel much outside the Americas. In the months I had been at Carbon, he had not been anywhere international for business purposes. The primary geographies for Carbon's capital deployment included parts of Asia, which I had never seen him visit. He invested globally from his Aeron armchair in Manhattan.

Focus for Fund V. Carbon intended to deploy Fund V as swiftly as possible—in the extreme (slowest) case, over two years. A VC fund would normally take two to three years to deploy and sometimes up to five. Carbon hoped to do everything in about one or less.

Focus. Compared with other VCs, Boone was hands-off when it came to his portfolio companies. He did not take board seats. Boone seemed to believe that his and Carbon's edge was more in picking the right companies with the right themes rather than in helping with operations. This, and not traveling for business unless his physical presence was absolutely necessary, freed up hours, days, and weeks for him to do higher-return-on-time work.

Boone had asked me to do an exercise to determine my return on time: On an average workday, log what you're doing by the minute. Tally, analyze. Then add up all the minutes you might save from when you were being inefficient or suboptimal and see if you can't do both more and higher-quality work. There was a constant awareness of how much time a task should take and whether you could perform the task at the same quality but faster. There was also a constant awareness of whether you needed to do the task at all—how was it contributing to the Firm's return? For this reason Boone hated inessential meetings. He hated unnecessary socializing, galas, and events. No wining and dining. No happy hours. Only occasional golf.

Although Boone had given me (limited) access to the main fund, I was still shut out of Venture Fund V. I discovered, coming as a shock, that I felt very little connection to the long-term success of my firm. I could not reconcile how I felt about Boone with how I felt about Carbon.

More than one slide of the deck talked about on-demand transportation, which, according to Carbon, offered lower wait times, more customers, more money for drivers, and thus more drivers—what it called a *virtuous cycle*. Here, and in a few other places, I would read the text and experience a sudden stoppage of time, the flash-forward images in my mind's eye offset by an intense déjà vu. My thoughts flew back to my first week on the job when my peers wanted to order Sweetgreen, which was so new to the city that the chain famously (at least to the Midtown lunch crowd) did not offer delivery. Not a problem! an assistant said to me. We'll send a Postmate down to NoMad. Many months later, friends would ask me, "Have you heard of Postmates?" "Have you heard of Peloton?" As they explained these cool new companies to me, I would think not about how I had been Postmating and Pelotoning since I started at Carbon but about how the world that Carbon had envisioned—hoped for, could profit off—was here. The Fund V deck I held in my hand was the world Carbon wanted to come. It was one dominated by Amazon, Netflix; one of ubiquity; one of *virtuous* cycles of on-demand content and convenience and everything else. I was sure Carbon's world would come. I was not so sure if I wanted to live in it.

FUND V ENDED up with billions in total commitments, with over
95 percent of it from existing LPs and 14 percent from the Firm's
partners and employees (which was a lot of skin in the game). During a sit in the afternoon on the day the fund closed, Boone gave me
a voucher for a massage and a body scrub at the Mandarin Oriental,
along with a card saying *Have a relaxing weekend* and *Thank you for
all the hard work!* and *You rock ;)*. I wanted to cry. Though I did not.
This was right before bonuses. He was nice—so nice—as he worked
me to the bone.

I HAD BEEN TRYING to wait until after Fund V finished its launch
to bring up Katherine, but she had told me that her round was fill-
ing up and would likely be oversubscribed. She asked if there was
any way to move up the timeline. So, in a sit before the close of the
new fund, I asked Boone, "Remember my friend you met at Family Day?"

"Yes."

Boone was turned off by hard sells. He liked numbers, figures,
track records. My pitch: "She's founded her second company to dis-
rupt educational testing. She sold her first company to Insight. She's
raising a seed round for her start-up. Maybe you could take a look
at the deck and see if it might be appropriate for you or Carbon?"
Boone invested through at least three separate entities: Carbon, himself, and his foundation, with the best and biggest opportunities

going first and always to the Firm. "If you're interested, we can set up a meeting?"

"She's ambitious."

"I know."

"Sure, send it."

A DAY OR TWO LATER, in a sit, with no reminders necessary, Boone brought up Katherine.

"So, your friend . . ."

"Yes."

"She seems supersmart"—my heart sank, a ding was coming; for what reason?—"but we're not doing Edtech." I smiled and nodded and thanked Boone for taking a look. But I knew this was not true. Just months ago, Carbon had invested in start-ups like an online tutoring platform and a virtual marketplace for educators to share original resources. My discontent was partly about Katherine and partly about Boone but mostly about what this meant for the way the game was played—whether in the best case, the game could be called fair.

SELF-EVALUATION FOR **CARRIE SUN**
(DO NOT SUBMIT)

1. Key aspects of job
   a. Boone (150%)
   b. Gabe (50%)

2. Firm-related projects

    a. Many.

3. Most rewarding aspects

    a. The couple times Boone has told me he thinks I could do anything.

4. Most significant accomplishments

    a. I survived.

5. Most challenging, and how I dealt with it

    a. <u>Constant feedback</u>: Boone gives me diet tips although I have never asked him for any. One morning, he sent me a screenshot of an Instagram post (which he did not like) from the account (which he did follow) of the founder of Elisabeth's favorite fitness studio on the Upper West Side. The woman, who reportedly also trains Shakira, Kelly Ripa, and Sarah Jessica Parker, posted a photo of the cross-section of an iceberg. The part above water was overlaid with *30% WORKOUT*. The part below water, in an aggressive font: *70% DIET*. The caption: "Salad anyone??! #MondayMotivation Listen, there is no need to kill yourself at the gym if you're going to eat a pizza afterwards."

        i. I dealt with it by immediately craving a whole pizza.

    b. <u>Rhetorical questions</u>: Boone reads primarily nonfiction— *How Champions Think, The Art of Learning, Barbarian Days*. We would get books in the mail and he'd pass them to me with the instruction "Read it first and tell me if it's worth my time." Once, Parmita and I went to an event with an HBS professor, after which, ahead of the publication of her book, the audience received advanced reader copies. In a sit the next morning I mentioned I had a book for him from a talk I had gone to last night. "What did you think of the speaker?" he asked. She was very smart, I said, but I think her TED Talk may have captured a lot of the material. "Carrie," he said, "why would you give me a book you thought was only okay? Also, why would you give me a book that you haven't even read?"

    i. I dealt with it by not giving him the book and by acknowledging the shame I would feel after his rhetorical questions plus a death stare.

c. <u>More rhetorical questions</u>: Vince, the president and CEO of a major New York cultural institution, courted Boone through a warm intro. The institution needed money for renovations; it was hoping to better conserve its collection. Vince invited Boone to private tours and special dinners, all of which we turned down. "Why does Vince keep inviting me to things?" Boone asked. I think he wants your support, I said. It must have been obvious I was pushing my interests—creativity, learning; I wanted us to support the institution so I always floated Vince's asks straight to the top. Vince asked, again, if Boone wanted a tour. "At Carbon," Boone said, "we're trying hard to build the future. Why would I give any money to the preservation of the past?"

    i. I dealt with it by wondering if I belonged at this place, a place so hostile to the past that had provided Boone with the returns, compounded over centuries, enabling him to be where he was today.

d. <u>Stereotype threat</u>: Boone and I were in a sit and both on Instagram, though I cannot remember why; I hardly used the app. I requested to follow him. He accepted and did not follow back. He laughed. "Carrie," he said, still laughing. "You *have* to change your handle." Why? I asked,

wondering if I had accidentally posted something not safe
for work, but no: my account had zero posts showing my
face or body. Boone looked at me. "It makes you sound like
a . . ." What? Say it. Go on. Boone looked left and right.
His gaze landed to the side of me. "Like an escort service." I
maintained my composure, then went rational. I explained
that this was an allusion to an Art of Fiction interview in
the *Paris Review* I had been particularly fond of then; that
the word *mandarin* was not meant to refer to myself but
rather a sensibility of prose that was formal and complex;
that it was that pressure to conform to a rigid set of rules I
was wanting to escape in my life; and that, like Carbon,
this year, after Neil left, I was trying to get back to basics
by doing the simple things—like expressing myself—well.
"Doesn't matter," he said. "That might be your intention,
but everyone will think otherwise."

  i. I dealt with it by changing my handle, by noticing the
     extra burdens put on Asian women to conform or not
     conform to stereotypes.

e. <u>Waste</u>: The toilets at Carbon are auto-flush. There were
   issues with people (front office, men) leaving liquid and
   solid matters behind. So, Carbon hired a woman whose
   full-time job was to clean the bowls and seats after each
   use. The woman would spend her entire day in the unisex
   bathroom hall. I would smile and wave at her whenever I
   saw her. Sometimes we'd come into the office at the same
   time and ride up in the elevator together, and I would notice
   her high heels, her highlights, her extra-large bag, and her
   large phone that was always connected to her white earbuds.
   One day, it occurred to me that I had no idea what her
   name was—she was not listed on Carbon's internal contact
   sheet—so I asked our facilities manager, Luis. He told me. I
   said hello to her using her name until, after maybe a week

or so of not seeing her, I forgot it. I asked Luis again. Then I
forgot again. Then I was far too embarrassed to ask Luis a
third time, so I asked some of my work friends and found
that no one seemed to know her name.

    i. I dealt with it by double-flushing and wiping down my
       seat; by making sure, as I was in charge of our corporate
       gift to employees, that she, a contract worker, was
       included during the holidays; and by acknowledging my
       frustration at the men at Carbon not taking care of their
       own shit.

f. <u>Optics</u>: Sloane used to plan the holiday party, retreat,
Team Lunches, and more. When she left, Boone told the
assistants that he would spread out Sloane's work, asking
each of us to submit ranked preferences in an email. He
and I would count the votes. We would do this every year
so the responsibilities could rotate. There would be no
monopolies. He thought we would view this as a kind of
promotion, as though Carbon were doing us a favor by
giving us opportunities to get more and more involved. We
viewed it as added responsibilities for which no one had
any extra bandwidth. Because Sloane used to have first
dibs on everything—and it was this hierarchy Boone was
trying to shed—I could not be seen as receiving special
treatment. Everyone got her first or second choice (the least
time-consuming responsibilities went first) while I took
whatever was left over. "Next year," he said, "I will let
everyone submit their votes but arrange it behind the
scenes so that you get your first choice."

    i. I dealt with it by feeling grateful that what was left
       over was secretly my top choice—the Carbon fifteenth-
       anniversary celebration, next March—an event telling me
       that Boone did care about select histories, and by

understanding how Carbon was, indeed, all about performance.

6. What can I do better, and what can Firm do to help

    a. I used to be so good at tuning out whenever Boone would say something weird or harsh or possibly mean. What I can do better—*must* be better at—if I want to succeed at Carbon is self-surrender. Team over self. Be all in. Believe, and trust, that he knows best. But I am not sure anymore if that last statement is true.

        i. Firm can provide us assistants/women with the same additional resources so readily given to the investment team/men.

7. Goals from last year's self-evaluation

    a. I have hit all of them, per Boone's constant, instant feedback.

8. Goals for next year

    a. Stop prioritizing my work over my mental and physical health.

    b. Speak up—especially to Boone, even if it's not what he wants to hear.

9. How to improve as a team/Firm

    a. Let the assistants have a team meeting so we can organize our labor.

I remember watching the pulsing cursor as one part of me fantasized about typing this list of the real challenges of my job and how I dealt with them, while the other part of me noticed how, even within the private space of a blank page, even knowing I held the power to type and erase, write and revise, that I—still—did not feel free to say what I wanted. I could not summon the courage to submit a more honest self-review or the fortitude to even press down on those keys. I remember staring at the document and dreaming of the freedom to speak my truth.

I remember asking myself over and over: What is wrong with me?

I remember trying to answer that question and thinking back to the early nineties when Mom was a babysitter making six dollars an hour working for a couple—he, American; she, Swiss—who, at the time, had two sons, the eldest one my age. Mom would bring me to play with them; I loved it. Mom was nice at their house. When the boys climbed a tree and fell or ran and tripped and scraped their knees, Mom would rush over and ask if they were okay. At home, if I cut my finger or slipped or stumbled or in any way accidentally hurt myself, I would receive a verbal lashing. *Nǐ zěnme zhème bèn?* she'd yell, the phrase I heard most often. *How are you so stupid?* Then she'd wash my clothes or dress my wound while mumbling to herself about my idiocy.

I was six or seven when I asked her one evening, after I had had the best day playing *Super Mario Bros. 3* with the boys, "Mommy? Why do you love Andrew and Brett more than you love me?" I did not yet know about self-silencing. *Nǐ zěnme néng shuō zhème nántīng dehuà?* she said. *How could you say such ugly words?* She told me I was wrong. She loved me, not them; how could I not know this? I did not yet know about rhetorical questions either, so I answered her. "Because I feel you are nicer to them than you are to me." No.

My emotions were wrong. So wrong. My thoughts were wrong too. Why was I so dumb? *Nǐ luójí dào guòláile,* she said. *Your logic is upside down.* We were Chinese people. This was how Chinese families were.

When I was in elementary school, Dad's doctoral adviser, a jovial Italian American who had grown up in Milwaukee, whom I called Uncle Palermo, told my parents that I appeared to be a cold child as I did not smile or laugh or shout or cry. Mom and Dad blamed me for my coldness and asked me why I was so weird, why I *zǒng shì gēn biérén bù yàng.* By then I knew about rhetorical questions, so I did not answer why I was *always not like other people.* I remember, also around this time, how I would be so bored whenever I accompanied them on their trips to Lake Lansing or Grand River. They would be busy trying to catch bluegill to steam for dinner with ginger, scallion, and soy; I'd be busy staring at my legs. I was a mosquito magnet. I would sit on a bench and watch each bite and observe the sensation of my pruritic skin. I'd play a game with myself: Could I make the itch go away with my thoughts? I succeeded on the first try. It was too easy for me to ignore my body. To mentally Tiger Balm that which caused me to suffer.

From fourth to eighth grade, sporadically, I tried accessing my emotions again. I wrote them down in a turquoise My Heart 2 Heart Diary, then in a black notebook on the cover of which was a drawing of the Bridge of Sighs in Oxford, England. These were the journals, buried inside a drawer, I believed that Mom had found. In the first one, the last entry read: *I love my mom & dad. too much.* In the second, on the back cover of which I had written three sentences in pink and gold gel ink pens—*Why?*; *Why exist??*; *Life is hard*—the longest entry talked about my eight-night stay in the ICU for pneumonia. Another entry read: *Mom's already constantly complaining about how I don't have any work to do & I wasted my spring break by not studying. Sometimes I just get so tired of studying that someday, I'm afraid I'll push myself over the limit.* And another: *Many times during the last few years, I've thought about suicide. Not only to end my pain, but others' as well.* To end my pain of receiving unabating negativity approaching annihilation.

If I smiled too much, laughed too hard, a scream would come: *What do you have to be so happy about? You're so odd.* Then: *If you're too happy, people will come for you.*

If I spoke too few words, or shed a tear at all, a laugh would come: *You're a coward. You're useless.* Then: *If you're too sensitive, people will take advantage of you.*

I did not talk back.

If I worked and only worked and did not emote, maybe my mom would stop.

Senior year of high school I read *The Handmaid's Tale* in AP English Literature. I did not have the same reaction (or any) to Offred's story as my classmates. I worried I was evil, that my moral wires were frayed or cut. The main character's life under a totalitarian regime was fine. She was alive. The rules were what they were. What was so bad about following them?

Senior year of high school, at a Lunar New Year potluck, the mother of a classmate of mine from Sunday Chinese school told me how all my parents did when I was not around was talk about what a good daughter I was, how proud they were of me that I was going to MIT. "No *way*," I said, shaking my head, dashing to the bathroom. I stared at myself in the mirror, unable to embrace this data point so orthogonal to my set of lived experiences. This was the first time in my life I thought it possible my parents did not view me as a failure.

Mom remembers the exact moment when, she says, I became a total stranger to her.

I was twenty-eight. We were in Chicago for a mother-daughter trip. I had been having doubts about Josh and had just ended our (first) engagement. One of Josh's friends from Stanford had asked me out. I liked him; we talked about Alain de Botton, Rachmaninoff. I told Mom that I had begun seeing someone else. *Nǐ zěnme néng shì nàme yàng de nǚrén?* she snapped. *How could you be such a woman?* (She had said a version of this many times before: In my early twenties I would send her photos of my life in Boston and she would call me a *jìnǚ. Prostitute.* Because I wore tank tops and black eyeshadow.) "Stop it!" I yelled and screamed and could not stop, talking back to her for the first time. "Don't be so mean to me!" Mom told me to stop shouting. In Chinglish, she said, as calm as ever, "Nǐ néng bùnéng be nice. Be nicer duì nǐ mā." Then, in Mandarin, she added, "You are no longer my daughter. I am no longer your mother either and *never again will I be.*" But the effect of these words had long ago worn off.

I HAVE A COPY of the two sheets of paper on which I typed the self-evaluation I did submit, but I have no episodic memory of this review. My mind had been frazzled, in a perpetual state of distraction, from relentless task-switching. Boone preferred calls to emails; often I'd be on the phone with someone, with someone else on hold, as Jay would walk by and ask if Boone was free and I'd check Boone's

calendar and mouth a new time for him to come back while hoping
I did not say the quiet part out loud. Forces top, down, internal, and
external competed constantly for my attention, so I spent every second reacting to the world, reacting as though a virus had infected
my phone and toggled all the switches to allow notifications to
flash/buzz/sound all the time. If, as Boone believed, how you spent
your days was how you lived your life, then I was not in control of
my life. Boone did not merely influence my days—he owned them.
I could never choose to prioritize my needs over his unless he, he
who decides if and when, let me. Like the time he gave me courtside
seats to the US Open and because there was a rain delay, because
the match was rescheduled during market hours, I could not go, I
had work, time-sensitive work, and when Boone saw me typing furiously in my cube, he rang my office line, and before I could say, *Hi,
Boone*, he told me, *Leave. Now.* (I caught the final minutes of Serena
Williams losing in an upset.) I had urgency fatigue. I was the fox allowing Boone to be the hedgehog, fielding interruptions so he could
be in maximum flow. No one dared interrupt Boone so everyone
interrupted me. I carried the burden and displeasure of never being
the cause, never a complete action. Work felt like a series of nested
em dashes, living inside a sentence that could never reach its period.

I HAVE TWO more sheets of paper on which Boone typed my performance review in Calibri. *Great attitude. You show appreciation.
Good sense of humor / smile a lot. Take feedback well.* Positives took
up most of the first page. The negatives he had listed: *High standards all the time. Not sweating the small stuff.* Goals for next year

were to *Communicate quickly* and *Continue to increase proactiveness* and *Take feedback well—it's just intended to make us better.*

I HAVE A DEEP WELL of semantic memories of things Boone had said to me—facts, unmoored from time and place, scrambled because, as Parmita noticed, my reviews were *perfunctory* since I *get feedback 24/7*. He told me my standards might be slipping. (He had spent half of a recent Team Lunch drilling into us the only standard: world-class.) He told me he was extra hard on me because he wanted to see me succeed. He told me to be more aware of when others needed help. He told me to be nice, be nicer to everyone—to always take the high road and to let everything go. Stay pleasant, stay kind. Keep calm and keep on. He also told me: "Your Achilles' heel is that you're too trusting. You're too much of an eternal optimist about the good in people."

AFTER MY YEAR-END REVIEW, which evidently lasted fifty-four minutes because I Gchatted Parmita right after, I typed:

> **ME:** he was like, "i don't hold anything in"
>
> **ME:** "and it's bc i think you CAN take it"
>
> **ME:** "i like working with you and that's so rare"
>
> **ME:** "you/we are trying to win marathon not a sprint"
>
> **ME:** "there are very few seats at carbon in a position of influence, you are in one of them"

ME: "i would like you to be here long term and work on things you enjoy/are passionate about"

ME: the question is more difficult like

ME: do *i* see myself here?

How could I work on things I enjoyed and was passionate about if I could not get help with expenses? He wanted me to give first, be nice, help others—who was helping me?

THE NEXT DAY I had a sit with Gabe. I have no memory of this. I have Gchats telling me that Gabe gave me a *glowing review*; apparently he and Boone raved about my *ability to do research and help with everything*. Gabe mentioned Boone's only concern about me was that I would leave because I was too bored. At once, now, I recall several things: I recall thinking how boredom was so not the issue. I recall feeling anxious that Boone's eighteen-month hourglass was almost up, that I had two months left, and that if this did not work out, it would not be for the reason I had once given him. I recall a recent sit in which Boone had said, "You are clearly a learning organism," and I had thought, Yes. You're right. And for an organism to live it must be under an ozone layer and just the right distance from the star at the center of the system.

FOUR DAYS LATER, Boone called me into Townsend. No Jay. He handed me a sheet of paper.

"Plus the gift," he said, "if you'll remember. . . ."

"Yes, of course."

"And that's after tax. . . ."

"Yes, I know. Thank you." How could I forget the gift? Val and other assistants had mentioned to me that they wanted to petition Jay to let them invest in the funds.

"You're doing great. We're giving you a raise—we want to bring you in line with the top end of assistants here."

Ah, Lena. Lena, whom I would overhear murmur-chatting on the phone with her best friend in Iowa for hours at a time each week. I smiled and nodded and said, "Thank you so much."

"That's a large increase." He did the math, said the delta.

Was I not showing enough appreciation? Val, Parmita, Penelope— they had all told me I had the best job, coolest job, best boss, ever. Jen had said she had been searching for years, perusing thousands of résumés, to find, in her words, "the one": me. I was the luckiest. I should express more gratitude. I nodded with more energy and enthusiasm even as my heart felt guilty, my mind cloudy, and my soul empty. I had grown up poor, then middle class. I felt at fault for not wanting something someone from my background should want.

"It's," he said, "a *big* bump."

THE NUMBER GOT me close to what I had made as an analyst at Fidelity. This touched a sore spot.

Boone had told me that Carbon's culture was much more like a start-up's than a hedge fund's. Lean, flat, entrepreneurial. Everyone did a bit of everything. But many start-ups attracted talent—the kind of talent that would want to work all day, every day, in nebulous roles in support of some mission—because of a culture of equity. Which is to say: All employees shared in the success of the firm via stock or stock options. All employees, not just the partners, shared in the winnings and felt a sense of ownership because the access to the upside was transparent, agreed-upon, and—key in my opinion—geometric. It was multiplicative. And, over time, it compounded. This meant that when the firm's profits and valuation went up, the CEO's share of the spoils went up at more or less a similar rate as the janitor's. Your compensation was not a mere guessing game at the end of each of year as to how generous your boss wanted to be.

My bonus felt random. "It's complicated," Boone had said at our last comp discussion. "Many factors go into it." Boone wanted me to own my decisions and my work product. He wanted me to act and feel like an owner. Take the blame. Take responsibility. Really *feel* the hit. But he kept the fees. He paid me from his pocket. He paid me whatever he thought I was worth, and—given that I felt like I was doing at least five jobs: executive assistant, personal assistant, research assistant, project manager, communications consultant—I thought that I was undertitled and underpaid. Boone had a jammed finger and other broken body parts but pushed through his pain to work. Why should I push through my pain? Why work like him when I won't get paid like him?

I DID NOT GO TO Martin's holiday party. I did not want to go to ours either, I had zero left in the tank, but I was in charge of its planning—so I had no choice.

The party was held at a restaurant in Flatiron with gingham table runners and a West Coast–inspired menu that leaned adventurous: chicken liver, trout roe, raw beef, lamb neck. This past fall, when Matt was doing research on restaurants, he and I thought that before Boone decided to invest or not invest or short Chipotle, Boone should sample the product. One day at lunch, Matt and I walked into the library and handed Boone a burrito bowl. Boone jumped, pushed back his chair, and, hands in the air, asked, "What is this?" After he was done reading, hours later, I went back in to clean up after him. He seemed not to have touched a shred of cheese. So, when it came time to finalize the party's food, I presented Boone with a menu of items like "salad of kale" and "Little Gem salad" and "roasted cod," which he approved.

After courses of risotto with mushroom and rigatoni with Bolognese, Boone rose to give the speech that I had written for him. I knew that he was (although he would never admit this) anxious. The main fund would finish the year up in the high single digits. The performance was good, very good, especially in a year when the markets were flat: the S&P 500 total return, up about 1 percent; the MSCI World Index, down less than 1 percent; the asset-weighted return for the hedge fund industry, near zero. But corporate profits for the S&P 500 had fallen for two consecutive quarters year over year. Oil crashed, China crashed; investors were jittery.

Boone showed none of this anxiety, of course, during his speech. He got up, flipped through the deck I had made of Carbon's year in review (mostly professional photos taken at the retreat and the offsite), made a few jokes (one of which was about how an analyst's hair made him look like a nineties boy-band member), and mustered whatever positivity he had left to thank us for all our hard work. He told us to make sure to "have fun" next year.

THE DAY AFTER THE PARTY, a Friday, at lunchtime, I sent Parmita a distress signal on Gchat. I said I was *reaching a breaking point.* That I wanted to *quit tonight.* That I was *so mentally exhausted i don't know how i feel or think about anything.*

Parmita talked me out of doing *anything nuts.* She had been going through work issues herself. After she completed her final-round case study with one of the world's largest hedge funds (where she was interviewing for a business development role), the staff contacted some of her references on Thanksgiving Day; the time stamp on one of them was close to midnight. Then they called around to her former and current workplaces asking for references, after which she was forced to resign because Insight had not known she was looking elsewhere. All of the ten or so reference checks Parmita knew of were positive except for two, both from men: one said that she was a "self-entitled millennial," another "too aggressive." She got dinged for the job. Despite her stressors, Parmita was there for me. I had withdrawn, detached.

I used to talk to Yuna a few times a week. In December, I talked to her once, on Gchat, on the day she became a US citizen after thirty years in America. She said her life was *crazy and stressful.*

I used to not drink. When I did it was one beverage, socially. Since October I had been craving and indulging in one or two drinks after work most days. I had taken Adderall several times. Molly once.

Around seven p.m. Parmita came over for *wine + cheese + your couch*.

"I'm burned out," I said, reaching for the brownie Parmita had brought over in addition to a wide selection of Beecher's. "I'm drowning. Boone always says to people, 'Carrie will do this' or 'Carrie will do that.' He has analysts who cover certain spaces and still he asks me to come up with a list of questions for meetings or do preliminary research. I mean, I love it. But it's too much. Way too much. I can't say no. My performance is judged on my *yes* attitude."

"From my observation," Parmita said, reaching for the bread, "he's been *destroying* you. He's burning your candle at both ends. When was the last time you played piano? Or wrote?" As she tried to comfort me, my mind cycled through the reasons I might want to push through my pain: I did not have to worry about money. I did not have to budget. I had access to the Carbon network and its imprimatur; the combination of my educational background and my work history meant that I was given, in many situations, the benefit of the doubt. Above all, I gave him my word.

"Okay," I said. "I will talk to him about my workload issues in January."

BOONE AND I EXCHANGED PRESENTS in his office. I turned my head toward the park and, as there was no snow to reflect the moonlight, saw a field of darkness. I looked forward to nothing. "So," I said, "you know how every week you ask me, 'Where are the best places to surf this weekend?'"

He nodded as he unwrapped a small box with a piece of paper inside.

"And how both of us scour Magicseaweed for hours but it's all ad hoc because you have to click one by one on each location for the surf report? Well, I got you a website. It's just an address right now"—he swiveled his chair around and typed the URL into a browser—"so it's not live yet. But the gift is that in my spare time I'll build you a custom website that saves you time." It was to save time, his, mine; but it was also to automate watching the weather, its changing conditions, to make it easier for him to catch the best waves. I explained the product: You enter your zip code, how many hours you're willing to fly, and the website, using APIs from various surf-report aggregators, will spit out a list (based on your preferred forecasts) of the top surfing locations for the next seven days. If this sounded like a lot of work, it was. I had already hired and paid a developer in India to code this, but, alas, although the developer and I had multiple Skype calls and desktop-sharing sessions, language issues led to him building a website with a totally different functionality. I decided it would be much simpler if I did it all myself.

Boone smiled. "Cool." He handed me a gift bag. "Go ahead. Open it."

I pulled out a black alligator-leather clutch.

"Elisabeth loves this designer," he explained. "Alexandra—"

I thought he had said "Alexander," so I said, "Wang?"

"No." Pause. "Knight."

I unwrapped a Barneys box. Leather leggings from The Row. I knew instantly I'd have to return them because I had gone up two dress sizes and was no longer wearing pants. After my second running injury of the year, coinciding with the period of *nothing non-mission-critical*, I gave up caring about my body. Every other afternoon I ordered a sundae from Sprinkles: one large scoop of ice cream sandwiched between two halves of a cupcake, topped with fresh whipped cream and crumbled fudge brownies. Sometimes I would add a cupcake on the side, often I'd feel repulsed, always I would feel a high from the sugar, yes, but an even higher high from the briefest hit of an emotion I could not name, express, or place within my corporeal self as I looked around me and saw Pressed, Juice Press, Juice Generation, and salads with hard-boiled egg whites. Not lost on me: that Postmates was a Carbon-backed company, that Carbon's kitchen staff hand-delivered my indulgences to me. Carbon gave me my burnout. It gave me on-demand self-medication too.

I put the two-thousand-dollar leggings back inside the gift bag. I thanked Boone again and, smiling, said, "By the way, my boyfriend really enjoyed meeting you the other night." I had recently started seeing someone who was rather against type: blond, agreeable, encouraged me to eat past my heart's content. We had met through mutual friends.

Boone laughed. "Your boyfriend has the second-limpest handshake I've ever had in my life." He laughed again and added, "Second only to"—he named a peer of his.

WHEN I GOT HOME that evening, I read Boone's card. Words. A smiley face. A gift of ten professional in-home massage or private yoga or fitness sessions (my choice). He thanked me—twice—for *all of the hard work.*

Back in September, when I moved into my Flatiron place, Boone had sent me a gourmet food basket (which took up the entire counter space of my kitchenette) along with the most exquisite white phalaenopsis orchids (which were three feet tall). I put the plants on a windowsill with indirect sunlight, next to a terrarium Jen and Maya had also sent me as a housewarming gift. I was determined to keep the organisms alive so I set a weekly reminder to put a few ice cubes on top of the soil. Every day I'd come home from work wondering if this was the day that the stems would break: the plants worked so, so hard to produce their flowers, which made the stems vulnerable from the heaviness of blooming. The stems never did break. But sometime before the end of the year, the plants died. Something about their environment was inhospitable to life.

First Quarter

China rang in the new year with a crash. Drops in both the Shanghai and Shenzhen indexes triggered circuit breakers that had been installed after the bubbles burst last summer over fears of a slowing economy, devalued currency, and increasing market turbulence from retail investors. Nai Nai, Dad's mom, who held fast to what I thought of as the Chinese dream—or the restoration of greatness and power through the prosperity of a people, a nation— was one of these investors. Nai Nai *loved* the stock market. She was always betting her life savings on this or that deal, which I had long viewed as speculation, gambling. Recently, I was told, she had made a quick buck. She cashed out and paid off my parents' mortgage. I did not know whether to attribute these events to luck, skill, or something like fate and destiny, but what I did know was that I had to take a closer look at China. It seemed like the rest of the world thought similarly: After the previous June's crashes, global markets had taken weeks to respond. Now, on the first trading day of the year, China's sharp sell-off ignited wildfires of panic, with the S&P 500 and the Nasdaq off to their worst starts since 2001, the Dow off to its worst start since 2008.

THE POWERBALL JACKPOT climbed to a record of over one and a half billion dollars. I bought a bunch of tickets for Boone. Chinese, American—was the dream the same?

AT 9:27 A.M. DAD texted me asking to talk. Monday had been a market holiday, so my boyfriend and I had flown to Michigan to visit my parents for the long weekend. I texted Dad back: *How about we chat quickly during lunch today?* Dad replied: *Great and delete this message from your phone after reading.* I have no memory of this call. But I have Gchats with Parmita after:

> ME: his opening line
>
> ME: "dan is like a hollow ghost with a mask of gold"
>
> ME: he is a sick person
>
> ME: he is weak
>
> ME: and he has bad genes
>
> PARMITA: omg sorry so Chinese

PARMITA: SO CHINESE

ME: like for 15 min

ME: "your kid will be sickly"

ME: my dad can't hold back

ME: he was getting so upset

ME: "you are pretty smart girl, can't you find someone else in NYC?"

ME: YOU ARE GOING TO SUFFER WITH DAN

ME: i'm like, dad

ME: I HATE JOSH

ME: HE MADE ME SUFFER

ME: and they're like how?

ME: you look happy?

ME: i almost cried

ME: my dad is trying

ME: but like

PARMITA: Never tell Dan this btw

PARMITA: He just doesn't need to know

PARMITA: Look I have been sickly my ENTIRE life

PARMITA: Like Carrie the DAY I got diagnosed with liver tumors

PARMITA: Was the day the Goldman internship apps were due

PARMITA: My dad filled mine OVER THE PHONE while
I was in the hospital

PARMITA: Like everyone was freakin out and I was
like look

PARMITA: If I die, fine

PARMITA: But if I live and I have no internship

PARMITA: That will be worse

Dan, who was a bit younger than me, was not sick, not that I saw.
We did weigh about the same. He carried a seat cushion for his back
wherever he went and also slept with a continuous positive airway
pressure machine, which he had brought with him to Michigan. My
parents must have gone into my room, saw, then assumed.

In the afternoon I messaged Parmita again:

ME: today

ME: utter shit show

ME: omg boone

ME: i am going to shit

ME: SO MUCH SHIT

I have no memory of this either. Boone, still, had never once
yelled at me—but his feedback and asks, which were continuous
and non-repeating such that I could never cement a routine or
mechanize some aspect to make them easier to complete, had increased in intensity.

A typical ask: One of Boone's companies would be reporting

earnings soon. Analysts had been revising down the sales forecast for the company's main revenue source as global markets continued to tumble. A recent morning at around nine o'clock, Boone was fretting over a data point—maybe a warning from a supplier to the company about weak orders—and asked me to pore over sell-side reports to determine the *change* in sentiment on the Street. Collecting a single data point would require me to read not one but two reports. Each report ranged from one to twenty or so pages of dense text and charts. "I need it by the open," Boone said. "Preferably before. And I need you to be accurate." I had less than thirty minutes to read dozens of research reports and pull and synthesize data that might or might not affect a billion-dollar position.

After the close of trading, the first of Carbon's major positions reported earnings. Netflix, another billion-dollar bet for Carbon, the stock of which was down about 5 percent year to date, beat on earnings per share and international subscriber growth. Investors worried about slowing US subscriber growth due to an already-high domestic penetration but ultimately shrugged off the concerns, homing in on Netflix's expansion in 130 new countries, pushing the stock 10 percent higher in after-hours trading.

At 5:00, 5:17, and 5:28 p.m. Mom sent me a series of WeChats. *My heart cries,* she began. *Your life is ours. . . . Fate ties us together. Daddy tries to let you see the bitterness of reality that is hard to take, and as a mom, I like you to see that fate is irresistible and the reality is inevitable.* She continued: *Dan is so the one I have never thought of could be good for you to match you. . . . I pity all of his aspects and sorry for him. He looks unusually weak and I am afraid that any day he becomes sick.* She signed off: *Forgive mom. . . . please no Dan to see. . . .*

Please delete all my word when you finish the reading of it. She said she loved me—*love,* a word that began appearing in our written communications soon after I left for college—she included three heart emojis too, but all I wanted to do was forsake everything Chinese for the rest of time.

I also wanted to scream, but I was at work, so I walked to the bathroom. I looked at my phone, at the icon for Instagram, thought of my former handle—mandarinescape—and realized of course the *mandarin* referred to how I wished I could escape my ethnicity. I touched the WeChat app and, as I considered how by then I was not even that into Dan, responded as calmly as I could to Mom: *You can either accept him. Or I will live by myself with him.*

THE FOLLOWING DAY, Netflix gave up its gains. It would fall the rest of the week.

AT 9:49 A.M., two days after his *I would like to talk to you* text, Dad texted again: *Can you call me at your convenience during your lunch time today?*

I replied: *Sure, I have an extremely busy day as the markets are a bit crazy right now, but I can try to call you. I won't have more than 5 minutes though.*

Dad responded: *We can talk tomorrow or some other day.*

Up until a year or two before this, I had been unable to withstand my parents being upset at me for more than a minute. If a call ended with something not quite right, I was the one who would call them back and apologize. Just like when I was very little, when my mother took me to the mall, I was the one who walked behind her—who chased after her, not the other way around—and the couple of times I lost sight of her (the Disney Store, Aladdin's Castle) I was the one who would find the information desk and, on my tiptoes so I could see okay above the counter, ask the adults to please page Mommy over the intercom. Today, I did not follow up with Dad.

LAST JANUARY, A NEWS AGENCY published a story with a picture of Boone exhumed from the archives of his alma mater. Nothing public was an accident—or, if it was, it was remedied, like last summer when a couple of assistants asked me, "Carrie! Did you see the photo of Boone up on Goop's blog?" No, I had not. They told me it was one of him sitting next to Gwyneth Paltrow at a soirée in the Hamptons. By the time I checked the blog, the photo was not there.

A year later, the same news agency cornered the market on recent images of Boone when it published a story on how he and other hedgies were preparing to shelter during an impending snowstorm. Boone had traveled across town to support Elisabeth, who was being honored for her years of volunteer work at another acclaimed hospital in the city. The article was accompanied by a shot of him in a suit, smiling and standing behind his wife.

TEXT FROM DAD, 9:22 a.m. on Saturday: *What is your personal email address now?* A blizzard was pummeling the city and would drop 26.8 inches of snow in Central Park by midnight, forcing New

Yorkers to stay home during a citywide travel ban. I let Dad's text sit for now.

Less than an hour later, although I had not replied to Dad, he emailed with the subject "Your life and Love" and an attachment titled Note2Carrie.docx. In 14-point Calibri, he wrote:

1) Your WeChat message to Mom hurt us very much.

2) Although you are an adult, we as parents have the moral obligation to share you what we know about life and love.

3) Your IQ is 140 but your EQ is very low. In terms of "love," you are so naive. We wanted to protect you. In return, you abandoned your parents and call it for the sake of love.

4) In terms of family value, a person's value is 100 divided by # of persons being dated with the max value of 100. This is not a culture argument but a universal civilized human value. *Sex and City* for entertainment is OK. But it is trash in terms of family value but you take it as your life principles. It looks like it has poisoned your soul. Unbelievable!

5) I am shocked to hear that Dan is trying hard to make you happy. True love comes from the bottom of heart, it comes out naturally. There is no need to try. For us, we are happy all the time. Why do we need someone to try to make us happy? As long as someone is trying, eventually this person will be tired and stop trying. In terms of happiness, there is no definition. Since there is no definition, how can you get it?

6) The logic of life is like this: if you have no desire, you are happy all the time. If you have some desire, you are somewhat happy. If you have a strong desire and want others to make you happy, your

life will be miserable. Simply put it in Chinese: ZhiZu ChangLe (happiness comes out of being satisfied). Wong, Mark, Ruth, Palermo, and Beth all held/hold the belief that we need to try hard to help the less fortunate. That is why we were able to come here in the US in the first place. Nobody can make your life happy if you yourself don't feel happy. And if you don't feel happy and want other people to make you happy, then your life will be miserable.

7) There is no doubt that Dan is trying to make you happy. But how long can this trying last? One year, 5 years, or 10 years? We know he wants to try. But will his physical conditions allow him to try? Steve Jobs wanted to live and try to stay alive at the end of his life. What was the result? Intention doesn't mean physically capable. Image this: Dan's physical condition is falling very fast and lying in the bed in just a few years and you have to serve and nurse him. This is 90% possibility. Your gamble is simply too risky.

8) Bottom line: Dan will destroy both your career and life, of course unwillingly and unintentionally. Of course, it is a judgmental call. God is your mind and you are what you think. You control your life.

9) Above all, we can't be happy if you take this person who is going to destroy your life as your life partner. How can we?

10) In short, ultimate happiness of life is seeing your child/children growing up healthily and happily. This is the essence of life. A happy life is a normal life. A normal life is the one without worries. Life with worries is not a happy life. Trying hard to seek life happiness will eventually end up in vain (see below).

Dad ended his note with a koan. My chest burned, a fire ripped through me—no, I did not want to be normal. I turned my phone face down and reached for my Carbon water bottle.

I TRIED TO DELETE DAD'S note from my mind but could not. I have no memory of taking an IQ test, although I must have taken one when I was six or so because I have a vague recollection of Mom and Dad arguing over whether to tell me the results. (Dad said no; he worried it would go to my head; he won.) This timeline would also make sense because I have a vague imprint in my mind of my parents debating whether to move me from first to fifth grade. (Mom said no; she wanted me to develop social-emotional intelligence; she won.) But fate *is* irresistible—it is within: I rushed out of Mom's uterus weeks premature. I rushed through high school; I finished the math and physics curricula by sophomore year, then spent much of my days taking science classes at Michigan State and counting down the seconds until college.

Dad was somewhat correct about my EQ. One part of it, that which was directed toward others—observing their wants, needs, and emotions and how I might act to bring about a pleasing outcome—was high; these were the skills for which I was rewarded at Carbon. But the other part of my EQ, that which was directed toward observing and knowing myself, was worse than "very low." It was nonexistent. To have awareness and control of your emotions, you must first have a self, a self from which to notice, a self that begins with a body. If I did not have a body, then I would not have a soul that was capable of being poisoned.

REFLECTING ON MY IQ test made me think of a related one: the
Carbon Test.

In the early nineties, Martin wanted a systemized way for finding
those people who could help his firm, Argon—which had generated
compounded annual returns of over 40 percent net in its first eleven
years—keep on winning. With the help of a psychoanalyst who was
a senior adviser to the fund, Martin developed a tool to screen
people for traits that he thought made for a great investor, among
them high intelligence, a strong sense of ethics, an indefatigable
work ethic, an innate competitive impulse (expressly in sports and
fitness—no wonder most people here were lean, toned), but also a
natural aptitude to work well as part of a team. Carbon had its in-
terviewees on the investment side, in the final rounds, take the Test.
It was an initiation ritual (and not uncommon, this sclerometer of
the mind, at least among top firms on Wall Street). The details have
been shrouded in secrecy. I did not take the Test, but this is everything I know.

You show up to a mid-century modern apartment on the Upper
West Side. The space is clearly someone's home, not too large,
packed with furniture and books. You're there for half a day. Part
one: The woman who lives there, a traditionally trained psycho-
therapist, reads you classic IQ-type questions. You answer verbally.
Part two: A Rorschach test. You are judged on your personality, in
particular on your inclination toward narcissism. As he wrote in
his decades-old book on the subject, Martin's adviser believed that
every one of us had come out of the womb selfish; that in terms of

societal collapse, great wealth and productive achievement should not be held at fault; that you can be as rapacious a capitalist as you want so long as you learn to love and give and root out your narcissism. No matter your walk of life, as he stressed on the last page, whatever its outcomes may be, you have no one to blame but yourself.

The adviser tabulated your performance. He called Boone and reported the results with the suspense of a murder-trial verdict. Boone wrote down notes; I scanned them into our database. I had been asked by people who took the Test to tell them what I scanned. I never did. But I thought it uncomfortably asymmetric, how you would start a job with your employer knowing something about you that you did not know yourself.

TEXT FROM DAD, 11:32 a.m. on Sunday: *Hi Carrie, busy?*

I replied: *Hi Dad, yes. I am just very tired and exhausted and I want to have peace and quiet at home, so I am reading today.*

Dad: *I sent you an email yesterday. Please take a look. It is important.*

I did not respond.

EMAIL FROM DAD, 10:51 a.m., two days later, with the subject "Life and Happiness" and the body:

> *Confucius said: "You should be settled in terms of family at age of 30"—*

I stopped reading.

After the close, Apple reported earnings. According to its press release, Apple delivered its biggest quarter ever due to all-time record sales of iPhone, Apple Watch, and Apple TV. It achieved a significant milestone of one billion active devices; it beat on earnings per share. Despite that superb quarter, its CEO warned of unprecedented conditions, citing how global markets had broadly been affected by fluctuating currencies, sinking commodity prices, and decelerating economic growth. Down 5 percent year to date, Apple would drop another 6 percent in the next trading session.

A company can beat expectations and set all-time records and still be depressed.

TEXT FROM DAD, 11:34 a.m. the next day: *Can we talk a little tomorrow during lunch time?*

I did not respond. I wanted to be left alone.

ALL I WANTED when I was a child was for my parents to pay attention to me. They did not have time to play with me, certainly never during the week, so I spent my time playing by myself, flipping through my mom's GRE books, doing logic puzzles, reading, planning, and waiting for Saturdays. I would beg my parents to take me out. Anywhere. I did not care—laundry, groceries, post office, though something preferably not errands. I loved our local zoo and children's garden. "Saturday I'll take you," Mom would sometimes reply at night after an extra-long day, during which she cooked, cleaned, worked, studied, and often sewed new clothes for me from fabrics she had bought on sale. Saturday morning would come. I'd jump out of bed.

"Mommy! What time are we going to the zoo?"

Silence.

"Mommy?"

Silence.

"Mom? You said you would take me to the zoo today—"

"We're not going."

"Why?"

"I don't want to."

"Why?"

"No reason."

"But why don't you want to?"

"No reason!" I could not understand why she was getting mad and shouting at me when she was the one who broke her word. "Stop bothering me!"

As fast as I felt myself wanting to cry I would remember Dad's phrase: *Crying, there's not enough time.* But I never stopped looking forward to Saturdays. It was around then that I started to assign an extremely high value to the ability to follow through, to keep one's word. I started to suppress bodily urges too. Because, you see, I did receive tons of attention from my parents. I could not cough without Mom grumbling, "Put on a turtleneck." Could not take a step without her carping, "Don't drag your feet." Could not watch cartoons (with the volume dialed as low as possible) without her needling, "Don't sit so close to the screen. You're ruining your eyes." I set plates down softly. I closed doors gently. I tried to exist as soundlessly as possible. But my parents always found a way. When I was ten, my fifth-grade teacher gifted me a copy of *Seventeen* magazine. At home, as I was turning the glossy pages in silence, Dad found me and said, "You're permanently ruining your mind by reading this garbage." Mom and Dad never gave up. I spaced out to protect myself. Smothered and neglected was how I'd felt my whole life.

AMAZON, YET ANOTHER billion-dollar bet for Carbon, down 6 percent year to date, reported earnings. It missed on earnings per share and revenue; its shares plunged in the evening, opening the next day down around 10 percent. After blowout beats in the second and third quarters of last year, investors and analysts had, perhaps, been a tad overly optimistic. Amazon would continue to fall for seven of the next eight trading days. Even though Amazon came up short of expectations, its revenue grew 22 percent from the previous year, its operating income grew 88 percent, and its web-services business grew apace as the segment's net sales and operating income surged, up 69 percent and 186 percent, respectively, from the previous year.

A company can grow, but if it's not in the precise directions and magnitudes others expect from it, then it can—and often does—take a beating.

NOTHING MATTERED. I had no feelings whatsoever about work, parents, Dan. If I died, fine.

Any roars of anger I felt toward my parents were calmed, the second I noticed them, by whimpers of sorrow, compassion, and care, leaving me debilitated from the whiplash of emotion. "We are happy all the time" was such a lie—to me. To them, it was a statement they needed to be true. Mom maintains that her *xiàfàng* days, when she was *sent down to the countryside*, were the happiest, easiest days of her life. I do not remember a single instance when either of them said one negative thing about China, their childhoods, their parents, or the Cultural Revolution. I do remember the first prayers I made when I was seven or so. I would run out of our apartment as my parents erupted at each other, threatening violence. Dad liked to throw things. Mom liked to bring up death. *Wǒ sǐle jiù hǎole. Wǒ sǐle nǐ jiù gāoxìngle.* As a child I did not know whether *I should just die* and *You'll finally be happy when I die* should be taken seriously. I felt the stress—always—of a life-and-death situation. I would sit in the dark stairwell outside our home, press my palms over my ears, close my eyes, and whisper: *Dear God, Please let my parents be happy and stop fighting. For that I'm willing to sacrifice anything. Thank you. Amen.* Praying and self-sacrifice gave me an illusory sense of control. As did ambition: I told my friends at the monkey bars, and my parents, I was going to make tons of money and buy them all houses. I wanted to take care of the money so that my parents would not need to work as much, and thus would have energy left over to be kind and loving to each other and me.

IT WAS THE LAST DAY of January. Carbon was down, Boone was down. I could not kick him further by bringing up my workload issues—not now.

ONE OF GABE'S COMPANIES reported earnings. The stock of the high-growth tech company was down about 13 percent year to date. It beat on earnings per share and revenue. A key number, however, for investors in its business model was license revenue, which grew by 31 percent from the previous year but was much lower than the 60 percent year-over-year growth from two quarters ago. The firm cut its forecasts for the year. Investors and analysts had already been worried about the vertiginous valuations of software firms, as well as an increase in competition in the space from, among others, Microsoft. The stock tanked, dropping nearly 50 percent after hours and hitting an all-time low, down 66 percent from its peak. Gabe sat across from Boone in Boone's office. They had been together since the start of the earnings call. I dared not look their way.

Around eight, Gabe opened the door. I got up. He walked past me without a look or a hello. Boone motioned for me to come in. He was silent without any expression as I went over our items. At the end of this sit, he did not ask me, What else? So, then, I studied his face. The blood in his cheeks laced in a pattern I had not seen before. I wanted to help him feel better. I did not know what to say. Everything felt like a big risk. Finally I said something along the lines of "No need to beat yourself up for things outside of your control."

"No," he said. "I am owning this. There is no such thing as a slump."

BOONE AND I had a long sit. He told me I was witnessing history. I recalled Sloane's parting words to Boone that he had shared with me—*a front-row seat to some of the coolest things happening in the world*—and thought about how, like her, I appreciated the view from my seat. Carbon met with prime ministers, entrepreneurs, philanthropists, financiers, record producers, fashion designers, and sports commissioners. There were constant whispers of a PM at Carbon being involved in a major piece of financial news, orchestrating mergers of companies affecting the way the average consumer lived. Was this *cool*? Yes. But was it *cool* or was it vile to be making a living off the luck of having inherited, from Martin, a reputation, an association, one that was enabling Carbon to focus more on returns and increasing returns on time and less on public relations and building a whole new brand from scratch? I stopped my wayward thoughts, transfixed by his statement from yesterday he had just repeated again today—*I am owning this*—equal parts mesmerized by his taking of responsibility and repelled by the presumption that something as entropic as the markets would be within his power to possess and control.

I GAVE MOM A CALL. She had WeChatted me. We had not spoken since MLK weekend. She wished me a happy birthday, then asked, "Daddy's email, nǐ shōu dàole méiyǒu?"

"Yes, I did."

"Ránhòu ne?"

"And I thank you for your words. I have taken them into consideration. But my life is my life and I am choosing to stay with Dan."

She sighed a sigh so loud and heavy I almost felt her breath. In Mandarin, she asked, "Do you know him? How do you know him? How can you understand him in this short a—"

"Mom, I can't talk to you about this right now. I'm at work."

"You were once *so* obedient, such a good daughter when you were with Jo—"

I hung up.

Mom used that phrase again: *tīnghuà*. Which means *listen words. Obedient. Submissive.* The first time I told her I felt controlled in my relationship with Josh, she had said to me, "Good. You're a wild child. You need a man to tame you." I could not understand why she had seemed partial to Josh till now: it was not Josh whom she liked but who I had been when I was with him.

I went to my spam folder. I saw an email from Josh, sent at 9:06 this morning: "Thinking of you. The whole 'family' wishes you an amazing day. Wish I could spend it with you." I walked to the bathroom, closed my eyes, covered them with my fingers, then screamed and screamed and screamed—silently—into my palms.

MID-FEBRUARY. S&P 500 closed down 10 percent for the year, down 14 percent from its peak last May. We were in a correction.

Some of Carbon's portfolio on the long side and their performances year to date:

A payments company, down 20.67 percent.

A data storage company, down 25.24 percent.

An e-commerce company, down 29.03 percent.

A lending company, down 33.30 percent.

A home goods company, down 40.59 percent.

A bloodbath. But this blood loss would be less alarming if the short side of the portfolio dropped even more and made up for some of the losses—the whole point of hedging. I was reminded that stocks are a projection of the most human aspects of us: irrational exuberance, unexplained depression, inexplicable need to achieve external validation of intrinsic value and worth. You can diversify away many kinds of risk—country, currency, industry, asset class, and factors like company size and value—but you can't diversify away the risk of being human. And being human means that market conditions can and will affect you more than you know.

I BEGAN MAKING mistakes at work. Chrome was a hedge fund that had debuted with much fanfare a few years back. It struggled last year, ending in the red. Boone said he might want out.

Boone had me schedule a meeting for him and one of Chrome's founders, Troy, at a restaurant home to the power breakfast. It was weeks away. In these weeks, Carbon was not able to turn around its performance. Chrome was also down for the year, though by less. Arctic air had shifted. "I'm going to hold," Boone said. "But keep the meeting."

The day before the breakfast, I was, per usual, at work before Boone. At 8:10 a.m. Troy called. "Where's Boone?"

There are moments in life you fear not because the moment itself is so terrifying but because it will reveal something to you, about you, after which things will never be the same. To guard against my lone recurring nightmare coming true (wherein I forget to do work), I was fanatical about calendars—my own and, of course, Boone's. In college I could not hang out with friends or meet my boyfriend until I completed just about everything due in the next week.

Boone was at home.

He was at home because I hadn't told him he had a breakfast meeting.

I hadn't told him he had a breakfast meeting because it wasn't on the calendar for today.

"He'll be *right* there," I said to Troy, knowing Boone could walk over in eight minutes.

I called Boone. No answer.

I called his apartment's landline. No answer.

I called the housekeeper. No answer.

I called his cell again—no answer.

I called Jen, who answered; I told her it was an emergency. Could she tell me who of the staff might be at the apartment right now?

I called the laundress. No answer.

I called the chef. No answer.

I called the management office of his building and asked them for the cell number of whoever was on concierge duty that day.

I considered sprinting to Boone's apartment and banging on the door.

I called the concierge, who answered; I told him it was an emergency. Could he please, please, *please* go knock on Boone's door? "Trust me," I said. "He'll thank you later."

After a minute that tied for one of the longest minutes of my life, Boone called.

"Boone—"

"I'm playing with my kids. What's up?"

"Emergency, my fault, I'm sorry. Your breakfast with Troy is today and not tomorrow, so please hurry up. He's waiting."

Click.

I called Troy back. "This is one-hundred-percent my fault: I had the wrong date on the calendar. I take full responsibility—my apologies. Boone is on his way to you." Troy waited over thirty minutes for Boone. For the first time in my life I thought I was going to get fired. The emotion I felt at the acknowledgment of that thought: relief.

An hour later, Boone walked into the office.

I sprang up from my chair. "Boone, I'm so—"

"Don't worry about it," he said. "You never make mistakes; I'm not worried. This is not a systemic thing." Boone is nice, I thought. *Sooooo* nice. But I was not sure about the validity of his last statement. I looked over at Lena, who was looking to the side of me with a blank face. Whenever she made a mistake, she did not tell us about it. She did not have to. She would sit in Michael's office with her face apple red as the rest of us would watch, on mute, through thick glass walls, Michael deliver a monologue à la Alec Baldwin in *Glengarry Glen Ross*.

Lena tried to console me with statements about how everyone makes mistakes. Still, I could not get myself in a sunny enough mood to don the great attitude that Boone had listed as a positive at each of my two year-ends. I was no longer my aptronym self.

"What's wrong?" Boone asked me at our end-of-day sit.

"I don't know. I feel terrible. This morning—"

"Stop."

"But—"

"Don't."

"I just—"

"This morning was *ages* ago. Don't indulge your emotions. Get over it. Move on."

THE DOOR SHUT behind me as I found a seat in the back of the room. I took out my phone, created a new note, and typed, *If you want to WIN.*

Nick Saban stood in front of the lectern. He spoke; I wrote. Considered by many to be the greatest college football coach of all time, Saban had won several national championships, one with the LSU Tigers and the rest with the Alabama Crimson Tide, ending the most recent season by winning the conference and the national playoffs. In all polls, his team ranked number one.

Mindset.

Discipline to execute.

Can you make yourself choose what you have to do to be successful?

Weeks ago, the *Journal* had reported on our lack of success, noting that January had been one of the worst months ever for the Firm. Boone, who was sitting closest to the coach wearing a suit, had responded by doing business as usual. Don't panic, he stressed to me. Focus on the process, keeping to the process. If Saban was known for one thing, it was his process, which he called the Process. But February saw the spread of a virus through the Caribbean. The retreat, which had been scheduled to take place at a resort in Anguilla to which Saban, as the guest speaker, was to be shuttled on a private jet, had to be moved back to the Manhattan offices.

DO YOUR JOB.

Be responsible for your own self.

Because I fail is WHY I succeed.

I knew about Saban. If the Center held any meaning for Boone, Saban held meaning for me. In the nineties, Saban was the head coach of the Michigan State Spartans. Uncle Palermo would give us tickets. Mom and Dad would take me to the stadium on Saturday afternoons.

Relentless about winning.

Being the best that you can be.

If you're a street sweeper, sweep streets like Michelangelo painted the Sistine Chapel.

At first the games looked like men running into each other. Pushing and shoving. Attacking and defending. Over time I saw them as tradition, culture, and American history. The waves, the chants, the buff white man in a green breastplate whom crowds descended on, who turned out to be Sparty the mascot—I wanted to be near it all. I loved the coming together, the collective joy of uniting toward a common goal. I loved that my parents and I were rooting for the same outcome and whatever spat they had been in was now on pause. I loved the rules, the formal nature of which reminded me of my other loves: math, logic, board games.

Before Saban, the Spartans had not had a winning season in four years. Under Saban, in twelve months, they ended up with a winning season and a bowl game. Underdogs can—with hard work and great luck—become winners. Was this not the American dream? I begged my parents to buy the movie *Little Giants*. I wore a cheer dress on game days, sometimes eye black too. Years later I applied to college with an essay on how I had the mindset of a football player.

What's important now.

Success is momentary now.

Only as good as your last play, last game.

In the essay, I had mentioned grit, tenacity, and the ability to bounce back from failure. But I knew, today, hearing Saban speak, my pull toward the game was deeper than that. This was a game about playing through trauma, wherein you're rewarded for your ability to take it—hit after hit, tackle after tackle—and come out the other side smiling. A game of life or death, do or die, in which the risk of catastrophe, the adrenaline accompanying a fight-or-flight response, drowns out the noisy troubles of your days. A game of no past, no future; you can be anyone you want on the field as long as everything you do is about the moment, each moment that is but one point in time. The price of participation was an epistemic delay. You won't know the degree to which the game will leave your insides—heart, mind, and soul—in ruins, until it is too late.

Human condition: to survive.

Saban told us to take every opportunity to say thank you. Appreciate everyone with specifics, he said. Help others be more successful, and help players be better people. Yet I wondered: Did being a helpful person erase the consequences of the game, which were often damaging and invisible, like chronic traumatic encephalopathy, a disease caused by repeated blows to the head that can lead to early dementia, mood disorders, and suicide? Why did we celebrate a game that caused so much injury? During the Q and A, Saban talked again about the mind, the mind, and how he would schedule twenty guest speakers a year for his players to get the mindset right. But if the mind was such a priority, why were players so quick to attack the region of the head? Through a game I once enjoyed I had participated in the causing of harm. The cost of unity—of feeling like one with my parents, of being a member of a large and cheering family—was the mental and physical health of others. All this violence—to what end? To possess time, capture yards, and march into a territory that does not belong to you?

Challenge of keeping on: have to enjoy Process of keeping on.

I used to look away from the television whenever a player was injured on the field. I told myself it was not part of the game, the clock was not running. I was wrong. The clock is always running. As Saban just said, there is no off-season, and there are no off minutes. So you don't get to play without acknowledging the harm, the trauma, the burnout. The challenge of keeping on becomes about endurance, and some of the best ways to endure are to compartmentalize the inconvenient, sublimate the pain, and forget the past. All my life I had been trying to right my mindset—had even gotten good at justifying the systems in which I found myself—in order to keep on. But this was a defense, a reflex, a coping mechanism; it was not who I was or who I aspired to be.

So what, what's next?

Saban thanked us for the opportunity to speak. Applause spread across the room. I clapped, slowly, locked my phone, and stood up.

In March, Carbon turned fifteen. I had not been here for Carbon10 but was told it involved an extra-fancy meal at a Michelin-starred restaurant with special guests and festivities to which everyone, not just the front office, was invited. But Boone was not in the mood. The funds were way down. With excitement, people would ask me, What's happening with Carbon15? I'd shake my head and say, Nothing. Boone was in such low spirits that no one (except Michael and Ethan) would go into his office until they received confirmation from me that he was agreeable enough to approach that day and hour. Unlike everyone else, I could not avoid Boone.

I had sent Boone an email last night along the lines of "I know you don't want to celebrate, but I think it'll be good for company morale if we do something tomorrow. Maybe a nice lunch at the office?" He agreed. I contacted Nobu, but the staff did not get back to me in time. I contacted Tao. They said okay. The next day, I made sure the catering arrived on time and intact and that the front- and back-office kitchens were both set up, then put together a plate of lobster wontons and Chilean sea bass satays. Tao had been one of the restaurants made famous by *Sex and the City*. I thought of my dad, who had blamed the show for perverting my values. It was true, I did watch *SATC* on repeat during my late teens and early twenties. I even took a class at MIT titled *Sex and the [City] Institute: An Exploration of Gender Roles and Sexuality*. But what I loved about the six seasons was not a woman's right to shoes, or to have sex like a man. I was drawn to a woman's right to have a full, thriving life in a big city, in her thirties—a life that seemed to be divorced from her childhood. The women had no backstories. It was that possibility of a future with no past that appealed to me—Boone and I weren't so different after all.

I looked at the giant fortune cookie inside of which was the custom fortune I had asked Tao to write for Carbon and Boone. Something like "May the next fifteen years be even better."

I looked around the kitchen, then back at Boone. I made him a plate, although I had already made him a backup plate, which his chef had delivered half an hour ago. I set down the plate of Tao in his office, thinking: This is all a performance. He'll say this food is too spicy; it'll go into the trash. By any measure Carbon was a success. Early LPs had made seventeen times their money over the course of fifteen years. Carbon employees who had invested in the main fund enjoyed a 26 percent compounded annual return since inception. During these same years, the middle class shrank, real wages flatlined, and inequality ballooned. Carbon grew and became one of the largest hedge funds and most active crossovers with a do-not-fuck-with reputation on the Street. They set the price, and the pace. Boone became a billionaire. And yet, somehow, everyone around me at work was in misery. I was in misery. I might have been unduly influenced by Boone's unrelenting bad mood, but I needed to stop making excuses for Boone—and myself.

I TEXTED MY PARENTS, who had not called me since my birthday (nor I them): *Just want you and Mom to know that Dan is not the person for me. I am happier by myself.*

Eleven minutes later Dad replied: *You are 100% right. He may be a good person but not the type for you in terms of family. We love you, always!*

A THURSDAY. Outside, it was dark. I went to find Boone. The front office was empty. Everyone, including the middle and back offices, was in the kitchen watching March Madness.

"Boone?" I said, standing in the doorway of his office. "Come to the kitchen?"

He was sitting facing his desk, not his two screens, both of which were black. He stared at the stack of reading in front of him, then looked back up at me, and, after the faintest sigh, said, "I can't. I have so much work. I don't have time."

SOMETIME NEAR THE END of March: The main fund was down around 20 percent for the year. Boone called me into his office. Carbon had gone through so many changes that he did not want to test the patience of his LPs again. "No changes," he said. "But if I've learned anything"—I was waiting for this; what would his grand takeaway be?—"it's not that the bets were wrong. It's that the size of the bets could be better, more dynamic given market conditions."

Inspired by Boone and his reassessment of Carbon's portfolio, I reassessed my portfolio (of life choices) as well. My thought process went something like this:

Confront the brutal facts.

I have hit rock bottom. I eat normally at work every morning, but then, in the afternoons, I continue my habit of cupcake-sundae deliveries and later go home and close the door and rid myself of myself. I don't remember when it began. Probably sometime in the past two months when every minute of every day I've wished to leave my life behind. I am materials rich and agency poor: I feel starved of freedom, starved of the ability to do the self-constitutive activities that would make me me—so I feed myself, fill up and up and up. I have a set of memories with the same notes: turn on both hot and cold faucets because I hate the sound of my habits; purge; look over to the window where the dead orchids are sitting because I can't bear to throw them away (I'm hoping they'll spring back to life); purge again; brush my teeth; look at the moss and succulents in my terrarium and think of how they are still alive by being in a glass cage. I've gained thirty-six pounds since the start of Carbon. I can walk. But not run. I can't work out. Sometimes I will chew and spit. This will happen at the office with Dang Coconut Chips, but only in the afternoons when shit gets so crazy that all I want to do is—this is the word I've been typing to Parmita—*die*. No item in my wardrobe fits me anymore, so I wear only Rent the Runway dresses. My bruxism has returned. I can't sleep, I can't think, I can't cry.

Take note of market conditions.

Boone calls me into his office. "Martin has been talking up this analyst he wants me to meet," he says. "Let's set up a short meeting." Weeks later, Boone calls me in and says, "Martin wants me to put money into Noah's start-up." Boone forwards me Noah's deck and white paper and tells me to read them and give him my thoughts. In a long PDF document with small fonts, Noah's first sentence sticks out. He boasts about his résumé (not dissimilar to mine) with a self-confidence I only know of in my dreams. At our next sit, Boone asks, "What do you think of Noah?" Whatever I say will not matter; Martin has already given Noah his stamp of approval. So, I say, Of course there can be no doubt that he is an impressive person. Boone specifically asks me what I think of that first sentence. I tell him. But I'm right, it does not matter what I think: Boone invests. Noah's start-up helps students around the world gain admissions into elite institutions of higher learning. The values it espouses are achievement, prestige, status, merit, ambition, youth—his materials are peppered with youngest this, youngest that. Might there be more to life than getting into an Ivy League college? Katherine dropped out of Princeton; her start-up wants to widen the sources of talent to be more inclusive. Noah is trying to get everyone (that is, those who can afford his tutoring and admissions-consulting services) into Princeton. His start-up is tech-enabled. Another word for his industry: Edtech.

A cop stops Boone out east. He tells me he was racing to take his daughter to a Taylor Swift concert and going way over the posted limit, I think; he tells me to call his lawyer in the Hamptons. I know how this will (probably) end up. I have no reaction.

Soon after, I start to detect the flickers of a political consciousness. Until now I have been apolitical. I read the news; I know of (but do not engage in any) issues; I have never voted. Some of this is the result of an intentional deprioritization of politics; but most of it is because some other part of me knows how much I feel compelled to identify with winners, which scares me: I fear I might sympathize with the wrong team.

I notice this compulsion beginning in the eighth grade. Before then I had identified with the unheard and unseen. In elementary school, one day after recess, I raised my hand and asked the teacher, "Why is it okay to step on the grass? How do you know the grass does not have feelings?" I worry this anecdote might be a false memory, but I find confirmation of this frame of mind in my diary, when I write around the time of my near-fatal pneumonia: *All life created equal* and *Who is to say that . . . I'm more worthy than the life of a daisy?*

But later that same year, Saban left MSU, and even though both my parents went there for grad school, I was tired of feeling helpless and inadequate and small and down and lost and now I wanted to win badly: I switched my support to the Michigan Wolverines, the winningest team in college football. From then on I identified with the victors, the favorites, the people who stomped on the grass. It gave me a brief sense of control—a Hail Mary for future liberation—when I felt I had none. Because I felt so minimized at home, I imagined myself into positions of maximum freedom and agency. Fast-forward to today, to Boone, someone for whom speed limits do not apply. After reading about a different man who was approached by a cop on Staten Island, who was then choked to death for allegedly committing a most minor infraction, I realize, now, my fear has come true.

An author's sophomore book is about to be published. A private wealth manager to tech billionaires contacts our office asking Boone to host a book-launch party at his home for the author.

Boone is incapable of throwing a party not to *Vogue* standards, so he hires an event producer. I want to go. I love books. Boone knows this. But I know there is no way Boone will put me on the invite list that includes other rich and famous people who are Boone and Elisabeth's closest friends. On one of my walkabouts with Jen after work, I mention how, of all the finance and tech and fashion heavyweights who come through our office, a professorial author is who I most want to meet. "The East and West Coasts are very different," she says. "There was no upstairs-downstairs when I worked in the Bay Area, but that is, obviously, not the case here." Boone tells me to go order twenty copies of the author's book off Amazon, put it on the corporate card, and take one. A short while later, in a sit, Boone and I are again discussing books. I am still in awe of the writer, all writers, every single one of them and the entirety of book publishing, and I say, "Someday, I am going to write a book about you." Boone does not smile back. Nor does he give me his classic rhetorical question plus a death stare. Nor, surprisingly, does he say no. He responds instantly: "Well, I'd have to do something worth writing about first."

Adjust the size of the bets.

I must change my life.

PART THREE

In the future, as the bits get pieced
back together, who knows what
will come into view?

—DAVID GRAEBER
AND DAVID WENGROW,
The Dawn of Everything

Second Quarter

I sat in a window seat on my journey (back) to the west. To *měiguó*, America, the *beautiful country*. I had spent the past week taking my first solo vacation: two nights in Shanghai, five nights in Hangzhou, where my parents vacationed after they got married and Mom said she and Dad were once the happiest. I had gone to the lake where three pools mirror the moon to be alone and to change my life. According to my boarding pass, I had fifteen hours ahead of me before landing, so I removed my shoes, put on clean socks, and turned off the in-flight entertainment system. I looked through the plexiglass and thought of my parents, their American dream.

IN THEIR YOUNGER YEARS, Mom and Dad were the people who (to borrow a phrase from Edwidge Danticat) read dangerously. Mao feared a counterrevolution to his revolution, so he forced over sixteen million urban youth from their homes and exiled them to the country's remote areas to be reeducated. Anyone caught reading Western literature risked persecution, public shaming, even death. My parents were sent down to the villages. They did not go to school. They farmed, they labored. Wheat, rice. They carried rocks up and down high mountains to make reservoirs to harvest the rain. But on one important front, they did not obey. Dad told me they saved banned books and hid them from the guards, burying them in the dirt roads during the day and later digging them up at night, after lights out, reading them under dim flickers of oil reflecting shards of moonlight. This was how Dad—working over twelve hours a day, making one cent an hour, staying in a hut he had built using sun-dried mud-bricks strengthened with rice husks—continued to educate himself. In a different village, Mom exhibited such out-standing behavior that the peasants chose her to be the lǎoshī to their children. She requested materials on as many subjects as she could. This was how Mom—also working over twelve hours a day, making two to three cents an hour, now spending her days as a *teacher* in a hut she had built using the same method as Dad—kept her mind sharp. As the Revolution neared its end, my parents dug up their books, begged friends for more, and scrambled to study for the national college entrance exam, the single determinant of col-lege placement, which had been canceled for over a decade. Mom and Dad took the exam, and—competing with millions of test-takers, from young teens to people in their late thirties, most of whose coming-of-age stories had been ruptured, delayed, and re-written by the state—they passed. The pass rates for the first couple exams were around 5 percent.

Mom and Dad met at the oldest university in their province on the first day of the fall semester of the first year there was college after the end of one of the most turbulent periods in recent Chinese history. It was 1978. Mom was twenty-two, Dad twenty. They were English majors. After college, they married. Protest literacy is in my blood.

In the eighties, Mom and Dad taught English at separate institutions of higher learning in the city of Hefei, the capital of Anhui. Dad was selected by his school to be the translator/guide for two visiting scholars from the United States: Ruth (whom I could not bring myself to contact again after canceling on her) and Paul Wong, a third-generation Chinese American who was a professor at Michigan State. Ruth and Paul took a liking to Dad; they helped him come to America in 1988. Mom was now a single working mother, still teaching; she could not take care of me so I was mostly left with my grandmother and aunts. After many months of long airmail letters back and forth (Mom and Dad both saved them all) Mom received one in which Dad mentioned his thoughts of *zìshā*. *Self-kill*. During the Revolution, Dad had endured a grave loss of personal liberty, and yet, apparently, that was nothing compared to the pain of, as he wrote, the loneliness of being in America. The isolation. He said he missed her. He loved her. Mom wrote back immediately and said she would be coming to him. She traveled to the US consulate in Shanghai and pleaded her case but was denied a visa on May 24, 1989, eleven days before the Tiananmen Square Massacre. Mom was never one to take no for an answer. She went back to the same consulate not two months after she had been refused. Political dynamics had shifted. "I eagerly appeal to you for a reconsideration of my application," she wrote, after which she listed her supporting documents. On the second page, an explanation:

> *The first. My husband has worked well for his program. He has got some financial support from his MSU. As he has planned to complete his master degree program and begin a new program for his PhD degree, I have to decide to see him for once. We both miss each other very much. . . . I assure you of that my projected stay in the US would be temporary. If my application was passed, I would have to leave my 4-year-old daughter at my parents. . . . Though it would be a great suffering to us, We have to do it so.*
>
> *The second. According to the national rules of home-leave, my school ratified my application and allowed me just a half year for it. I am a teacher of university, and I know that I should obey the rules and keep my word as well.*
>
> *The third, the most. Your country is great and beautiful. I have a few American friends and correspond with them regularly. . . . I have got to know much of your great country. And I want to say: I will strictly observe the laws of USA. . . . So long as I met my husband and accompanyed him for a few months, I would be very happy and much satisfied.*

Two months later, Mom received a letter asking her to go to the consulate for an interview. There was a time, not long ago, when America believed in not separating families: the letter asked her to bring me as well. Mom was shocked but elated. Both visas were approved; I would no longer be left behind. I do not remember the interview, but I remember running up and down the aisles of a dimly lit airplane, imagining I was on the rings of a new planet. There were no nonstop flights between China and the US, so we went from Shanghai to Tokyo to Chicago to Lansing, the capital of Michigan. We landed in America on the first of January of 1990.

ON APRIL 11, 1990, when Mom and I had less than two months left on our tourist visas, President George H. W. Bush signed an executive order delaying the deportation of Chinese nationals who'd been in the United States after the Tiananmen protests. The directive gave temporary protections to some Chinese in America, who feared persecution upon their return; after all, they had shown allegiance to the enemy: democracy. They received employment authorization until January 1, 1994. Mom and Dad, knowing any day we might have to go back, decided to stay.

MY PARENTS NEVER involved me in their money worries, but I knew: they were extremely law-abiding yet would soak stamps off of incoming mail and reuse them; I had free lunch at school.

Mom signed me up for piano lessons at the age of six. At first, I did not practice. I was not interested. One day, Mom screamed at me, screamed that I was wasting her money. She knocked, knocked, knocked on my forehead as if one more knock would crack the code to my bad attitude, then pulled me by my ear—I felt sure my ear would peel off my head like a sticker—and dragged my body to the piano. I learned to yield to authority.

Then one morning when I was in second grade, as I was pouring milk out of a bag into a bowl of corn flakes, I spilled some of it. I blinked, froze, and found myself on the floor. Dad did not say a word. Mom was out. Because I was (and still am) in the habit of avoiding mirrors, I did not see the bruise that had developed across half my face. The face, Mom has said, that's where Dad would always hit you. I felt no pain. I said nothing to my teachers. But the police showed up at our home that evening. They told Dad if he did this again, he would be sent to jail. Dad said we had just come from China; he did not yet know American laws and customs. Mom got home right as Dad was signing some attestation. Purple yam, Mom later told me, was the color of my cheek. No one apologized to me. No one told me what Dad did was wrong, or that his reflexive response to my inability to hold steady a pitcher cradling a bag of Quality Dairy was perhaps a displacement of *his* trauma—of everything lost when he and Mom went from being teachers at universities surrounded by their large, beloved families to being a dishwasher, a yard worker, a handyman, a maid, paying out-of-state tuitions in a country where those who knew them best did not know their real names. Call us Lou and Lily, they would tell people. So the lesson I learned here was that this was my fault: I had to be perfect. If I was perfect and careful and did not waste money, no one would be hurt. Most important, if I was perfect, Dad would not have to go away.

ON OCTOBER 9, 1992, President Bush signed into law the Chinese Student Protection Act, which gave green cards to Chinese nationals like me and my parents. Mom and Dad, whose goal had never been to emigrate in the first place, decided we would try to make a permanent home in the United States.

DAD LEFT WHEN I was ten. Mom was out. I came home after school. He hugged me—this is my first explicit memory of us touching—and when he let go I saw tears dripping down his cheeks for the first time. I was certain this was the end of the world. He told me he couldn't live with Mom anymore. "You're too young to understand," he said before he walked away carrying nothing; his bags were already in the trunk of the car. I knelt on our sofa, put one finger between two thin blinds, pulled down on the vinyl, and watched him drive off in our brown Honda Civic, the car getting smaller and smaller until it was no more, disappearing behind a building.

A war raged inside of me: Whom to believe? Dad, who had said that he was not leaving me? Mom, who had told me ever since I could remember that Dad had never wanted to have me? Or myself, who had witnessed Mom and Dad arguing again and again over—their biggest source of disagreement—me? Dad thought I was spoiled and that Mom was too nice, too lenient, too giving toward me; his default was *no*. Mom secretly spent her meager earnings on me so I could buy a 29-cent doughnut or rent a 99-cent video. I was convinced that Dad had left because of me.

When Mom got home, she seemed unsurprised. She did not cry. Between yells of "Your daddy is so stupid!" and "He is so not capable!" I pieced together what might have happened. Something about Dad using their money to gamble in the stock market, maybe. He had lost some or most or all of it, maybe. This was the money they had been saving for a down payment on a house after using their first chunk of savings to pay back Ruth, who had given them funds to start their lives over in America (although she had insisted that they not return her gift). Dad felt controlled; Mom felt like she was doing the right thing by taking over the family finances. From then on I told myself that when I grew up, I would never depend on anyone, especially a man, to live.

A week or two later, Dad came back. He told me on a different day, when Mom was away, he had come back for me, to provide me with a stable home and *jiāting. Family.* I was so unbelievably happy and felt certain there was a God that I instantly started crying. But as much as I wanted Dad here, with us, I was also confused and exhausted from hearing Mom's and Dad's shouting punctuated with silent treatment; from being Mom's little confidante given Dad's repeated stepping outside their marriage; from fantasizing about the day that Mom—with my help, with my unwavering love, kindness, promises, and attention—would be strong enough never to need Dad ever again; and from thinking that Dad no longer wanted to be with Mom because he'd wanted to be in a childless union. Every time thenceforth my parents fought I would feel my organs turn into lead with the weight of responsibility for Dad's unhappiness.

And then there was Mom. At five years old, I saw *Creepshow 2,* a film of short stories by Stephen King; for about a decade I was terrified of moving bodies of water, including the toilet, especially the flush. At six, I saw *The Rape of Doctor Willis*; I wondered what *rape* was. Mom believed in exposure therapy and shielded me from very little, immersing me in culture from *Red Azalea* to *The Rape of Nanking* to Eugene O'Neill's plays. When I was still writing back-stories for my Polly Pockets, Mom told me in another world I would've had many brothers and sisters. She had had multiple forced abortions after she gave birth to me because of China's one-child policy. Then the government mutilated her body with an IUD. In Michigan, Mom went to check on her contraceptive. The doctor told her that the device, which had been altered to be more difficult to remove, was so out of place, so embedded in her uterus, extracting it would require surgery. Mom, for much of her life, had no control over her body, her womanhood, the place whence I came. I'd watch her keel over in pain and suddenly yelp, wince, and shrink. I'd ask her if she was okay and wait by her side. She would look to the side of me and tell me to go away.

THINGS CHANGED AFTER Dad left and came back. I began to wish for a broken home. Broken would be an equilibrium. Our family was in the process of breaking and breaking, and as a result, I felt consumed by an anxiety of not knowing if Dad would be there after I got home every day.

MY PARENTS NEVER pressured me to do well in school, but they did not have to. I figured out the only way to dilute the potency of their constant commentary on me was to study. When I studied, they criticized me less, and I wouldn't have to do chores. I studied all the time—I loved it.

But freshman year of high school I loved it a little less. Classes were easy. Dad saw me spend time with friends. One day, he sat me down in our family room after dinner. "We came to America for *you*," he said, pointing his finger at me and speaking in English. "We stayed in America to give you opportunities your mom and I never had. Do you know how much we suffered? We suffered so much and it was all for"—Dad's voice broke, and I thought this might be the second time I would see him in tears—"you." He sighed. "And what do you do? How do you thank us? You waste *all* the opportunities we give to you. Your life is *so* easy compared to ours. But," said Dad, looking down, shaking his head and still pointing at me, "your life is your life. You do whatever you want. If you fuck up now, it is *your* future you're fucking up, not ours." I thought of their suffering. How my mom's nails were thickened, her hands and feet swollen, permanently, from being soaked in water all day as she toiled in the paddies stepping on night soil, with leeches crawling up and down her bare arms and legs. How my dad hated eating fish, although he still went fishing, because when he was little, there was no food, and he would have to catch fish in the local rivers not to starve. I will never know the extent to which they suffered, not really, and I will never know the dreams and sorrows and hopes and despairs they carried along with their sickles into the fields, with each new dawn, as the roosters crowed and the birds chirped, but I knew then—as I do now—their journeys would live on in me.

"Dad," I said, "I promise you: I won't waste my life." From that night on I spent zero effort socializing or making friends. No time for crushes either. I went all in on my education.

Mom became a US citizen in 2000, Dad in 2001, me also in 2001.

By the time of my high school years, my parents' finances had improved. I had had braces. I'd moved up to reduced lunch, then regular lunch, then when I turned sixteen my parents bought me a new car. Dad would wake up early and fill the tank for me before I went to school. Though Dad worked as an IT specialist doing database management and programming for the State of Michigan, he could not help but pick up coins he saw lying on the sidewalk. Though Mom worked as a researcher doing statistics and data analysis for the University of Michigan, she could not help but demand we flash-showered one after another so the home water tank would have to heat up only once. My parents unscrewed half the light bulbs that came preinstalled in our house because the brightness, they said, was wasting electricity. They would save the soapy water from doing dishes to do more dishes; and, as they did, I would search the fridge for an American dessert, prying open the lid of a tub of cream puffs only to find eggs from their latest brine, rice from their latest fermentation, or raw perch, pike, and bass from their latest haul.

My parents became highly active and cherished members of their Chinese community. Many weeks we would go to potlucks or game nights at other families' houses. We would bring my mom's famous spring rolls, renowned for their soft, juicy fillings wrapped inside thin, crispy shells. Mom had been awarded favorite teacher, several times, at our Sunday Chinese school, where I saw her be soft and oh so kind to every single kid she taught; I wondered why she could not be that way with me. (Mom *loved* kids, and education; she donated money, even when she had next to none of it, to support the schooling of children in remote Chinese villages.) I had thought that my parents would be nicer to each other and to me once their lives were less of a struggle, once they had settled into their desk jobs, but my homelife improved marginally, at best. One of the ways that Dad lovingly referred to Mom—and I could never tell whether she objected to it—was *dǎng. The Party.* As in: the only party that mattered.

The one thing I detected that gave my parents a touch of joy—that caused them both to relax, smile, and sometimes even laugh—was when their investments made money. They invested in single-name securities. They loved casinos. They loved watching sports and playing cards with their Chinese friends (with whom they traded stock tips). I considered their favorite outdoor activity—fishing—a kind of casino too. It baffled me how my parents, whose jobs were both quantitative in nature, could find thrilling and happy and blissful what I perceived to be a combination of uncertainty and luck. I had been reading Burton Malkiel on the efficiency of markets. He argued that the "stock market is so good at adjusting to new information that no one can predict its future course." But after experiencing firsthand what monetary good luck could do for families, I decided I would try to prove him wrong: I would try to find a pattern in the stock market and share it with the world. This would be my contribution, my theory of everything.

I applied to MIT early action because it seemed like the best place to learn how one might go about achieving that goal. At the same time I played piano and was coeditor of my high school's literary journal. I loved music, I loved literature, but I never believed a career in the arts or humanities was a possibility for me. I never believed it was in my power to tell the story. So I graduated as co-valedictorian in a class of 393, undecided between the sciences. My parents and I had moved into a four-bed, three-and-a-half-bath, 3,392-square-foot beige-brick house with a professionally landscaped garden during my senior year. After the last day of classes, our house was TP'd and vandalized. Mom and Dad were horrified, mostly about the lawn, which had been spray-painted with letters and numbers spanning the whole front yard: *FUCK YOU 4.0.* The paint killed the grass. The other co-valedictorians' houses weren't targeted, not that we knew of, so Mom and Dad saw this as a hateful, perhaps racist, act, especially since I had been called a chink on some classmate's blog a few years earlier.

Dad spent a day on a ladder removing toilet paper from the trees. Later, Mom and Dad went to Home Depot to buy materials to reseed the area underneath the message. I asked to help, I felt this was not right; they told me to stay home and *bié dòngshǒu. Don't move hand.* The new grass grew back in no time, but it was never the same color or texture as the rest of the lawn.

SOMEWHERE OVER THE PACIFIC OCEAN, I decided I was not ready to leave Carbon. I had agreed to give Boone five to ten years and could not bring myself to break my word.

"How was your vacation?" Boone asked. We were in a Monday-morning sit. He looked tan from being in the Caribbean for a week with his family.

"As you know," I said, "I went to China. I saw my great-grandmother, who's one of the oldest people in Shanghai."

"Really?"

"She was just in her local newspaper for being something like the second-oldest living person in the district of Xuhui." I thought of how astonishing it was, given China's long history of female infanticide, that my family on my mother's side had four living generations of *first*born women. When I was growing up, Mom would tell me to always remember that coursing through my veins were *chāoji nǔ jīyīn. Super woman genes.*

"How old?"

"One-oh-eight this year. No heart disease, no Alzheimer's, no high blood pressure."

"What's her secret?"

"Her heart is calm; she doesn't worry. She's lived through two world wars, a civil war, famines, revolutions, and she fears nothing, not even death."

Boone chuckled. "Guess I'm in trouble."

My mistakes continued. Each task added a variable risk of interruption; each interruption broke my concentration by five or ten or thirty minutes. Before I could return to where I had left off, another interruption would come, and I could never get back to the thing I needed to do.

Gabe was away on a research trip. He had back-to-back meetings before heading to the airport for a return flight; I forgot to check him in online. I was in the middle of several tasks requiring focus when my calendar reminder went off and I snoozed it. By the time I remembered, it was after the cutoff. When he arrived at the security checkpoint, there was no way for him to board the flight. I called and called—travel agency, credit card, frequent-flier program, all the luxury concierge services for Carbon and for Boone—but having status could not rewind time. I got him booked on another flight, a disruption of about an hour for him.

The next day at the office, Gabe did not yell at me, though he was even more silent than his normal taciturn self. After I finished apologizing, he said, "This cannot happen again."

"I know; there's no excuse. I will set even more reminders for myself."

"Maybe you need to do less work."

As Boone was signing papers in his office, I said, "*Billions* invited me to their writers' room."

"Really?" He stopped his pen and eyed me. He had told me months ago that he was watching the series. "The actual show?"

"Yeah."

A small shrug.

THE ROOM WAS ALIVE, flooded with the kind of effervescent midspring sun that tapped you on the shoulder and invited you to go outside. Eight or so people sat around a table looking at me.

"Does he know you're here?" Brian asked.

"Yes," I said. "He trusts me."

Brian smiled. I had met him last month at a dinner party. He had asked me if I watched the show, if I thought it was accurate; I had said yes and that N18HF, the helicopter one of the main characters took at the beginning of episode two, was a tail number with which I was much too familiar. He had tapped my shoulder twice and said, "We must chat."

Sitting next to Brian today was David, a co-creator of the series and Brian's longtime writing partner. Together, they had written *Rounders*, a cult classic, with lines like "If you can't spot the sucker . . . then you *are* the sucker." The movie came out before the poker boom of the aughts, a craze they had helped feed by giving the Hollywood treatment to the underground world of illegal high-stakes gambling.

After some small talk, Brian got down to it: "We invited you here because we're thinking of bringing a character like you onto the show. A chief of staff, right-hand-man or -woman-type character for the next season. Let's start at the beginning."

I took a sip of water. Brian and David asked nearly all of the questions.

Where were you born?

How did you come to America?

Where did you grow up?

What was your childhood like?

What were your parents like?

Where did you go to college?

What were your majors?

Why did you graduate early?

Did you have difficulties with friendships?

Did you have difficulties in relationships?

How was it difficult being a young woman working in finance?

So, much of your life has been about underselling yourself and your abilities not to make others around you feel bad, right? Especially the men? Now you've got this highly adaptable and chameleon-like quality to you . . . which is why you were probably drawn to Carbon in the first place because there you felt like you might finally be free to be your full, ambitious self?

Let's backtrack a little: How did you get the job?

Aren't you overqualified?

Walk us through your typical day.

What do you mean by triage situations?

What do you mean by his eyes and ears?

How's your relationship with his wife?

Why are you not his type?

There must be friction between you and other assistants, right?

What about you and the COO?

How well are you paid?

Do you have the power to fire someone?

We would ask you what you do outside of work but there is no "outside of work," is there?

As I answered the writers' questions, I could see new ones forming in their heads, queueing up like ping-pong balls in a lottery machine waiting to be read. I was prepared for all of them except this next one.

"So, tell us: What are you going to do after you leave Carbon?" Brian asked.

I looked at him, silent, shocked at his phrasing. I reached for the bottle of water and took a second sip.

"You can do anything you want in this world," he said. "Where do you go next?"

HOURS LATER, Parmita and I met up for our first double date: her and her new boyfriend, an MBA candidate at a top business school, and me and Josh, whom I had started seeing again.

Yes. I know. None of my friends were happy about this. After I finally replied to one of Josh's emails, one with an Edna St. Vincent Millay poem, he had sent me another one: "Prospects" by Anthony Hecht. The poem, which talked about setting out for the sublime, revived parts of me that I had let die at Carbon: the want of softness, pleasure, beauty, joy, dreams, play, song, and—my most guilty admission—*ease*. I wanted my life to be easier. I was exhausted by my job existing for someone else, doing whatever it took to make Boone's life easier. I wanted someone to want to take care of me. Josh said he was traveling between Florida, London, and Michigan but would fly into New York for the day to meet me wherever and whenever. I chose a restaurant near my apartment at five thirty p.m. on a Sunday.

Josh teared up the second he saw me. He asked the hostess to give us a table in the back. He apologized for trying to control me. If I wanted to work forever at Carbon, he'd love me. If I wanted to write books, he'd love me. He loved my drive, my strength. We have all the time and money in the world, he said. I reminded him of the specifics of that control: making me negotiate my diet with him for one dessert after dinner every other day; telling me to fix my skin; telling me that I had anger management issues; telling me that he did not like or love the parts of me that would get passionate, animated, emotional. "I regret *all* of it," he said. "I was so stupid. I never thought I could love someone as much as you, and the more I loved you, the more vulnerable I felt, the more I took my insecurities out on you. I've really grown in our time apart."

I was at my lowest. Josh felt bad and familiar. I did not believe him. But one day later I heard myself trying to talk myself into giving him another chance. He had never, despite our many arguments, raised his voice with me. He had never seen his parents fight or yell or say anything mean to each other (they'd been happily married for decades), and so he believed that all speech between couples should be civil and sincere, without any hint of negative valence. He would ask me about my inner life (even if he did proceed to invalidate my reality), and, if I felt anything less than great, he would want to hear every last thing I had to say, as long as I said it with, in his words, a "Pooh voice." To him, I was never a bother. He had never once forgotten my birthday. Whenever I fell sick or cut my finger cooking or in any way accidentally hurt myself, he would rush over and hug me and ask me if I was okay.

Now the four of us sat down to dinner at an Italian restaurant in

SoHo. Parmita had come straight from her new job as a director of business development for a fast-growing Series A start-up. She had gone into those interviews as assertive and aggressive as ever and surfaced mere hours later having closed the deal. No longer in finance, she seemed much happier, much less anxious. Before we received our menus, Parmita squealed, "Carrie! *Billions*! Spill!" She turned around and hung her bag on the back of her chair. "Tell us everything."

I gushed about how brilliant I found the writers, how I thought that they were all probably secret psychics. "I hardly told them anything. They deduced everything."

"So exciting!" Parmita said.

I gushed about Brian and David, who seemed to understand not only the technical side of hedge funds but also the complex psychologies and intricate relationships of everyone working at a fund. "And at the end," I said, "Brian asked me, 'What's the secret to being a billionaire?' That's what everyone wants to know."

Josh shifted in his seat.

"I told him the big secret is that there is no secret. Boone sent me four books in the mail before I started and his so-called"—I made air quotes—"'secret' is that he executes those simple concepts exceptionally and consistently well. But I think that is literally the hardest thing to do. Of course, he has *help* executing them; that's the whole point. It's all about the hidden help, the people to whom you can farm out tasks covering every inch of your life so you only spend your time in total devotion to your"—I pinched my right thumb and index finger—"tiny little hedgehog thing." I thought of how Boone had not once been interrupted at work by his kids.

Josh took a sip of water, looked away from the table.

"Finally," I continued, "when I got up to leave, Brian said, 'You're so interesting. We were going to make this character a man, but now I think we'll have to make her a woman. Can we make her Chinese too? Is that too obvious?' I told him, 'No, go ahead.' And you know what the most shocking part of the whole experience was? They just assumed *I* was going to leave Carbon. It wasn't an issue of *if* but *when*."

Parmita's boyfriend, Anant, had not said a word—understandable; we had just met. Parmita and I both looked at Josh, who had not asked me a single question or expressed any enthusiasm during the conversation. He shifted, again, in his seat. Parmita and I glanced at each other before she turned her body toward Josh and said, "So, Carrie tells me you're spending half your time in New York?" Josh parted his lips and started talking about himself.

AFTER DINNER THE FOUR of us went to a lounge with velvet booths for a digestif. When Parmita and Anant went up to the bar to order their drinks, I turned to Josh and asked, "What's wrong?"

"Nothing."

"Why are you sulking?"

Silence.

"Why are you not interested in my lunch with *Billions*?"

Silence.

"You said you would be supportive of my career, and I need to be able to talk about my work, whether that's *Billions*, Carbon—"

"Can you stop saying *Billions*?"

"*Billions* the number or *Billions* the television show?"

"I don't want to hear about Boone."

"You don't want to hear about Boone, *Billions*, or Carbon? Which is it?"

"All of it."

Silence.

"Are you jealous of Boone?"

"Stop saying his name!"

"But he's my boss."

Josh paused for half a beat. "He's not even a good investor, you know. He got lucky."

"Please stop—"

"He got lucky on timing and low interest rates and rode the tech wave."

"You're wrong."

"Facebook? C'mon. Anyone with half a—"

"*Stop.* Boone is a genius."

A waiter came over. I scanned the menu as Josh ordered his wine. "I'll have this one," I said, pointing to a rosé cocktail; then, with my index finger, I traced over the menu to the lower right-hand side. "And a cookie plate. Thank you." The waiter wrote down our order and left.

"You're getting dessert?" Josh asked.

"I am. Do you have a problem with that?"

"We just had a full meal at Charlie Bird."

"Yes . . . but we only had appetizers and entrées and the razor clams were teeny tiny and I'm still hungry and want to have something sweet to go with my drink."

"Uh, that's a lot of calories."

"Are you kidding? You literally promised me days ago that you would stop with this."

Parmita and Anant returned. I asked about their summer plans. As they talked, I thought back to the emails Josh had written me after we reconnected. Subject: "I'm Certainly Glad to See You Again." Attached was a link with an explanation: "I was just as overcome with emotions seeing you at dinner. My hope is we can avoid the sad mistakes that Gatsby and Daisy made after such an incredibly promising reunion." Then, in a follow-up email, Josh shared how he had "come to know jealousy among peers" and had "mostly overcome it," naming his best friend from college, who had quit a hedge fund job to start a tech firm and thereafter landed on the cover of a major financial magazine with the largest IPO ever in his industry.

Josh and I returned to my apartment. As I hung up my keys on the hook next to the door, I drew my bottom line: "If you ever try to control me or my eating again, I'm out." Josh apologized. He did not know what had gotten into him, it was the alcohol, he wouldn't do it again. "And I won't let you shame me about my work," I said.

"You know you're just a glorified secretary, right?"

"How would you know? You don't ask about my job or what I do and you never want to hear me talk about Boone—"

"Don't say his name!"

I breathed in and out and in and, evenly, quietly, said, "You never want to hear about Boone or Carbon, so you don't know anything about what goes on during the day."

"I don't need to know any details to know that you're getting paid to make him feel better about himself."

LATE SATURDAY NIGHT. I was at a friend's birthday party in Murray Hill. Boone texted me asking me to do something work-related. Then he sent another text, fifteen words—a flippant, dismissive remark that was personally insulting to me.

So. In the very next instant I watched my thumbs tap-tap-tap and then tap the blue arrow to send a reply in less than a second:

I *totally* understand what you mean!

A new low.

Instead of telling him he must watch his words—that this was a callous way to talk about me and those I love and represent—I had agreed with him. Not only that: the speed and ease with which I had abandoned myself and my people for the sake of Boone, to help *him* feel good, to help a man who did not believe he was a subject worthy of a book feel better about himself—

I accepted his unreasonable requests as reasonable ones.

I told myself I was just doing my job, executing orders, being a professional.

I put my own needs aside for Carbon and Boone because I had believed that serving my employer meant serving humanity. I had believed in the prestige of Carbon, which, to me, lay not in any zeros after commas but in the moral legitimacy of the enterprise. I ignored the fact that individual portfolio managers at Carbon used individual private jets. I ignored how each of those private jets contributed to climate change and government revenue shortfalls via tax breaks. I ignored the carried interest loophole. I ignored the fact that many middle-class workers paid more in taxes, percentage-wise, than hedge fund managers or private equity execs. I ignored the very real privileges of everyone, including me, working at Carbon, how people treated us differently, how they tripped over one another to make *our* lives easier: they answered our calls; we jumped the queues; they gave us discounts and freebies and—what killed me—they saved their best behavior for us.

Something was wrong with this setup. I knew it. I think he did too.

I HAD BEEN WONDERING WHO, if anyone, Boone thought held any power over him. If his spokesperson called, he returned the call with no delay. If Ken Griffin or Henry Kravis or Martin asked to meet, he told me to "make it work." None of this was unexpected. Boone cared about any person or institution who could change the game on him.

What I did not expect was for Boone to be so accommodating of entrepreneurs in need of capital. When we planned his last trip out west, during which he met with, among others, the founders of two of the hottest start-ups in the Valley, Boone told me to defer to their schedules. One time, a founder came to visit us and asked to be helicoptered into the city to avoid traffic. I asked Boone, thinking he'd say no. "Put him on my personal account," he said. Another time, a founder wanted to show Boone a deck but could only, for scheduling reasons, do it in downtown SF, away from his offices. Boone told me to book a boardroom at the Four Seasons, spending like four thousand dollars to see this one hour-long presentation. He even got to some of these meetings early and waited. Whole minutes. He met founders on their terms. These might seem like micro details, but, to me, they represented a reversal in the circuitry of the type of venture capital I had grown up reading about. They also represented a fundamental reversal in the meaning of money: What if you gave someone your money and did not take control?

Another reversal: Boone appeared to be less interested in moonshots. About Katherine, he had later said to me, "Too ambitious." About other start-ups, he had said, "Technology too difficult." Most venture capitalists went after tail events, those very circumstances that might produce extreme, outsize returns precisely *because* their end goals were so ambitious and difficult. But Boone—instead of spending most of his time swinging for home runs and hoping for grand slams—consistently and methodically swung for singles and doubles and triples, loading the bases so that any future hit would bring in a run and increase his team's score. His Investor Day quote (about the imperative to "take note of all that which time—years and years—will make obvious") had been a dead giveaway: the kind of change that would take many years to become obvious was incremental, not radical.

When Boone told me that he had not yet done anything worth writing about, at first I thought, Is he too humble? Then I thought, He's telling me everything.

While rarely bothering with board seats, Carbon did add value to a portfolio company beyond access to financial capital. They provided access to their vast network (they could get a founder on the phone with anyone in the business world in no time) and access to intellectual capital (they might, say, connect a founder to additional expert resources). In the frame of reference of venture capital, it was indisputable, especially given the internal rates of return, that Carbon had added value. In the frame of reference of hedge funds, it was also indisputable that Carbon had added value. Fifteen years of good-to-great performance with one down year was almost surely attributable to skill, not luck. Carbon was much written about in the financial press. Ergo, the frame of reference of his statement had to have been, in fact, the world, inside of which he had yet to achieve something of value or do something of note—which would make his statement an indictment of the entire industries of venture capital and hedge funds.

Boone harbored no illusions about the game. This was, perhaps, his ultimate genius. I saw how the belief that the game was about more than just money was my fallacy, not his. I had fallen for his diversions, those repeated instructions to be "super nice" and "thoughtful" and "kind" and to "give first." I had fallen for them most readily because a large part of me was motivated to believe the lie, the myth—that a big, powerful crossover fund could care about something else, something greater, like morality or being a net positive to society; that the financial system could be fair and driven by something other than greed and self-interest. I used to think that Boone was driven by a love of the game, whatever the game was, and that making money was a side effect. No. There was only money. Everything *else* was a side effect.

It all went back to what he had said to me in my first month at Carbon. Running a fund involved two aspects, explicated best by the two buckets of fees: performance, management. PMs must not only pick winning companies but also manage their funds; it's a balancing act that, depending on the size of your fund, could tilt either way. For Boone, even as Carbon surged in AUM, he and Carbon appeared to focus only on the performance. Carbon liked to hire young, hungry, and moldable, but it did not really invest the time or the money to develop our talents and help us level up. Carbon did not have HR. No one in operations beside the CFO and his assistant (who also split her time supporting the entire team of traders). True, there was the back office, but that's because they were there to support the performance. Boone did not schmooze. He and I had never had a drink or meal or coffee together, the two of us. He despised office drama, did not want to get involved in any of it—he had called it "brain damage." He seemed to believe that the human aspects of the Firm would, if the returns were high enough, self-sort. If you have the highest returns and the highest pay, nearly everything will solve itself because the people—internal workers and external LPs—will convince themselves that they want to be a part of your mission. Greed is good because it makes things predictable. No need to coerce or enforce or foist any delusions when you have people volunteering to do the labor of self-persuasion.

Case in point: Carbon was down over 20 percent and did not lose investors.

Money can solve nearly everything.

Nearly everything. The real enemy of a hedge or venture or crossover fund was any person who was not in the room and who could not be persuaded to want to be in the room. Put differently: someone who could not be fueled by money.

SOMETIME IN JUNE, our chief compliance officer called me and asked to get in to see Boone. Jeff never talked to Boone. We were never not in compliance.

Jeff came over and sat down with Boone. After a few minutes, he got up, shook hands with Boone, and left. In a sit that afternoon, Boone told me Jeff was leaving for another job. A memory slipped into my mind: Boone and I are walking through Central Park; I'm on my second interview with him, when he, after staring into space, tells me that no one from Carbon has ever left on their own. It was hard to believe. But I had believed it. Last month, a friend of mine, a smart and hardworking Asian woman who did accounting in the back office, left to go to business school; she had told me she saw no upward movement for herself at Carbon. Half a year ago, another friend, a brilliant math major, an Ivy League graduate, who had been one of only two full-time Black employees I knew of at the Firm, left to switch jobs, maybe even careers, because he felt that there was no upward path for him either. "The head traders are young and won't leave their jobs for a while," he'd said. "I'm paid extremely well—for what? Why?"

I returned to my desk. I set down my notepad, put down my pen. I felt ready to leave.

July 1 – September 26

Boone had told me over and over that as long as I was a team player, he'd always have my back. Which was why I almost never spoke up. I let things go. The first time I had spoken up, about Courtney, I felt I was hung out to dry; I wrote it off as a fluke.

Sometime in July I decided I would have to speak up again. I dreaded (I knew) this would not go smoothly, so I had delayed and delayed until after I felt ready to leave. My issues with IT were coming to a head. It had been almost two years. I simply wanted them to do their jobs. In a sit after Boone got back from this year's Sun Valley conference, I spoke up about my feeling a lack of support from Ted and his team. I came armed with documented examples—and felt beyond petty doing this, but Boone responded positively only to proof, data. I mentioned it was not just me; all the assistants, like Lena and Val, shared similar stories with one another every few days. "I'm not trying to blame IT," I said. "I'm really not. But I need help doing my work. Other assistants feel this way too. I've reached a point where I'm unable to keep picking up the slack from IT and also be able to perform at the level of perfection you expect from me."

He nodded, then said, "I understand how this might be frustrating for you." He was thinking and deciding. Perhaps hoping I might just drop it. "But these guys are the best we can find. Ted and his team, they're not perfect, but they're the best we've got."

Since the previous fall, Boone had been chiding me about my standards being too low, telling me every other day some version of "Do *not* mention *any*thing to me until you have thoroughly vetted it as *the best in the world.*" What happened to this mindset? Why was it selectively applied? "I'm so sorry, Boone," I said, watching my tone, "but I can't let this go. I have multiple examples of IT not doing their job. You're telling me you're okay with this?"

"Fine. Should I involve Jay so it's anonymous between you guys?"

"Sure."

"I don't want to get involved."

It was then, in an instant, I understood: Everyone was merely trying to get by. Me, IT, other assistants—everyone was overworked. Or, as Val had texted me, *Everyone's been unhappy.* Boone was right, I would face resistance. The responsibility, however, did not lie with me to be nicer or more likable and not with Ted or Courtney or any of my colleagues to be more helpful either, but with Boone, the fund owner, because the dominant mindset at Carbon, a firm making billions, was one of scarcity. I was on my own. Again. I rose up from my chair and walked out of his office, hoping that my even gait would steady my wild and breaking heart.

GLOBAL MARKETS HAD BEGUN the year in decline. After February, the public equity markets and oil prices rebounded but the IPO market remained soft. For Carbon, things were down and stayed down—public equity funds, private equity valuations, Boone's mood—except the amount of work. To many of us it felt like it increased; this was the Twenty-Mile March.

Boone seemed to take more meetings this year than he had the previous year when Carbon was more actively deploying capital. He also spoke words I had never expected to escape out of his mouth. "Too expensive," he said when he and Val and I sat to review the budget for Family Day. "What can we cut?" When he saw that not a single person at the office budged from their desks at four p.m. on Family Day, he gave me a direct order: "Round everyone up." Seven minutes later, our butts soldered to our chairs, he told me to send an email to Carbon-NewYork-All telling everyone to drop everything and go down now. It took me forty minutes to dislodge four people from their work. Lena did not go. Neither did Erin (who had kept her seat after Kelly, a mother now, came back and quickly transitioned over to Ethan's family office). I imagined Val, who had planned this event, alone at Victorian Gardens, waiting an hour for her colleagues to show up.

The rain had stopped. But the air was still wet. The venue felt like a deserted schoolyard. No kids, barely any adults. The paint on the tugboat and crop-duster planes looked dull and faded and the gardens had a revolting quality to it, a place where clowns, balloon twisters, popcorn scoopers, and other low-wage workers readied themselves and forced smiles to entertain absent plutocrats. I looked up at the gray sky and felt hope. Clouds spread the light and softened the rays so that no one on the ground today would have to walk in the shadows of Billionaires' Row.

AT 6:59 A.M. I texted Val: *This is all I am thinking about.*

Twenty minutes later she replied: *Same!! I'm so anxious to get it off my chest.*

It was Friday, the week after Labor Day. I chose the half hour before lunch when Boone would be free. I walked into his office and asked if Val and I could talk to him. He nodded. I told him to meet us in Meru. We did not want the whole front office staring.

Val and I speed-walked to the conference room so we could have a few seconds to settle in and pump ourselves up. She had been expressing to me that she could not take the stress of her job anymore. She was getting migraines, her face was breaking out, her hair was thinning.

Boone arrived a minute later. He sat at the head of the table, between me and Val. I began: "Hi, Boone. Thank you so much for taking the time to hear us out today. We wanted to talk to you about how the Firm might be able to help us do our jobs even better. We've been feeling increasingly overworked and burned out and we wanted to talk to you about how to make our situations at Carbon feel more tenable."

He nodded.

I looked at Val.

"Carrie and I both work so hard," she said, "and it's extra hard when we have so much work to do and we see people—I won't name names—but there are people around us who take personal calls or gossip in the kitchen for hours. They're also never at their desks, so we have to pick up their lines and take messages for them. I am so overworked, I've literally been having daily migraines"—Val's voice cracked; her eyes watered, and her tears, one by one and then a torrent of them, fell—"and even when I'm out on vacation, I get constant emails. I'm constantly working on the weekends. The problem is that we have to respond to everything instantly, so we are always 'on,' we are never 'off.' We feel completely drained."

Boone looked at me. "Do you feel this way too?"

"Yes. A hundred percent."

Boone looked back at Val. "So . . . what is it that you guys want?" Val and I glanced at each other. We had rehearsed this. Boone went on: "You might not want the same things, so, separately"—he looked at me—"tell me: What is it that you want?"

"For me," I said, "I would like a reduction in workload. I need help. I've been making mistakes and they are unacceptable. And while I know everyone makes mistakes, I feel mine are indicative of the intense and unbearable *volume* of responsibilities."

Boone turned to Val. "And you?"

"I agree with Carrie on the volume issue. But, for me, I would prefer one of two things. The value I bring to this role is very high, and, given the amount of work I do, I would like to be more fairly compensated with, hopefully, a raise. And if that's not possible, then based on the type of work I do for Ari and Jacob, I would like, hopefully, a title change. From an assistant to something like a research coordinator or research associate."

He nodded—though barely, not in agreement but in thought. "I hear you," he said. I examined him for tells, but I could see none. "First, let me thank you two for working your butts off and for speaking up. Give me some time to see what we can do for you. Maybe like, get you guys invested in the fund or something. But . . . give me some time."

We nodded, smiled. Boone left the room. Val walked over to my side, which was closer to the door. "Carrie, I didn't look stupid, did I?" she asked, wiping her wet cheeks with her palms. "I can't believe I cried. I feel so stupid."

"No," I assured her, wishing I could cry myself. "I know Boone. If anything, this worked to your advantage."

THE SECOND BOONE saw me arrive back at my desk, he called me into his office. "So," he said, as he motioned for me to close the door, "what's really going on?"

Slowly, I shut the door and sat down on a plush leather armchair. I was wearing a black rectangle of fabric that made me look like a king-size pillow. My weight remained up over thirty pounds. I was wearing flats, the single pair I had been living in for the past half a year—they were so stretched out that I was unable to take a step without the soles exfoliating the carpet. I looked at Boone. "I feel like I am underwater and cannot last another day. What's really going on is exactly what Val and I said to you in Meru."

"But what's the real issue?"

I held myself back from rushing to repeat it all. "I feel extremely stressed. I feel like I am responsible for too much, and it has been taking a toll on me physically, mentally, emotionally."

Boone looked me up and down.

I explained my physical ailments.

"You look great to me."

"Leaving how I look out of the equation for a minute," I said, "I am telling you that I am feeling overwhelmed. The first year I said nothing because I was new and had a lot to learn. I thought the second year would be better, but it wasn't. I have given everything to this job, I just had my two-year work anniversary, now I'm starting my third year here and—"

"Have you tried taking breaks?"

"I don't think this is about breaks."

"I think you should experiment with taking breaks. Fifteen, twenty minutes, in the afternoons. I do it most days. It really helps."

"But I can't, there's so much work. If I take a break that same work will still be there, plus twenty more minutes of piled-up work."

"Taking breaks will help you better cope with your stress."

"It's not about the breaks."

Boone's hands were resting on the table. Inch by inch he raised them up high. "Stress," he said, pressing his palms down in one sudden swoop, as if to keep something from rising, "is a hundred percent mental. It's all about the mindset. It's been a very difficult year for Carbon—for me too. That's probably why you're stressed. I think you should try a few more stress management techniques. Get some professional help or something."

I could not believe it. I kept cool, went rational. "I've already tried all sorts of things: acupuncture, exercise, meditation. I've also tried breaks. Boone, I've tried them all. Of course I have. It was the first thing I tried; it's not working. I'm asking for help. I need help."

"Take the afternoon off."

"What?"

"Right now. Leave. Don't worry about a thing."

"But I have so much work to do today."

"Don't worry. Go de-stress."

I sighed silently. "Okay. Sure. Thanks so much, Boone." I took my notepad and pen and walked out of his office, back to my desk, where I stared at my monitors and sat inert. I looked around my cube as if it were one of those word-search puzzles in which whatever jumped out at you first would be the solution to your life's problems: *Superbosses*.

My work phone rang.

I picked up.

Boone told me to come in.

I went back in and sat down.

"I got you an afternoon at the spa," he said. "It's at two p.m. today, at the Peninsula." A swell of tears sloshed inside of me and I observed how I had no energy left to suppress the innermost parts of myself. I thought this might be my virgin lachrymal moment at work. It wasn't.

Boone gave me things. Things that did not help. I longed to live and work in a perfect, beautiful world where good intentions would be enough. I longed to feel more gratitude for the spa days, shopping sprees, vacations, private fitness sessions, but the truth was any gratitude I did feel was totally eclipsed by a desire for a change in process. I needed not individual solutions (like breaks) or materialist pleasures (like scrubs) but structural, procedural, systemic changes. I thought of the deep-tissue massage and deep-cleansing facial that I would receive soon and realized here was the problem: solutions advertised as deep only touched the surface.

WHILE I WAS AT THE SPA, Val sat with Ari. She texted me at 4:55 p.m.:

> Ari called me into his office and we had an amazing convo. He agrees with us even more than BRP agrees with us. He was like it is way more clear than you think and boone and I are both spending the weekend to think it over but we want you and Carrie to both be more than satisfied
>
> Without you I wouldn't have the balls for this. Honestly
>
> I thought I must be wrong if no one else feels this way
>
> Thank YOU!

In truth it was I who had Val to thank. Were it not for her, I would have continued to believe that my burnout was in my head and all my fault.

MONDAY CAME. TUESDAY CAME. Val and I were ecstatic and bouncing with energy, at work early both days. Every assistant supported at least two people; that was the rule. At nine a.m. Val left

the office to go to Jacob's apartment to wait for a furniture delivery.
Two hours later, she and I texted:

> Between us if things don't change I
> can't keep doing this job. I'm giving it
> until year end. Ari just emailed me a
> bunch of stuff he wants by when he's in
> the office at noon. I told him I'm at
> Jacobs until lunch time. He just doesn't
> care. No one cares they just want what
> they want.

Okay between us ME TOO. End of year.

> I literally can't it's killing me. We are
> going to live short lives

THE NEXT DAY, Boone told me to tell Val to go into his office. I
mouthed *Good luck* as she walked by me. Theirs was a short conversation. Val walked out and did not look my way.

In the afternoon, when Lena and Erin were away from their
desks and Boone was out on his daily break, Val came over to my
cube and said, "He said no."

"Nothing?"

She shook her head.

"So, literally, no changes? No investment in the fund either?"

"No. He said if they give me a raise and other people hear about
it, then everyone will start asking for one; then he said if they give
me a title change, other people will start asking for that too; so they
can't give me anything. But he said my efforts don't go unnoticed."

I so wanted to believe this, I knew how much Boone cared about us, but this seemed to me like a sad, tragic, imperfect process, at best—to sit around and wait and hope that your boss and your boss's boss notice all the work you do. At Carbon, we were encouraged never to say things like "That was me" or "I did that." But how would anyone know the work you did and the efforts you put in if you did not advocate for yourself? What if your supervisor was too busy to notice? (Or, simply, less than omniscient?) Was your worth only what your boss could see?

HOURS LATER, BOONE called me in for our end-of-day sit.

"You heard from Val?" Boone asked.

"Yeah," I said, wondering when he would answer my request for a reduced workload.

"What do you think?"

"It is what it is, I guess."

"People always think the grass is greener somewhere else. They leave, they find out: it's never greener. This is how most funds are. This is what it takes to survive. If they don't like it, then they can leave. We know our pay is among the highest on the Street. People are paid well; some are even overpaid. Money is the only reason anyone is here anyway."

I SAT IN a suite at Michigan Stadium watching the Wolverines play the Nittany Lions. I could not get into the game. At least Boone had gotten back to Val; he had not gotten back to me. It had been a week since I told Boone I needed immediate help, a week since he told me to take breaks and deal with stress better, a week since he blamed me for my inability to handle my workload. A week was at least two eternities in hedge fund time.

Days earlier, I had begun therapy because Boone had told me to get professional help. That was his suggestion to address the issues created by his workplace. I had flipped through hundreds and hundreds of profiles until I saw one and thought, *Yes, you!* The therapist seemed like a good fit given her background in East Asian studies and her own experience with career change. She agreed to see me for two hour-long sessions to start. At the first session, I described my physical symptoms, including repeat colds, headaches, allergies, fatigue, acid reflux, indigestion, dry eye, eczema. I described how for months after a bad ankle sprain I could not walk right. I described my disordered eating, although I said the worst of it was over and I had mostly stopped. I described my emotional issues. How I felt on the precipice of collapse. "Why am I so bad at dealing with stress?" I asked her. "I used to be the person who could do anything, *nothing* fazed me, and now I can't even do this *one* job. What is wrong with me?"

Without pause my therapist said, "Nothing's wrong with you. Your job is killing you."

The following day, I had my second session. As I was packing up to leave work, Elisabeth called to offer support. Her voice was gentle, cheerful—motherly, one might say. "Sometimes, we have bad days. We just need to calm down, not get worked up, and not overreact," she said. "Like yesterday Ryan came up to me and was like, 'Mom, I'm having the *worst day ever*' and I told her, 'We all have bad days, honey, it's okay.'" Elisabeth was trying to empathize with me.

She was trying. Really, really trying. "Boone is having probably the worst year of his life since Carbon began. It's been *very* tough on him, so I know it can't be easy for you. It's been hard on me too." I did not know what to say. She went on: "You know, I didn't have much help at home until like our second kid. He was like, 'You don't work. What do you do all day? Why do you need help?' And I just had to be patient with him"—I gasped silently into the receiver—"and explain to him all that I do as a full-time mom with two kids. Over time he understood and agreed to get me more help. But, some days, I still think he doesn't get it."

I wanted to extend my arms out and hug, hug, hug Elisabeth, who helped me realize that I no longer wanted to spend my days proving my worth, justifying my humanity, defending my mental and physical health, and patiently waiting for her husband to "get it."

Because I did not know how to get off the call I ended up being late to my three-hundred-dollar-an-hour therapy. When I arrived I talked a mile a minute about how I felt paralyzed by the need to make some big decisions. "I want to quit my life," I told my therapist. "But I promised him five to ten years. I'll feel like a total hypocrite if I break my word."

"You made that promise," she said, "with all the information available to you then. And now you have new information. You are allowed to change your mind."

THE PROCESS BY WHICH I changed my mind—also known as Bayesian inference, or the updating of priors upon receiving new information—was broken. I had a vested interest in not letting it work. One of the first beliefs I held was that my parents loved me. I did not update this belief every time my father forgot my birthday or every time my mother said that she wished she had never had kids. I got in the habit of not changing my mind in the face of overwhelming evidence. I had a happy, easy, and normal childhood—Mom said so.

In college I interviewed for a research role with a quant shop in Chicago. I made it to the superday and walked into a room with blank walls and no windows, where I was handed a derivative pricing problem. (I can't remember what it was, something about options.) I did my computation on a piece of paper in front of the interviewer and looked up when I was done. "So, it's trading far below that right now and the price is falling," he said, after which I doubted my calculation and retraced the steps of my work. "What do you do?"

I felt so dumb, but I shoved my feelings aside and went rational: Something was wrong and the possibilities were that I was wrong, the model was wrong, or the market was wrong. I did not think that the model, for which two people had won the Nobel Prize, could be wrong. I checked my math, did not think I was wrong either. It had to be others, vague others, others whose behavior did not fit the model. "Well," I said, "it appears, then, that this is underpriced."

"So what do you do?"

"I . . . would"—fighting my instincts, betting on logic—"buy more?"

"That's right! You double down."

The interviewer was testing the basics of my financial knowledge, but the real test was of my default moral and ideological position: that those working in finance—its academics, practitioners, and experts—were right; everyone *else* was wrong. An adaptive habit of mine—ignoring evidence and doubling down on some prior belief; one might also call this having a thick skin—was rewarded: I received an offer of employment, which I turned down for Fidelity, even as I continued to wonder how much evidence it would take for those in power, those making the models, to update *their* beliefs.

This habit of mine was further ingrained at Carbon: the countless times Boone had told me not to let anyone or anything get to me. Ignore the press. Ignore the world. Keep your head down. Do good work. The ways in which I had adapted to survive my early years—repression of character, frozen memories and beliefs, playing dead to stay alive, cultivating a bulletproof heart and mind—had made me the perfect handmaiden for financial capitalism.

THE NEXT BUSINESS DAY, sometime after Team Lunch because I did not want to interrupt his Monday-morning flow, I walked into Boone's office. "Hey, Boone, can I talk to you?"

He was scrolling through Page Six. He gave a nod and swung his chair around.

I slid the door shut and sat down.

"Don't tell me you're leaving me." He laughed.

I delivered my rehearsed lines, devoid of emotion. I feared if I let myself feel anything at all, there might be a possibility I would back down. "And so, for reasons I'm happy to get into if you'd like, I've decided it's best for me to transition out of this role and move on."

His square shoulders, flat eyebrows—all of it betrayed no emotion. Several seconds later, he asked, "Are you joking?"

"No. I'm serious. I'm beyond grateful to have been given the opportunity to work at Carbon and, especially, to work with you so closely, and I thank—"

"What's the matter?"

My eyes watered. I raced to wipe away any tears before Boone could see. "The matter is that I feel overworked. I am constantly stressed. You tell me to ask for help, and when I do . . . I feel I've received no help in reducing my workload."

"There must be something else."

"I'm telling you I'm burned out."

"Carrie." The tone in which he said my name meant a lesson was coming. "When I founded Carbon, I was burned out for a *decade*." He looked up and away. "No. *More* than that." He looked back at me. "If I can take it, I think you can too. You're tough; you're among the toughest I know. Want a sabbatical? If so, take it, and your job will be here waiting for you because finding your replacement will take a couple years at least."

A pause.

Then he asked, "What do you want?"

"What do you mean?"

"Tell me how to fix this; I'll do it. Anything."

I had written down notes prior to this meeting about what I wanted: to leave on good terms as I immediately reduced my responsibilities and to fully exit by Thanksgiving, around two months from now. I was less than three months away from year-end bonuses but could not make it. I could not make it one more day at the current pace. Given everything I knew about Boone, I had not entertained the possibility that he would try to convince me to stay. I thought about his words as a chorus of critical voices hissed in my ear, one of which was telling me to speak faster, another of which was telling me, as for my burnout, its fault was mine and mine only. I let my gaze fall to my lap, took a deep breath in, and, looking back up at him in the eye, said, "I want to be heard. I want my concerns not to be dismissed and ignored. Right now, that means less work. I cannot cover Gabe. And I need help—immediately. At least a part-time assistant, preferably full-time, someone I can turn to on a whim and ask for support."

"Done." He stared hard at me. "Actually . . . let me get back to you on both items. First I have to talk to Michael. Everyone here supports more than one person, so if word gets out and we give Gabe to someone else, we don't want a wave of people asking for less work. On the additional hire, the optics aren't great if you have an assistant. But maybe we can do a work-around, like have her sit somewhere else, not at Carbon? Maybe at the family office?"

"I would strongly prefer it if my assistant sat at Carbon, with me."

Boone continued to stare. At last, he said, "If we end up making these changes for you—and you understand that these are *huge* changes—you have to promise to give this a fair chance. You have to give it some time to see the effects of the changes. Do we have a plan?"

We held our first ever assistants' team meeting on the Friday after I tried to resign. Jay was present; Boone was not. I had suggested something like this in both of my self-evaluations. We were eight women, none of whom had kids, all of whom were trying to survive in a gendered office culture that prized the ability to put work above everything else.

As I made my way to Meru, I thought of Elisabeth, who had called me again after I tried to quit. We talked for ninety minutes. "I get it," she said. "It's still the most catty, intense girl-fighting culture, right?" I thought of how Val and Erin were not on speaking terms and avoided each other in the halls. I do not remember what had caused their fallout, but I realized then, with each step I took, that we, the assistants, were not to blame for our infighting. I had thought that maybe Sloane and Courtney were my adversaries—no, it was the Carbon culture that pitted us against one another. We did not share information. Institutional memory was siloed. We had zero standardization across roles (except being in charge of calendars). We received no central messaging. We had no channels to resolve work issues, like how our jobs mean the willingness to do anything at any time and with a smile. The supervisor-feedback form was littered with *goes above the call of duty, eager to help, persists, volunteers*. We could never say no to our superiors so we said no to one another. Carbon could easily give us more resources and yet we fought over arbitrary limits, like receptionists' time. Carbon's executives had told us they did not want us gossiping with one another out of privacy concerns. I now saw this as a cover for the fear of what would happen if we came together and talked.

We arrived in the conference room and sat equidistantly around the large table. I looked at Jay, whose hair was uncombed. I looked at Lena, who had been complaining mere hours ago about being exhausted yet unable to bring herself to say anything. I looked at Val, who had told me, after Boone agreed to my load-shedding, that she planned to send an email to Ari saying "ok now let's cut back the work." Before she sent it she spoke to one of the traders who'd been with Carbon since the aughts. "Why stop now and get a lower bonus," he had said to her. He advised her to care less, do less work, not make it known that she was dialing it back. So this was how *he* had survived, I thought. Smart, very smart, but it was easier for him to divest emotionally; he was not being paid to put on a happy face, not being evaluated on his easy, buoyant personality. Besides, I helped him with his pulling back by giving him (and everyone else at

the Firm) a quick call, a heads-up, to minimize tabs and chats before Boone would walk over.

The meeting began with a long silence. Jay, annoyed at our reti-
cence, said, "You guys wanted this meeting—so speak up! How can
the Firm help you?"

We asked for increased transparency on our performances through
some standardization of responsibilities and compensation, as well
as for the ability to see our supervisor-evaluation sheets. Hannah,
an assistant who loved the Patriots and who sat at the opposite end
of the front office from me, spoke up. "Jay," she said, "I think we
should be allowed to invest in the funds. I think—and I don't think
I'm the only one here who feels this way—it's unfair that we're ex-
cluded. We want to have access to what we spend most of our days
working on."

Jay threw his hands up in the air. "Those are SEC rules," he said.
"Not mine."

No one believed him. Someone asked, "Which rule?" Others
joined in concert. Lena and I stayed silent.

"I mean," Jay said, hands in the air again, "I'll see what I can do."

Jay left. We looked at one another. "Yeah, that means no," someone said.

AFTER THE MEETING, I had a sit with Boone. He asked me how
it went. I told him Jay remained hated by the assistants. "Why?" he
asked.

"Because he always says no. No to any changes, no to more resources, no to seeing our supervisor-evaluation sheets. Probably no to being invested in the funds too." I did not want Boone to think I wasn't grateful for being an exception, so I added, "For the others, that is."

He gave me a look, the same fold of his eyes and crease of his mouth as he had had that one time he told me about Neil at Sun Valley.

FINALLY, I USED my three-thousand-dollar gift card to plus five-hundred-dollar spa credit at the Mayflower Grace, both of which Boone had given me for my birthday months ago. I had hoped for a week's leave, but given how my request-for-time-off conversation had gone with him—he had asked me "How many days?" not "How many weeks?"—I preemptively dialed it back. I brought with me a hardcover I had borrowed from Carbon's library—*Pain, Parties, Work*—fully intending to read about how, according to the jacket copy, Sylvia Plath "arrived in New York City" and "was supposed to be having the time of her life. But what would follow . . . changed the course of her life" and laid "the groundwork for . . . *The Bell Jar.*" I got through no more than ten pages before falling asleep around eight on my first night at the resort.

On the third and final day of my sabbatical, Val, who was covering for me, texted me at 9:15 a.m.:

> Last night when BRP left it was like 6:20
> and no one was left in the office but me
>
> He was like I just wanted to thank you
> for everything and making this so easy

I think BRP gets it. I just don't think BRP
has the energy—especially this year—to
rework the system

"I REALLY NEED to talk to you," Josh said as he and I were finishing up dim sum on an overcast Sunday. "I need your advice." We had planned an indoor afternoon at the American Museum of Natural History on the Upper West Side. I offered to talk to him if he'd come with me to get a dessert first. We walked to an ice cream shop, where I ordered a waffle cone with a single scoop. Then we made our way to a small park next to the museum and sat on a bench.

"I don't know what to do with my life," Josh said. His gaze, through his glasses, burrowed in its usual corner: off to the side of me and down.

"What do you mean?" I asked, my central vision on my Caramel Moose Prints.

"I have no idea what to do."

"You mean career or—?"

"Career."

"What do you want to do?"

He talked about his past several years working at his family's company. "It's fine? But it's not challenging." Josh was one of the most gifted people I had ever met. At Harvard, he was elected to Phi Beta Kappa his junior year, after switching majors, nonetheless. At Stanford GSB, he was named an Arjay Miller Scholar, even though—and I know this because we had spent a majority of those

two years arguing about the future, ethics, my diet and exercise—
he barely put in any effort, reading his case studies in the hour before class.

"Do you want to do something else?"

"Maybe."

"Then why don't you? You had a ton of interests when I first met
you." I thought back to the moment when Josh and I met. We were
strangers sitting at adjacent tables at a sushi restaurant in Boston.
He was on a date with a woman from Michigan whom I knew from
college; I was on a non-date with a man who incidentally knew
Josh's date. The four of us said hello and went back to our separate
conversations. The next morning, Josh, who had gotten my name
from his date, friended me on Facebook and sent me a message: *I
think you can do better. Dinner is on me.* He listed his religion as Bo-
kononism. We met up for dinner two days later and I fell quickly for
him. I never knew why—and, over the years, many people on his
side would accuse me (though never to my face) of being a gold
digger; they were unable to understand why I was drawn to him,
which, admittedly, I did not understand either—until now.

For our first date, Josh took me to the fanciest restaurant in
Boston, where he suggested we order tasting menus and champagne.
Between courses of seared foie gras and langoustine wrapped in
kataifi, he shared his story with me: During his senior year of college, he'd applied to and gotten into Stanford GSB, which he deferred to work at a hedge fund in New York. Then he got bored
and quit. He began taking math and physics and film classes as a
non-degree student at elite universities and was seriously consider-
ing getting a PhD and becoming a math professor. He'd been a

philosophy major before switching to econ. He did not party in college; he'd gone all in on his studies; he carried textbooks when he traveled and would read them cover to cover. For four years he kept deferring. Stanford was going to pull its offer if he did not attend that fall. But he felt paralyzed by indecision. He felt controlled by expectations (his dad wanted him to get an MBA) and also ambivalent about finance. Not just finance as a career: money, consumerism; he'd wanted to live a life of the mind. I was stunned at how someone whose background was so unalike from mine—his ancestry was a mix of Irish, English, Polish, German, and Italian, he'd said—could be at exactly the same fork as me at exactly the same time.

Fast-forward six years after our meet-cute and here we were, again, agonizing over finance or not finance, business or not business. I had wasted my life. Not because I began on this path, but because I used to tell people that giving up Wharton—for myself, so I would not be constrained to any specific career paths post-MBA—had been the most freeing moment of my life. No one believed me. Everyone, including my friends and family, told me how I was blowing up my career for a man I had just met. Self-doubt crept back in. Soon, I started to believe that others knew who I was and who I wanted to be better than I did myself.

"My dad," Josh continued, "expects me to take over the business when he retires in the next, I don't know, two to ten years? I don't know how to say no. I don't know *if* I can say no."

"Do you want to say no?"

"I mean, I don't think I can do that to my dad. The job I have in the family business is easy and I will inherit a lot of money, soon." I thought about the vague phrasing of his net worth and realized that, on this, I felt much closer to Boone than I ever had to Josh, who, after many years, several of which we were engaged, could not tell me any specifics of his finances, not even rounding to the nearest hundred million. I did not ask. I did not care.

My ice cream was melting fast. "If you're going to inherit everything soon, why don't you go ahead and do the thing you want to do?"

"Because I'll feel guilty inheriting something I didn't work for. I think if we, you know, you and me, if we have a future, if I work a few more years at the company, then we will never have to worry about money ever again."

"So, if I'm hearing you, you're working at your family's company to lessen the guilt you feel for inheriting your parents' wealth?"

He paused, then said, "Basically. Yeah."

"You used to talk about starting this or that or— You had dreams. What happened to them?"

"It's not just money, though. It's a *lot* of money."

"Yes and no—"

"Uh . . ."

"Yes, it's a lot of money. But it's also *just* money. I am confident that you and I, if we remain together, with or without your inherited wealth, could make a living. The only thing in short supply is time."

"But to live the lifestyle we want—"

"Don't factor me into this."

"What do you mean?"

"I don't want that lifestyle, I really don't. In fact, I hate it."

"You don't care about having hundreds of millions of dollars for our future?"

"It's your inheritance, not ours, and certainly not mine. Also, the New York apartment is owned by your family's trust, not even you."

"But if you're married to me, then it *is* ours."

"That's the thing—*only* if I'm married to you. I want to have things, own things, have equity in things that are not contingent on you. I don't want to live in *your* house."

"I'm offering you the chance to never have to worry about money again in your life."

"And I would rather live in a half-a-million-dollar house that I own than a ten-million-dollar one in which I'm squatting."

"So, let me get this straight: You don't want to live in our, uh, extremely luxurious Manhattan apartment many people would die to live in?"

"No. And"—I was going say something about values and priorities when a peace flooded my soul, a thought barged into my mind, giving way to a clearing so total in its domination of all my senses that it made me forget my original point—"I want to start over."

"What do you mean?"

"I don't want to sound ungrateful. You are offering me a lot. Thank you. I mean it, *thank you*. But this talk of inheritance, it's . . . not what I want. I want to start my life over."

He fell silent. So did I. I heard the crunch of fallen leaves and the happiest barks of unleashed dogs in a nearby dog run. Slowly, quietly, Josh asked, "You would give up hundreds of millions of dollars for the freedom to do your own thing?"

I looked across the street at a neighborhood deli and thought of my parents. The first thing I remember telling myself I wanted to be when I grew up was "the opposite of my mom." I had been so intent on defining myself as the antipode of her that I failed to see how that mindset shortened the umbilical cord I had tried to cut loose. She yelled; I would be calm. She judged; I would be tolerant. She saw danger; I would know no fear. She changed her mind randomly; I would be so consistent and logical and rational—and thus, unchanging, because how do you reason and decide your way into insight, revelation, becoming a whole new person?—that I would drive myself into paradoxical corners from which I saw no escape.

But the unconscious mind is an ocean where the conscious mind is a wave; I'm much more like her than I'm not. My parents gave up their birth country to start fresh in America and give me opportunities—opportunities but not *freedom*. I had felt unfree most of my life. Not free to fall down. Not free to spill milk. Not free to disobey or be a child and, above all, not free to cry or be sad or in any way unhappy, because being anything less than happy would disturb the fragile terrarium of our beliefs, delusions included, that made it possible for us to keep on. All my parents wanted was to give me a chance at a better life and yet everywhere I felt in chains. All I wanted was to make my parents proud and happy and—what did I do? The one line from Dad's email with which I completely agreed: "We need to try hard to help the less fortunate." I had plunged headfirst into helping the rich. I was so disgusted with myself—the self so preoccupied with psychic safety that on exactly two occasions, both to Josh, once in front of his Harvard friend when they were talking politics, I had heard my voice utter the words, "I also don't have a ton of sympathy for poor people," for which the reasons we gave were all related to the American dream, the aliveness of it, the robustness of it—so disgusted with the abhorrent views lying inside my mind and body that some part of me wanted to go all the way and starve, binge, purge, spit, chew, drink, and roll myself into the contemptible person I believed I was.

Alas: I am their daughter. Resilience is in my blood. My parents are extraordinary. They had suffered enough for many lifetimes— famine, violence, and totalitarianism during the Great Leap Forward and the Cultural Revolution; poverty, racism, and ageism as Chinese immigrants in mid-Michigan during the eighties and nineties—but they were also very lucky, so lucky my mother has always believed she had been blessed with a guardian angel. It took me thirty-one years to realize and maybe accept that they had (and still do) hurt me, but that hurt, that narcissism of survival, did not absolve me of my moral responsibilities.

Looking back at Josh, I knew if I wanted the freedom to do my own thing, I would have to give him up—and give up Boone, and, in a sense, my parents. I would have to give up all the gifts they continued to offer me because a gift weighed down by the imposition of gratitude becomes an expectation; over time, it becomes debt. "I have wasted my life," I said. "But it's okay. I will begin again. My parents did it in their thirties and if they can do it, so can I."

I stood up from the bench to throw my sticky napkins into a green trash bin. Josh got up after me. Together we walked to the other side of the park. Josh looked at me with both hands in the pockets of his Loro Piana coat, one foot on the steps, and asked, "Do you still want to go in?"

I looked at the stairs to the museum, a white limestone structure with soaring columns in front of which stood a statue of a white man with money charging forward on a horse, supported, on foot, by two people of color. The stairs that had led to Carbon's Casino Night two years ago. "No," I said, and knew it was time. I decided then to tear down my life. "I'm all set."

WE HELD ANOTHER ASSISTANTS' team meeting in Paget three and a half weeks after the first one. Again it was us and Jay, no Boone. Jay spent half an hour giving a speech on how much Carbon valued us and how we were integral to the success of the Firm. "You are here because you are the *best* on the Street," he said, after which Val texted me: *And now he's going to tell us why we can't get what we want.*

Jay said no to any standardization of job responsibilities.

He said no to a more transparent, standardized compensation structure.

He said no to seeing our supervisor-evaluation sheets.

He said no to allowing assistants to invest in the funds.

IT HAD BEEN more than four weeks since Boone made me promise to give this a fair chance. I did. I no longer supported Gabe—he was given to Charlotte, the first person I had met at Carbon's offices, who had since moved up to an assistant—but, on the second part of my request—my own assistant—there was no movement.

FRIDAY MORNING. Around nine I walked into Boone's office and asked if we could chat. Not giving myself any time to back down, I blurted out my prepared lines: "Boone, you asked me to think it over and I've thought about it a lot. I've been going to intense therapy twice a week, at your suggestion, actually, to see how I can better deal with my stress. I appreciate everything you've tried to do for me. I have decided it is best for me to transition out of this job."

No reaction. One, two, three, four, five seconds later, he asked, "Is it your relationship?"

"What? No."

"If you're deciding whether to work or not work, I think you'll be bored not working."

"This has nothing to do with my relationship. I don't think I will ever not work. I may or may not have a day job again, but I love working—too much, in fact. That's the problem."

"Then what is it?"

I didn't know how to answer.

"What changed?"

"I think I've voiced my concerns to you in one way or another by now."

"There must be something you're not telling me."

I kept silent.

"You know, I didn't go searching for your replacement the minute you expressed doubt."

"And I didn't go searching for a new job either. I've never even so much as entertained the thought of another job, and I get plenty of recruiter emails. I can show you texts if you want, between me and Val, saying how I had always planned on giving it until year end, to reassess everything then, but, honestly, every day, *still*, I feel"—unheard, unseen; tired of waiting; that I like you as a person but not so much you in the system, but who is the system, and who has the power to rework it, if not you?—"burned out."

"Why didn't you ask for help earlier?"

"I did. Or tried to, at least."

"This could've all been avoided if you had spoken up. Why didn't you speak up sooner?"

MY FACE WAS INCHES from the communal toilet, but I did not care. A foreign substance was inside of me and I wanted it out before my stomach acid destroyed what I hoped would be evidence.

Minutes before, I had been in a dorm room with my friend Sarah and a few upperclassmen, mostly men, most of whom I did not know. Earlier in the night, Sarah and I had gone to our dorm's winter formal, and I was wearing a floor-length magenta dress that my parents' friends in China had given me as a high-school graduation gift. It was my first semester of college; I was eighteen. At some point everyone else in the group left to smoke on the roof. I did not smoke, was not into weed either, so I stayed behind—as did he. A man several years older than me, a basketball player, who, the moment the last person in the group left the room and shut the door, came over to me and pulled down the top of my strapless dress. He lowered his head to my breasts. I opened my eyes wider and wider because closing them was something I might do for pleasure. The first words I spoke to him were "No," "Stop," and "Please stop." I voiced these words evenly, absent all emotion. He got up and exposed himself, grabbed my hair, pushed down my head. Later that night I googled *Is forced oral penetration rape?*

Some people during a traumatic event go into a rage, others go numb; I went rational. I wanted to recover evidence and also wanted him out of me. This was the first time I tried to make myself throw up; I did not succeed. I knocked on the door of a peer health advocate in our dorm and asked for an emesis-inducing medication like ipecac, used for treating poisoning; she said she did not have any. I found Sarah and told her what had occurred. "Are you sure this happened?" she asked. I knocked on the door of my resident advisers, a kind couple from Texas. I did not want to bother them past midnight, but I needed to recount as many details as close to this incident as possible. I felt nothing. No anger. No fury. No tears. I was calm and on autopilot, following the rules. Since I could not get his semen out of me, I focused on getting the smell of him and the odor of his smegma out of my mouth. I went back to my room and ate and ate and ate and ate, but no amount of chips and cookies could cover the taste of violence.

While the incident was bad, the aftermath was worse, much worse. I woke up the next day with the campus police at my door. I had asked my RAs to let me sleep on whether I was going to report this, and they had said, "Okay, sure, but only until morning." I don't blame them for changing their minds—they, too, were following the rules—but I felt betrayed; my life was over. The police told me that the university had already moved him far away from me, somewhere on the other side of campus. I was told he had lawyered up that day. For weeks I doubled down on being normal: I ate, I drank, I went to

class, although I was unable to concentrate for more than a minute. "Slut!" I heard one day on the steps of the student center, turning around to see one of his friends. I continued being intimate
with other men. I asked men and women if they wanted to have
threesomes. I commented on my female friends' breasts. When the
university assigned me a counselor from student health services, I
balked. Why must I be further punished by wasting time in therapy? I thought. I am totally fine.

I hadn't decided whether I would file a formal Title IX complaint. I feared not him, but the process. I feared not the reporting,
but the social suicide and long tail of shame that would come after
the reporting. I feared learning the ugly truth about ideals like justice, about whether an institution focused on minds and hands
(MIT's motto) would believe that my mind (which had thought and
said no and told many others about the incident within the hour)
and my hands (which had tried to push him off me) mattered.
Above all, I feared learning my mother had been correct when she
said, "When you grow up, you'll learn: no one cares about you except your family."

Over winter break, I went to see my British literature teacher
from high school. It was in her class that I did a book report on *Tess
of the d'Urbervilles.* I told her what had happened. "Carrie," she said
with no hesitation, "you *have* to speak up. You have to speak up for
women everywhere and try to prevent this from happening again. I
know you," she said, squeezing my shoulders, "and you are tough. If
there's anyone who can go through with this and stand up for what's
right, it's you." I thought about the rumors: Sarah had joined a so-
rority and told me several of her sisters had told her that they knew

of women who'd also had nonconsensual sexual encounters with the same basketball player. But no one wanted to come forward. I thought of my parents, especially my mom, who just wanted this ordeal to be over, asking me, "How could you not know better?" and telling me, "You should never be alone with a man at night." And—what made my soul die a little bit—"All this could've been avoided if you had been smarter." I walked back to the parking lot of my high school and sat in the car and cried and cried because being tough, being strong, having the thick skin I had been developing since my earliest memories of neglect and negation, so overgrown was the skin that often I felt like all callus and defense and no heart, was a curse. Then I stopped crying. There was no time. There was work to do.

When I got back to my parents' house I began writing the formal complaint.

Soon, there was a hearing. I told my parents not to come to Cambridge. I faced the Institute alone. He got up and told the committee on discipline, which included professors and administrators, that I had come on to him, he had tried to push me off. Any sounds people might have heard were my moans of pleasure. He was the victim. I was seeking revenge as a woman scorned. His friends got up and corroborated his lies and told stories about my promiscuity, how I had engaged in sexual activity before and after the incident. I got up and recounted my truth—I said no; he continued thrusting his penis inside my mouth until he ejaculated—and then the questions started. This was the only time in my life I became hysterical, inconsolable. I felt like *I* was on trial—I felt like the women on the committee were the hardest on me, as if projecting themselves into my situation, imagining how they would have performed the part better.

The questions, more than the rape itself, destroyed me. I was forced to explain why I didn't bite him, why I didn't fight back more, why I didn't run out of the room, why I didn't act more distraught or yell or scream. But my cool, calm response to intense, painful experiences was itself (although I did not know this then) an automatic, conditioned behavior that I had long been developing. Why must I defend my behavior when someone else committed a wrong? In this case, a crime? Why are my words not enough? It took me quite a while to realize that believability is a major currency of good fiction. Crafted lies are easier to believe than actual truths. It is much easier, much less painful, to believe that a woman would be vengeful than it is to believe a woman would clearly state, "No," "Stop," and "Please stop," and then be ignored, violated, and raped. Women did not want to imagine themselves in my situation because it would mean an affront to their agency. They did not want to imagine that they could, through no fault of their own, end up in a situation in which they were absolutely powerless and totally helpless, so they blamed the victim, implying that the victim could have and should have responded differently. This blaming gives them a sense of control, a causal structure to the world that makes sense.

Truth in trauma is what it is. It is not concerned with believability or sense. It is a rupture to a plot, a deviation from script. It is someone else's mind writing the arc of my narrative for me, someone else's hand yanking the thread of my life story from me. Of course his unoriginal lie with perfect lying witnesses was easier to swallow than my unbelievable truth.

"Not responsible" was the decision about him from the committee.

Determined not to let a man or an institution slow me down, I sped up. I spent not one additional second thinking about it. I tried to forget it, tried to forget as many details as possible, including his first and last name, but I could never forget the curl of his pubic hair or the stench of his scrotum. It was right after this, during the spring term when undergrads had to declare a major, that I settled on a path. Up until then I was undecided and had entertained everything from astrophysics to radiation oncology to neurosurgery; I wanted to understand how the universe worked by finding order amid chaos, maybe even try to control the chaos by killing malignancies to help heal the brains and lives of others.

The experience of reporting a sexual assault was a point in time that set me off on a specific vector in space. I felt that MIT had shamed me for the way I reacted during and after the incident, for behaving in ways that had hurt my own credibility. My toughness was my undoing. I felt a compulsion to go into a field where I'd belong, where my sangfroid would be not only welcomed but also rewarded: finance. Which happened to satisfy my middle- and high-school interests and my need to be independent from my parents as quickly as possible. I vowed I would never again allow myself to be trapped. I turned my incompletes into grades, took extra classes, did behavioral economics research, and fell in love, at the start of sophomore year, with a man whom I ended up dating for three years. He was eight years older than me. He told me he had heard of my reputation, had even been warned by others to stay away, but he believed me and my story without asking me to explain myself (he'd been a soccer player at MIT and knew the culture, he'd said) and I fell instantly for him. I spent nearly every night at his place, off campus; I never had to set foot on the grounds of MIT save for some classes with mandatory attendance.

Optimization, a required class for the finance major, was my favorite because it gave me a mathematical process for something with which I had struggled for decades: decision-making. To choose a point and the next point and the point after that, to form a literal string of choices that coiled into a tapestry one might call a life worth living. If I did not have visceral data to help me choose and decide, I could at least lean on rational, intellectual processes that made sense. But to that class, and many others, I showed up high. I took ecstasy many, many weeks, on weekends and weekdays, to feel alive. I celebrated being done with college by rolling for five days straight.

Over the years, people have told me I must have been crazy-ambitious or a genius to graduate from MIT with two bachelor's and a minor in three years. I smile, say nothing, while feeling my skin crawl because what I want to say is: *No, I was trying to get out of hell.*

BOONE WAS WRONG about me. He was also wrong about his other employees. Everyone was here at least partly for the pay, but many people were here because they wanted more. When they did not get more—upward career mobility, or the feeling of having contributed something positive, however small, to the world, the feeling that their work mattered—they had no choice but to leave. They prioritized their want of more above the pay of Carbon. I felt hope for humankind.

After Boone told me that I should have spoken up sooner, I continued looking at him and, as calm as ever, said, "I did, Boone. I did speak up. I spoke up about my workload issues right after Labor Day, which was over a month and a half ago. I also spoke up about my feeling of a lack of support from Courtney, and IT . . ." I could not bring myself to finish the sentence.

"You'll stay on for the transition? Until we hire your replacement?"

"I'm prepared to give three weeks."

"You've *got* to be kidding me."

I kept silent.

"After all this, you're hanging me out to dry?"

"I don't believe I'm hanging you out to dry."

"This is terrible timing for me."

"It is for me as well."

"Is your decision final?"

I nodded.

"I'm shocked," he said, moving his head slowly from right to left, left to right. "I'm rarely ever shocked. But I am *completely* shocked at how big this pendulum swing is."

I did not apologize.

"Can I get back to you? I have to think on it."

I nodded, thanked him, and walked out.

At lunch, Val and I headed to the kitchen to catch up. I told her how it went. "What?" she said. "What do they have to get back to you about? *You* quit!"

LATER THAT DAY, after Boone had spoken to Jay—whose assistant, Courtney, asked me what in the world was happening because Boone had been in their area for an hour looking like he had seen a ghost—Boone called me into his office. "I blame this entirely on your relationship," he said.

I gave no response. I put up zero fight so I would not get into yet another debate about whether I was blowing up my career for a man I had just started seeing again—a man I had once loved with my whole heart, whom I knew I would have to be leaving soon.

"But we've agreed to let you go."

November 18

I woke up at six a.m. I journaled. I wrote. Each word felt like chaos. I could not commit to an "I," an "I" with a stable point of view; I was so afraid of putting something false down that I hadn't put anything down, over the past two years, until now. My therapist had assured me that I wasn't lying—to myself or to others—because how could you lie when you didn't know the truth? Then my head would start to hurt, and I would think of my mother.

All my life, when Mom would see me agonizing over any and every easy or hard decision, she would say, *Bié xiǎngle*. Which translates to "forget it," but the actual characters mean "do not think." Mom would say, *Xiǎng butōng. Think no through*, always in the context of how you can't think your way through life's problems, which was always followed by *chē dào shān qián bì yǒu lù*. *When a car arrives in front of a mountain there must be a road out*. The key was the *dào*. A verb meaning to "arrive" or "reach" or "go to" or "get to" but also a punctuation mark—an en dash, meaning a range, a passage of time, a movement. You can't think your way through a mountain; you must move. I admit every time Mom said these words I would think, So, logically, why must it be the case that there will be a road out?

But I had missed the point.

When I told Yuna I was quitting my job, she had said, on Gchat, *Im so excited for u literally im like shaking my legs for joy*. She, too, wanted to quit her job and work *all the time* on her photography and blog, which she had not *opened to public for being afraid its not good enough*. But both her parents had become *jobless*. She could not quit, not yet. I knew the immensity of the privilege I had—the freedom to leave a situation and be more or less okay—but I believed that this should be a universal right. Yuna and I bonded again over our struggles to understand ourselves—or, as she put it, *Its like outside is all calm running course of life. . . . and inside freaking battle field*. I told her that Carbon had said, after my departure, they would be splitting my responsibilities into two full-time positions, and that was after a 30 percent reduction in workload they had given me back in September. *No fucking way*, Yuna said. She told me she and Jason had finally decided to take that trip to Seattle, a city she'd been wanting to visit for years and scout as a possible place to live. She was tired of Kansas. She had been working to pay off their debt and, months ago, for the first time in her adult life, became debt-free. I could hardly contain myself, my legs bouncing as my heart soared, imagining Yuna on a plane, moving high above the clouds.

At eight thirty a.m. I shut my laptop, showered, got dressed, and walked out the door.

I STEPPED ONTO THE SUBWAY in my ballet flats, bringing with me a change of shoes in case I was feeling daring again. I had not believed my therapist when she said that my eating disorder was caused by my environment—"overdetermined" was the word she used—but, with no restriction of diet or added exercise, I had dropped almost ten pounds since the day I informed Boone of my decision. I lost my cravings—stopped eating as resistance, stopped using food to distract me from my injuries, physical and moral. Today I wore a navy shirtdress from the diffusion line of one of Elisabeth's favorite designers, the one from which she and Boone had given me a much too expensive coat at my first year-end.

Carbon had immediately begun a search for my replacement. Boone had asked me what I thought of one of the other assistants, Allison. Boone liked her because she had been the chief administrative officer at a female-founded hedge fund before joining Carbon to support IR and another one of Boone's analysts. Days later, Allison contacted me to talk about the role. The job is extremely stressful, I said to her. "That's not what he said," she said.

Earlier in the week, I had had my exit interview with Jay. I met him outside his office and together we took the back stairs down one floor. Carbon had recently signed a new lease for a portion of forty-five. Even in these supposedly dark times, we had the resources to grow.

"This is from the previous tenant," Jay said as he watched me looking around the floor. He led me to a bare conference room. No abstract paintings, no credenzas. Only desks and chairs, which looked different. Instead of leather, the seats were fabric. Instead of metal, the frames were plastic. Instead of hidden cords and wires and sockets, everything was exposed. Jay took a seat at the head of the table and motioned for me to sit next to him. The afternoon sun flooded the room. All of Carbon's external conference rooms on the main floor faced the park, so I had never had to deal with the sunlight making me or anyone else boil. Jay pulled out a manila folder. "I hear you're leaving us," he said, handing me one of two sets of papers.

"Yeah." I paused, then rushed to say, "Jay, I'm so sorry for any inconveniences this will cause and—"

"Look, you don't need to apologize to me. I get it. Our jobs are more similar than you think. You know Penelope?"

"Of course."

"She used to do everything. I mean *everything*. Only after Elisabeth had her second kid or something like that did Penelope ask for help. She asked me to help her convince Boone, so then I had to come in and assess the situation and say, 'Okay, look, Boone, you need a family office. You need help, *she* needs help.' He warmed to the idea. But . . . slowly."

"Wow."

"Yeah, Carrie, I get you. I'm in the same position. It's never-ending. I'm not sure Boone gets how much work I do either, but you owe it to *yourself* to call for backup."

"Maybe I should've asked for help sooner. I believe I did, though. I tried."

"It doesn't matter now. It is what it is."

THE SUBWAY CAR made four local stops before I got off at Fifty-Ninth Street / Lexington Avenue. I emerged from underground and, on my way over to the building, walked past a bronze sculpture of a bull (or moon or bird) that soared over fourteen feet high but today, I knew, I was taller.

I swiped my badge at the lobby checkpoint and took the elevator up.

TEXT FROM JEN, 9:27 a.m.: *Good morning Carrie! Missing you already.*

MY ONE GOAL for the day was not to cry. I sent a thank-you-and-goodbye email to Carbon-NewYork-All, mentioning that I was leaving to "embark on some new adventures" and how "immensely grateful" I was to have been a part of the organization. I sent a personalized email to Elisabeth, who sent the kindest note back. I found Luis, who, when I gave my badge back to him, told me the truth. He had taken me to sit for a photo for building security on my first day and, after that, I would see him every so often, roaming the halls. "Carrie, wow, yep," he said after I told him about my burnout. "I remember your first day and you looked *so* amazing . . . and now I see that Carbon has ruined you!" I had never felt so good about being told I looked so bad. I deleted Boone from my Favorites, then changed my phone's settings so that Boone's contact would never ding again and would no longer bypass everyone else.

The day before, I had given up my seat outside Boone's office. Jay had taken over the hiring process for my replacement from Jen. He and Boone interviewed several candidates, but no one, including Allison, seemed to advance. So Jay pulled Zoe, the receptionist who had gone to Yale, over to cover the bare minimum of responsibilities as they continued on their search.

I HAD NO more work to do. I spent the morning reading the news, having the time and energy again to care about the world outside. The media still appeared to be focused on just one topic, which made me wonder how Boone might have voted. He donated both ways. He and Elisabeth had had dinner with Jared and Ivanka earlier that year. What made me think he probably went blue was an exchange months ago when he was informing me of his goal to keep his latest real estate purchase out of the papers. "Got it," I had said. "So like, the opposite of your apartment now?" Silence. No recognition. "There are multiple articles about your current place."

"You know, those aren't photos of *my* apartment."

"No?"

"What do you think?"

"It's . . . extremely ornate." Boone's apartment, before he and Elisabeth bought and redecorated it, had belonged to the widow of a publishing scion. That space had been full of drama and old-world opulence, calling to mind the Renaissance, designed by someone whom the *Times* once called "the Architect of Illusion." But Boone was all about the modern, the stealthily extravagant. His homes were styled by a starchitect of luxury retail. To me, though, his apartment had most of the same walls, same floors, same land—same stage—only different furniture.

"No," he said, laughing. "I'm not Donald Trump!"

The day after the election the office had felt no different. No one cried. No one celebrated. It was business as usual, like it was after Brexit—I had heard from coworkers that we had been well hedged for either scenario.

TEXT FROM PARMITA, 11:40 a.m.: *LAST DAY!!!!!!!!*

I CANNOT REMEMBER what I ate for my last meal. Probably dim sum. Seamless still paralyzed me, but I couldn't waste time at the office like I did at home, so I would default to ordering Chinese.

The second thing I remember telling myself I wanted to be when I grew up was someone who worked in a big city and ate *xiǎolóngbāo* for lunch. I was eight, on my first visit back to China, in Shanghai at the home of my great-aunt who would steam tiny little store-bought frozen dumplings for breakfast daily; I became obsessed. In the nineties, soup dumplings were nowhere to be found, at least not in the Mitten where people claimed to go cow tipping. I begged my parents to drive around hunting for them. On our family's road trip to New York, after visiting Ruth, I made my parents take me to Joe's Shanghai. It was 1995. Joe's Shanghai had recently opened up a second branch, in Manhattan (the first branch was in the Chinese immigrant enclave of Flushing, Queens). My parents indulged me on my quest. I have the most vivid memory of waiting outside the restaurant with them under a green awning on a petite side street in New York City's Chinatown. After someone called our group, we sat down, ordered, and waited. After ten minutes that felt like ten thousand years, the dumplings arrived. My parents told me to eat first. Whatever goodness they happened upon, however small the package, they gave it first and always to me. I bit into the dumpling and slurped and said, *Pí tài hòu. Skin too thick.*

Not a day went by at Carbon when I wouldn't have a fleeting thought about how I had achieved a childhood dream of mine. Mom's and Dad's tongues were sharper than knives, and often I felt like their honing steel, but their hearts were—and have always been— softer than tofu: they put *everything* into giving me a shot at the American dream, the one and only way I saw and felt their love. Even when I did not have the time or appetite to eat lunch, which was most days, and even during the period in which I was bingeing, I needed the psychic comfort of having the dumplings there at my desk, just in case. My orders expanded to include *shumai* and *hargow* and *jiaozi* but no wontons. Hated wontons. I kept ordering and ordering and wasted a lot of food. I had gone from free to reduced to regular to overindulgent lunch. I would think of my mom, whose father's rule at mealtime was never to leave a grain of rice uneaten on the plate; and of my dad, who would stay out past midnight delivering Domino's pizzas during icy, snowy Midwest winters, in hopes of more quarters in tips; and of myself, again, my thoughts returning as guilt and self-loathing, so nauseating were the emotions they would only make me want to binge more.

But it wasn't just me. When doing due diligence on restaurant brands, Carbon would order catering portions, most of which, because it was fast food (including Domino's), Boone would eye and judge and not touch and later the kitchen staff would flip whole boxes and trays into the garbage. Boone's personal chef would prepare, cook, package, and hand-deliver his lunch to me for me to plate at the office, but, often, because his schedule changed at the last second, Boone would not eat it. His chef would message me: "Please don't throw it out!" or "Please someone eat it, it's soba with miso dressing and a bit of grilled steak!" I started to view all the *xiǎolóngbāo* I had tossed as a symbol of the collective time wasted, the dreams deferred, for the profit and prosperity of billionaires. How big was this pile of discarded dreams? What else could we do with this energy?

It's easy to tell a story about how I had worked so hard to get up to the forty-sixth floor of a travertine tower in the middle of a big city where I could, in fact, order soup dumplings daily. Yes and no. I did put everything into my work and education. But the dream I'd made during the summer between second and third grades was realized only by the help I received along the way. Since the mid-nineties, aside from the help from my parents: Tastes changed. Culture changed. Menus changed. The restaurant industry and technology and supply chains changed. This is to say: The world and its systems outside my control conspired to deliver my dream to me. Boone had tried to guilt me by telling me I was hanging him out to dry. I had answered with a reflexive denial, but, in the intervening weeks, I had realized yes, I was, and I did not feel guilty. He was a billionaire. He could buy another dryer or hire another laundress.

Besides, for Boone to achieve his dream, how many people were he and Carbon hanging out to dry—and, up until recently, with my help? I was at last making a choice not driven by necessity or a need for survival: I was choosing to prioritize the dreams of others, including myself, over that of Boone.

But it did not have to be this way. Months ago, in a sit, I had asked Boone, What would you do if you weren't a fund manager? What was your American dream? He had answered with such alacrity, such honest delight bursting onto his face before his mind even staffed his lips with words, that I found myself overtaken with a familiar grief. "Spinal surgeon," he had said. Boone, too, had deferred a dream for the profit and prosperity of a billionaire—Martin. Martin, who, in the years before he founded the hedge fund that started it all, had wanted to be a novelist. Me being me, I asked Boone, So then what happened? He looked down and to the side of me. I waited. He looked back up, and the moment was over.

TEXT FROM VAL, 1:03 p.m.: A photo of a card I had given her that she had pinned next to her monitor with the caption *Official spot at my desk haha*.

BY THE AFTERNOON I had finished answering a flurry of texts and emails. Since I had cleared my desk the day before, I had nothing left to do. I sat at a workspace designed for a floater, although during my tenure we had not employed a single one.

The assistants surprised me in the kitchen with two dozen

cupcakes from Sprinkles that spelled *THANK YOU CARRIE*. They further surprised me with fuchsia dendrobium orchids and a Sprinkles cookbook, the inside cover of which was inscribed:

Carrie,

Best (sweet) wishes! We'll miss you!

Love,

Erin ♥

Charlotte

Val ♥

Lena

Allison ♥

Hannah

Xoxo, Courtney!

Emma from IR came over and gave me a card. I could not read it while she was in front of me because I found myself on the brink of tears. I spent the rest of the afternoon browsing Page Six, Bloomberg, Shopbop, anything that steered me away from sentimentality. I sent IMs back and forth to my coworkers and realized that this marked the end of an era: the last AOL instant messages I would send in my life. I thought about how hard it was even for Carbon—a nimble and fast-moving crossover fund betting billions on technologies that were transforming the way people talked and shopped and worked and played—to change something as simple as its own system of communication. In AIM, at Carbon, I saw a pattern hidden in plain sight: A small decision weighed down by repetition becomes a massive habit. It becomes inertia.

I thought of other patterns hidden in plain sight and realized, for billionaires, the distraction of others was the point. To keep my—and our—attention twisted inside games of little to no consequence to them; this was by design. I had been misdirected by Boone's morality plays, asking myself over and over, Is he a good billionaire? Is he a good person? Not only did I not have an answer (although if I had to give one, I'd say that he tried quite hard, succeeded sometimes, and most often chose the path of self- or organizational preservation, which would make him, well, human), but this line of questioning was irrelevant. Every delay—every stalemate, TBD, or indecision about billionaires' lives, their management styles, their tax avoidances or excessive influence—was a win for them. They were the ones with the luxury of time to wait out storms in palatial shelters, while the rest of us, with no areas of refuge, watched the weather to stay alive.

My problem was never with Carbon or Boone but with his kind. (I thought he was the best of his kind.) After years of trying to find a pattern in the stock market, working at Fidelity and Carbon, I shed most of my beliefs and gained this one: the only patterns that mattered—the ones billionaires wanted to keep the public's attention away from—were so simple and obvious that the investor class employed creative diversions because, otherwise, the secret would be out.

Compounding. Boone had a quote about it in his office. Stay in the market as much as possible. Have it, invest it. Wait out any panic and let it ride, let it grow. (Exponentially.) It gets easier to compound the richer you are. You can borrow to live. You never have to touch the principal. You never have to lock yourself into a price you don't like.

Risk/reward trade-off. Because the rich are so rich, they are able to risk a higher percentage of their net worth *and* invest in riskier assets. These two effects multiply and allow for the potential of much, much higher returns. This is why billionaires love crises. When others are sidetracked, they can scoop up assets on the cheap, take on extra risk at a time when everyone else is playing it safe, then wait for the world to return to a new normal.

Access. Companies used to go public at an earlier stage in their life cycles, making their hyper-growth phase accessible to the average investor. But large and larger pools of capital came rushing in, which gave start-ups an option to stay private longer, delaying their IPOs. This was often a win-win: a start-up might not want (or be ready for) the pressure of public financial reporting; private investors might get special access to the period of highest growth. Access is edge. Constraint is destiny. The loser, then, and always, was the retail investor, who most likely did not have the privilege to invest in the start-up or in the private fund. Carbon, in my view, was occupying a territory of the market to which all of the public should have access.

The final pattern, which took me decades to see, was alienation. Another way to say "continuous improvement" is *never enough*. Another way to say "team over individual" is *self-subjugation*. "Fact-based decision-making" is a process that discounts emotion while "forward-looking decision-making" is one that undervalues history. Carbon felt like home: an environment in which the institution is never wrong; you are always wrong; you have no one to blame but yourself. The ways in which I had adapted as a child—dissociation, alexithymia, fragmentation, compliance, and an overreliance on rationality—had enabled me to adapt with ease to Carbon. Without

visceral information, my morality inclined toward the amoral, sometimes utilitarian, whatever made logical sense. But I became in-
terned in a reality in which succeeding at Carbon took me further
away from the self I had longed to set free. Now: As the world burns,
as life gets more difficult for everyone outside the 1 percent, I worry
that those in precarious situations (often women, people of color,
and other marginalized and disadvantaged groups and, especially,
their children) will develop an increased sense of alienation—from
themselves, and from society. An alienation that is then exacerbated
and exploited, as Karl Marx predicted, by the system that is capitalism. The trauma plot and the capitalism plot are increasingly the
same plot. Each one rewards you for staying inside the other. What
will it take to break free?

AROUND FOUR THIRTY P.M. Boone sent me an IM. I walked
into his office. I sat down and could not look at him so I looked toward the park, over which the autumn sun was setting fast.

I burst into tears. The more self-conscious I felt, the more I cried.
The more I thought about how I was crying, the more I could not
stop a single tear. I felt consumed by a full-body experience: death.
For years I had been passively waiting for a part of me to wither
away so the other part of me could replace it and become my truest
self. But my old self, the one that had grown up in the harsh ecolo-
gies of family and school and society, the one that was so completely
and winningly personified by Boone—my mirror, my once mentor—
held on; my assembly of selves, after all, shared the same resilience.
In front of Boone, I mourned the passing of not only a prior self but

every future self I had once imagined. My past self did not die by some miracle, no; that would be too easy. My future self had to apply external force, had to make the decision to stop giving my past self oxygen. I was acting with agency from the self to which I had aspired and now, at long last, felt that I embodied. I'd always believed in the possibility of change, real change, because of my father, who, since the day he signed the attestation, never touched me with hostility again. I let go. I felt a rush of sadness, forgiveness, regret, fear, grief, hope, love, and relief. I felt seventeen years of suffering the world over to which I had been insensitive, the pain of every blade of grass I had chosen not to see and not to hear and ignorantly stepped on. I felt at the end of a vector, full stop. At the end of that mindset into which I had transitioned that first night in the hospital, before which I felt suicidal and after which my survival instinct kicked in and all of a sudden I cared *only* about the future, about maximizing my future—and, with that, growth, accumulation, and the pursuit of success. I realized my fear of wasting my life had nothing to do with the waste itself, not the time or money or any sunk cost, not even the act of apostasy or the wrath of my parents, and everything to do with what would come after: a period of being lost. For the first time in my life I gave myself permission not to know the path.

Boone reached for his box of Kleenex and handed me a few tissues. I handed him a card and a gift bag.

"Should I open it?" he asked. I nodded. He read the card and looked up, smiling. I cried more. He reached inside the bag and pulled out a book. A novel with a protagonist in pursuit of his personal legend. I verbalized what I had written, something like "You believed in me and saw my potential. For that, I will feel eternal gratitude." I meant what I said, I mean it to this day: it was only against someone as sharp and smart and high conviction as he, someone who held fast to his beliefs, staking billions on them, enduring the mental torture of being second-guessed and disaffirmed whenever the market moved away from him, making him doubt his everything, someone who in those moments stayed truest to himself while challenging me with experiences demanding my full heart and mind that I was able to unearth—and create—my self.

But I did not grow in the ways that he or I had expected. I don't believe I grew at all. I changed—radically. I transformed. I did not swing from one side of a pendulum to the other; I removed the pivot. This could not have been a total surprise. As every Carbon document would remind you in the footnotes: past returns are not indicative of future results.

"What are you going to do after Carbon?" he asked.

"First I'm going to take some time off and recover physically. Then . . . Well. You know how I've always wanted to be a writer."

"Can I give you some advice?"

I did not expect this. Maybe he had come around, maybe he finally got it, maybe he wanted to help me realize my dream and give me some words of encouragement and inspire me—wow. So I said, "Of course."

"I don't see you as a writer. I know you. You're too much of a doer."

My tears dried. I smiled and smiled because I did not know what else to do with my face.

"You have," he continued, "too much of a math and engineering brain."

I maintained my equanimity. I felt no impulse to go rational or to explain myself. I took a deep breath in and, letting it all out, said, "Yes, Boone, you are right. I am a doer. And I do have a math brain. But I also have many parts of me you have not yet seen."

He said nothing.

I said nothing.

I broke the silence with "I guess we'll see."

We stood up.

I reached out to shake his hand.

He stepped closer to me and widened his arms and we hugged— we touched—for the first time since I had become an employee.

I went back to my floater's desk. The kitchen staff were the last people I called. They gave me a cardboard box to help me carry my things—the cookbook, the orchids—home. I could not say goodbye to them, or to Val; so I picked up my box and walked straight down the hall, turned my head to the right, toward the kitchen, where a line of leftover cupcakes with sweet, sweet frostings in chocolate and vanilla sung to me, and I stood still for a second, for only one second, smiled to myself, and continued on, in heels. I walked to the elevator and pressed the button. As I waited, I looked at the dot. Silver like the wall and no bigger than a split pea, it was where you would tap your badge to get in. To anyone who did not know it was there, it was imperceptible, hidden. But it was there; I could not unsee it. Then I stepped into an elevator and went down to the street level. I walked out of the building and into an Uber. The car revved and stopped and swerved amid a mountain of traffic as we drove down a highway in this city of dreams, lit, and incandescent, with the possibility of reinvention. I was moving once again.

EPILOGUE

July 27

I reach forward, open the door, and pull out a blouse. Tomorrow, eight years will have passed since the day I headed uptown to meet in person with Peter and then Jen. When I went to exchange the coat that Boone and Elisabeth had given me once, the store did not have any more in my size, so I had exchanged it for a basketful of half-off items. I reach forward again and grab some pants, try on the outfit that on occasion I have wanted to shred—an outfit that I have not been able to wear since my first few months at Carbon, when I put my dreams on hold. It fits.

What's more: I feel peace.

I walk from the bedroom to the bathroom and, dabbing sheer concealer onto my face, look in the mirror. I used to think my most shameful secret was that I did not know myself, that I lacked conviction: what to eat, whom to date, who to be, how to live. Working in an industry that trafficked in conviction, wherein ambivalence was costly and seen as a weakness—an invitation for others to take control and dominate, an effect that's especially pronounced for women—made me feel like a fraud. Everywhere I went, decisiveness was valorized. Doubling down. Seeking closure. Being sure, settled, concluded. I sold a lot of conviction and to my surprise was not terrible at it—which made me feel like a liar. Mom was right. My logic was, in a way, upside down: I relished the feeling of *having* decided, to avoid feeling the full and crushing opportunity cost of each and every moment; I searched for clues on how to approximate an optimal choice, then tried to force my tardy emotions to fit the path I'd already selected. This did not work. Over and over I'd have to rewind, revise. I have been uncertain my whole life.

But—have I? Before I went underground and hid from the world and myself, in the third grade, I wrote my first book, a novel—six chapters; 2,349 words, one of which was *billionaire*. I took my project extremely seriously: illustrated the cover, blurbed myself (*Exciting! Easy too!*), stamped a colophon of a water bird (flamingo), and punctuated justly (seventy-seven exclamation points—I thought that was how everyone talked). The main character was a girl who happens upon a tree growing money instead of leaves. She uses the leaves to help her mother, who's trying to feed her family but cannot because the pipes are frozen and they do not have enough money to dine out; the girl treats her parents to Old Country Buffet. That night, two men stalk the girl, steal the tree from her home. The girl bursts into tears. Her mother gets mad. There's a diary; there's Boston; there are bullies, all of whom are boys. Lately I've been thinking my most shameful secret is that I knew all along the life I wanted to live, and did not have the courage to live it.

I walk to the other bedroom. I call out to my husband, who's composing where the piano, violin, flute, and trumpet are, and ask him to please be quiet for an hour. Sure, my love, Chris answers from his studio as I shut the door to mine. Here, in a room of my own in Brooklyn, working seven days a week most weeks and nine hours a day most days, I wrote my second book, a memoir—a prologue and thirteen chapters; 88,221 words comprising my journey toward self-knowledge and -liberation, ending with me leaving my job. I sent the manuscript to my agent, who submitted it to publishers. In just a few minutes on Zoom I will meet someone who I hope will see me as a writer. I feel the unmistakable ecstasy of possibility. I get excited, I wish, I dream. Again. I sit down at my desk, in front of a laptop, and, after reading through my prepared notes ("Everyone will ask you what's happened since," my agent said) I close my eyes and whisper:

> *The world they wanted to come did come. And though I*
> *redeemed in full (right after my departure, lest I ever be*
> *accused of a conflict of interest), I wish them well. They've*
> *increased their philanthropy and hired a head of HR.*
> *People tell me his assistant, who also has her own full-time*
> *assistant, is required to do far less for him than I was—I*
> *could not be happier for them. After my resignation I had*
> *given myself one year to get on a new path. But I needed a*
> *day job. The firm that reached out to me about Carbon*
> *reached out again, about working for a founder of another*
> *big fund in New York. I asked Boone to meet; he made*
> *time for me the next day; we met for tea in the lobby of a*

hotel near the building. When I started the new job—the only one I've ever taken purely for the money, to save up so I could go all in on my writing—my new boss told me that Boone had given me the absolute highest recommendation. I quit that job ten months in, the week I got into MFA programs, the same week Mom and Dad seemed to finally accept my—our—fate: Mom told me ever since I was three, even though she had vehemently denied it to the other parents who, after they saw me playing happily at the park by myself and not with their kids, had called me qiánwèi *(a term with a politically dangerous connotation in China), she knew that I was* forward guard. *Avant-garde. Or, as Mom translated it anew:* special.

A reminder went off—it's time for work. I open my eyes, look forward, and breathe.

ACKNOWLEDGMENTS

Thank you to Melissa Flashman, the most extraordinary agent. From our first meeting, the first semester of my MFA, you've believed in me; I am truly the luckiest.

Thank you to Juliana Kiyan, my brilliant, phenomenal editor. I am beyond grateful for your vision, which has shaped this book into a far better one than I could have written alone.

Thank you to the rest of the awe-inspiring team at Penguin Press. To Ann Godoff and Scott Moyers for seeing me as a writer, giving my debut a home. To Linda Friedner for believing that the stories in here can and should be told and heard. To Victoria Lopez for meticulous help with edits and production. To Stephanie Ross for designing a genius, stunning cover. To Christine Johnston for championing this book in such a sharp way. To Danielle Plafsky for creative promotions that help me reach an audience. And to the numerous other people who worked on making this book a book, from production to sales to design—I could not have dreamed of a better publishing experience.

Thank you to Alexis Kirschbaum, my incredible editor at Blooms-bury UK, for excellent edits and unwavering support.

Thank you to Vanessa Mobley for the many hours of deep conversation, and for reading my story as one of self-emancipation.

Thank you to Whitney Peeling for understanding why this book matters and finding those readers who might feel the same.

Thank you to Jason Richman for noticing me as a storyteller and helping me amplify my voice.

Thank you to Bennett Ashley, whose wise counsel made possible the journey from an idea to a proposal to a book.

Thank you to Peter Rahbar, whose keen insights and expert counsel imbued in me an authority of voice by which I now speak my truth.

Thank you to Maja Oeri and the Laurenz House Foundation for granting me the perfect environment—a year in Basel, Switzerland—in which I completed this work.

Thank you to Dr. Hilary J. Beattie, my ever-exceptional and tough therapist, for helping me—at last, and always—become me.

Thank you to all my teachers, especially: Jeremiah Chamberlin, who told me if I wanted to be a writer, I couldn't half-ass it, after which I ran off to get a day job; Honor Moore, Robert Polito, and James Miller, who gave me a comment, a question, and a critique, respectively, that changed the way I understood my project for the better; and Brenda Wineapple and Mychal Denzel Smith, whose classes challenged me to refine what it was that I wanted to say.

Thank you to Jenna Birch for telling me long ago *you have to be a writer, Carrie*—for being a good friend, noticing when I felt my most alive and free.

Thank you to Christopher Cerrone, my first reader, my best friend, my love. Our daily (hours-long, sometimes too-long) conversations about art and life have made me a much, much better writer and person. This book is what it is because of your beautiful mind and kind heart.

Thank you to my father. Over time you expanded your definition of *love* to include me; I felt it. I know it wasn't easy, that the hardest years of your life were the earliest years of mine, but you tried, you never stopped trying—thank you for inspiring me and understanding my struggles, for showing me that it is possible to break the cycle.

Thank you to my mother. What I formerly thought of as blaming I presently understand as teaching me self-reliance. Because relying on yourself was the only way you had survived. All your love and sacrifices and endless hours at your jobs, including those at home, have given me a life that is no longer a question of brute survival. And now—forty-five years after you declared a major when you took the *gāokǎo*, when you wanted to declare (Chinese) writing and literature but didn't because the revolution had just ended and you felt that you had to choose a more pragmatic path—I am living the dream. Our dream. Thank you. You mean the world to me.

And to you, dear reader: thank you so much for your time.